Praise For
Paco Underhill
and
Why We Buy

"The Dalai Lama said, 'Shopping is the museum of the twentieth century.' Paco Underhill explains why. Brilliantly."
—Faith Popcorn, author and Future Forecaster

"*Why We Buy* is useful as a how-to for retailers, but shoppers will discover a Vance Packard for our times, on the trail of our century's hidden persuaders."
—Hardy Green, *BusinessWeek*

"For retailers, this book should be mandatory. . . . For the rest of us, it's just plain fun."
—Harvey Schachter, *The Globe and Mail (Toronto)*

"No matter which point of view you're coming from, shopper or shopkeeper, you'll find Underhill's tips are often funny, sometimes provocative, and almost always usable."
—*The San Diego Union-Tribune*

"What Underhill offers in this delightful and engrossing book is a primer in the science of shopping. . . The effect of reading this book is that of being alternately entertained by hilarious stories and enlightened by trenchant observations."
—*Newsday*

"Underhill's way of looking at how we shop may revolutionize the industry. . . . In this day of heavy competition, advice from this book could give a retailer the edge needed to survive. . . . This book provides an excellent method for retailers to examine their own store space and look for what may draw customers in, as well as what may be causing them to leave without buying."

—Teresa McUsic, *Star-Telegram* (Fort Worth)

"The guru of retail consulting offers a wealth of insight into what makes a successful shopping experience for both buyer and seller."

—Craig Ryan, *The Oregonian*

"A fascinating voyage through the mall that will open your eyes to the psychology of modern retailing—and especially to the new dynamics of consumer shopping."

—G. William Gray, *The Tampa Tribune*

"Ostensibly a business book aimed at merchandisers, Why We Buy will also appeal to consumers who want to understand the art of shopping and the science of selling."

—Justin Adams, MSNBC

"Paco Underhill is Sherlock Holmes for retailers. . . This sleuth makes shoppers view stores with more critical eyes."

—Trish Donnally, *San Francisco Chronicle*

"A remarkable business tool, a distillation of all those notes and tapes, packaged in a way that is useful, witty, and loving."

—Keith H. Hammonds, *Fast Company*

"A readable, entertaining study of the behavioral science of shopping."

—Adrienne Miller, *Esquire*

"Intriguing for both lovers and haters of the game of visual stimulation."

—*Booklist*

"This lighthearted look at shopping is highly recommended to anyone who buys or sells."

—Rob McDonald, Amazon.com

ALSO BY PACO UNDERHILL

Call of the Mall

Why We Buy

THE SCIENCE OF SHOPPING

Updated and Revised for the Internet,
the Global Consumer and Beyond

Paco Underhill

SIMON & SCHUSTER PAPERBACKS

NEW YORK   LONDON   TORONTO   SYDNEY

Simon & Schuster Paperbacks
A Division of Simon & Schuster, Inc.
1230 Avenue of the Americas
New York, NY 10020

Copyright © 1999, 2000, 2009 by Obat, Inc.

This Simon & Schuster trade paperback edition January 2009

SIMON & SCHUSTER PAPERBACKS and colophon are
registered trademarks of Simon & Schuster, Inc.

For information about special discounts for bulk purchases,
please contact Simon & Schuster Special Sales at
1-800-456-6798 or business@simonandschuster.com.

Manufactured in the United States of America

20 19 18

The Library of Congress has cataloged the hardcover as follows:
Underhill, Paco.
Why we buy: the science of shopping / Paco Underhill.
p. cm.
Includes index.
1. Marketing research. 2. Consumer behavior. 3. Shopping. I Title.
HF5415.2.U53   1999
658.8'34—dc21   99-12125
CIP
ISBN: 0-684-84913-5
ISBN-13: 978-1-4165-9524-3
ISBN-10:   1-4165-9524-4

DEDICATION

Who knew when the first keystrokes of this document were made in the spring of 1997 that ten years and twenty-seven foreign translations later this book would still be alive? I am grateful that in the summer of 1999, when this book came out, my father, Francis Underhill, got to see it. I don't think he really knew what I did even after reading it. He had a lot of interests, but shopping wasn't ever among them. He died that fall. I was there. I made him a martini and helped him get comfortable in bed. He went, sleeping next to my mother, his wife of more than fifty years. I still talk to him.

AUTHOR'S NOTE

For some of you, the book you hold in your hands may be an old friend—given as a gift, bought in an airport, secured through Amazon or assigned at a school or training progam. Thanks for picking it up again. Most volumes stocked in the business section of a bookstore have a short shelf life. They zoom and crash and are forgotten within a year. This book has lasted ten years and is available in twenty-seven foreign editions. I had no idea when pen first went to paper back in 1997 that my story would appeal to so many readers.

From Russia to Japan, from Spain to Thailand, I've had visits and e-mails from readers just wanting to say hi, many looking for a job and not a few telling me their own stories. University professors from China, a Marxist minister in the Bengali provincial government, a jewelry designer from Spain—the list goes on. My favorite pieces of correspondence came from a man who ran a septic tank cleaning business in Missouri. The letter was handwritten on lined paper. I don't know how many letters that man writes a year, but I know I was privileged to get one of them. He'd read the book and wanted my advice on what color to paint his truck.

In 2007, I reread *Why We Buy* and realized that parts of the story had progressed and that some of the examples I'd used were dated. The book needed freshening and that's what it's gotten. If you liked it the first time, you'll like it even better the second. If you're picking it up for the first time, whether you love or hate shopping, this is a good, entertaining read, and you'll never look at the world of shopping and consumption the same way again.

Paco Underhill
January 2009

CONTENTS

I

INSTEAD OF SAMOA, STORES: THE SCIENCE OF SHOPPING

1. A Science is Born   3
2. What Retailers and Marketers Don't Know   28

II

WALK LIKE AN EGYPTIAN: THE MECHANICS OF SHOPPING

3. The Twilight Zone   42
4. You Need Hands   50
5. How to Read a Sign   61
6. Shoppers Move Like People   77
7. Dynamic   89

III

MEN ARE FROM HOME DEPOT, WOMEN ARE FROM BLOOMINGDALE'S: THE DEMOGRAPHICS OF SHOPPING

8. Shop Like a Man   102
9. What Women Want   121

10. If You Can Read This You're Too Young   137

11. Kids   151

IV

SEE ME, FEEL ME, TOUCH ME, BUY ME:
THE DYNAMICS OF SHOPPING

12. The Sensual Shopper   171

13. The Big Three   194

14. Time   201

15. Cash/Wrap Blues   208

16. Magic Acts   213

V

SCREEN SAVERS, JET LAG AND WHIRLING DERVISHES:
THE CULTURE OF SHOPPING

17. The Internet   227

18. Come Fly with Me   254

19. Windows of the World   268

20. Final Thoughts   280

Acknowledgments   293

Index   299

I

Instead of Samoa, Stores:
The Science of Shopping

ONE

A Science Is Born

Okay, stroll, stroll, stroll . . . *stop.*

Shhh. Stay behind that potted palm. Get out your clipboard and pen.

Our subject is the fortyish woman in the tan trench coat and blue skirt. She's in the bath section. She's touching towels. Mark this down—she's petting one, two, three, four of them so far. She just checked the price tag on one. Mark that down, too. Careful—don't get too close—you don't want her to see you. She picked up two towels from the table-top display and is leaving the section with them. Mark the time. Now, tail her into the aisle and on to her next stop.

Thus begins another day in the vineyards of science, specifically the science of shopping. But let's start by addressing a fundamental question: Since when does such a scholarly discipline even exist?

Well, if, say, anthropology had devoted a branch of itself to the study of shoppers in situ (a fancy Latin way of saying shoppers out shopping), interacting with retail environments (stores, but also banks and restaurants), the actual, physical premises, including but not limited to every rack, shelf, counter and table display of merchandise, every sign, banner, brochure, directional aid and computerized interactive informational fixture, the entrances and exits, the windows and walls, the elevators and escalators and stairs and ramps, the cashier lines and teller lines and counter lines and restroom lines, and every inch of every aisle—in short, every nook and cranny from the farthest reach of the parking lot to the deepest penetration of the store itself, *if* anthropology had already been studying all that . . . and not simply studying the store, of course, but what, exactly and precisely—scientifically—human beings do in it, where they go and don't go, and by what path they go there; what they see and fail to see, or read and decline to read; and how they deal with the objects they come upon, how they *shop,* you might say— the precise anatomical mechanics and behavioral psychology of how they pull a sweater from a rack to examine it, or read a box of heartburn pills or a fast-food restaurant menu, or grab a shopping basket, or react to the sight of a line at the ATMs . . . again, as I say, *if* anthropology had been paying attention, and not just paying attention but then collecting, collating, digesting, tabulating and cross-referencing every little bit of data, from the extremely broad (How many people enter this store on a typical Saturday morning, broken down by age, sex and size of shopper group?) to the extremely narrow (Do more male supermarket shoppers under thirty-five who read the nutritional information on the side panel of a cereal box actually buy the cereal compared to those who just look at the picture on the front?), well, then, we wouldn't have had to invent the science of shopping. In 1997, when this volume was originally written, the academic world knew more about the marketplace in Papua New Guinea than what happened at your local supermarket or shopping mall. Twentieth-century anthropology wasn't about what happened in your backyard.

In 1997, I'd been fighting for what I knew was right for more than ten years—and since then, a whole lot has changed. Companies across the world are now employing anthropologists to staff what have been popularly titled shopper and consumer insight groups. Ethnologic studies (that is to say, a science that breaks down humans into races, cultures and their various obvious and not-so-obvious characteristics) are part of mainstream market research. But when I first hung out my shingle, my academic colleagues thought I was selling out, and the marketers and merchants I sought to serve looked at me as an alien from a distant planet.

Down the hall from my office then and now is an equipment room with more than one hundred cameras. Eight-millimeter video cameras, direct to hard drive, digital, even a few ancient Super 8 time-lapse film cameras. To keep track of them, every camera is assigned a name—the video cameras are named after rock stars, the digital stills are signs of the zodiac. We find giving a camera a name rather than a number helps it last longer, and when Jimi Hendrix feels poorly, he gets to the shop faster than if he were camera number 26. In that same equipment room are piled cases of blank eight-millimeter videotapes, two hours per tape, five hundred tapes to a case. Across the world, we have now shot more than fifty thousand hours of tape per year. We also have dozens of handheld computers, or PDAs, on which we painstakingly jot down the answers from the thousands of shopper interviews we conduct; there are laptops in there, too, plus all manner of tripods, mounts, lenses and other camera accessories, including lots of duct tape. Oh, and many well-worn hard-shell cases for everything, because it all travels. A lot. The studio next to the equipment room has two complete digital editing suites and eleven stations at which to watch all those tapes—because everything we shoot, we look at. We have more than enough gear in that room to make broadcast-quality documentaries and, while we're at it, to equip a good-sized university's school of social anthropology or experimental psychology, assuming the university has a deserved reputation for generating tons of original research gathered from all over the globe.

Even with all that high-tech equipment, though, our most important research tool for the past thirty years remains the piece of paper we call the track sheet, in the hands of the individuals we call trackers. Trackers are the field researchers of the science of shopping, the scholars of shopping, or, more precisely, of *shoppers*. Essentially, trackers stealthily make their way through stores following shoppers and noting everything they do. Usually a tracker begins by loitering inconspicuously near a store's entrance, waiting for a shopper to enter, at which point the "track" starts. The tracker will stick with the unsuspecting individual (or individuals) as long as he or she is in the store (excluding trips to the dressing room or the restroom) and will record on the track sheet virtually everything the shopper does.

Befitting a science that has grown up in the real world, meaning far from the ivory towers of academia, our trackers are not stamped from the usual researcher mold. In the beginning we hired graduate environmental psychology students, but we found they were often unsuited to the work—more often than not, they came to the job burdened with newly learned textbook theories they wished to prove or disprove. As a result, they didn't possess the patience necessary to watch many shoppers at great length to see what they actually do. Creative people, however—playwrights, artists, actors, novelists, a puppeteer—have proven to be perfect for this work. They have no theories to uphold or demolish, just open minds and boundless curiosity about what people do and how and why they do it. They are dispassionate yet avid observers with no agenda except for wanting to accurately document how human behavior plays out in the retail arena. They manage to see the forest, the trees and everything in between.

When we find someone with the temperament and the intelligence for this work, we first put them through a training session in our office. There's a lot to learn—how do I watch and simultaneously take notes, for instance, or how can I tell whether someone is reading a sign or just staring at the mirror next to it? We have to teach the most important tracker skill of all: How do I stand close enough to study someone without being noticed? Because it's crucial to our work that shoppers don't realize they're being observed. There's no other way to be sure that we're seeing natural behavior. Fact is, we're all still surprised by how close you can stand to someone in a store and still remain invisible. We find that positioning yourself behind the shopper is a bad idea—we all pick up on the sensation that we're being watched. But if you stand to the side of a shopper, his or her peripheral vision reads you as just another customer—harmless, in other words, and barely worth noticing. From that position you can get close enough to see exactly what a shopper is doing. You can be sure that he's touched, say, nine golf gloves, not eight or ten. Then we throw the tracker-hopefuls out into the real world, into a store setting, to see them in action. Most of them wash out at this point—you can teach technique, but not the smarts or the slight case of fascination required to do this work well. It's weirdly addictive, and many of our trackers have been with us for a decade or more.

John has been doing fieldwork for my company, Envirosell, for more than ten years, in between working as a kindergarten teacher. Trained to monitor five-year-olds, does he have patience? Oh, yeah. He also just completed his two-hundredth fieldwork assignment. He's of medium height, with brown hair, a spare build, crinkles in the corners of his eyes and big broad feet. He has no trouble standing all day. In our tracker pool, we also have rookies who are still getting twenty trips under their belts, intermediate-level trackers, master trackers, team leaders . . . and Noah, who, after thirteen years of tracking and team leading, now directs the forty-plus members of our tracking staff based out of our home office in New York City. We found Noah in Nashville. He was a last-minute replacement, a struggling music student who three hours into the job had found his calling. The first time he walked into my office he was dripping with nervous sweat (he'd never been to New York before). Thirteen years later, I still can't break him of the habit of calling me Mr. Paco.

In addition to measuring and counting every significant motion of a single shopping trip, our trackers also have to contribute incisive field notes describing the nuances of customer behavior and make good inferences based on what they've observed. These notes add up to yet another, this time anecdotal, layer of information about a particular environment and how people use it. Our trackers crisscross this continent, as well as the globe. As of 2008, we have offices in Mexico City, São Paulo, Milan, Bangalore, Moscow and Tokyo, and each office has its own tracker pool. All across the world, Envirosell trackers spend more time in stores in a month than most people do in several years. They visit every kind of retail business imaginable, from banks to fast-food restaurants to high-end fashion boutiques to hangar-sized discounters.

Since 1997, we've worked hard to expand our repertoire of field sites, adding concert halls, stadiums, train stations and airports as well as libraries, museums, hotels and websites (more about those later). But our sweet spot remains what we've always done. Of the world's fifty largest merchants, we've worked with approximately half, and in the U.S. alone, our clients include more than a third of *Fortune* magazine's top one hundred corporations.

As for the forms our trackers use? They're also marvels of data gathering. They have evolved constantly over the three decades we've been doing this research and are, without a doubt, the key to the entire enterprise, a great achievement, if I may say so, in the art of information storage and retrieval, nondigital division. We have tried scanning systems, exotic software packages . . . and we keep going back to the same old system. It works, it's flexible, and thanks to Wite-Out and a copy machine, it can be changed on a dime and on the fly. Our ability to react to what and whom we find walking through the door of wherever location we go is critical to our success. I'd guess that at least one third of the time we go on location, we end up finding something very different than what our client told us we'd find. The store has six aisles and not seven, the shelf layout has been mysteriously reversed or that interactive machine we were hired to study arrived at the store nearly a month ago and hasn't worked since.

Our earliest track sheets were able to record maybe ten different variables of shopper behavior. Today we're up to around forty. The form is reinvented for every research project we undertake, but typically it starts with a detailed map depicting the premises we're about to study, whether it's a store, a bank branch, a parking lot (for a drive-thru project) or just a single section—even just one aisle—of a store. The map shows every doorway and aisle, every display, every shelf and rack and table and counter. Also on the form is space for information about the shopper (sex, race, estimate of age, description of attire) and what he or she does in the store. Using the system of shorthand notation we've developed over the years, a combination of symbols, letters and hash marks, a tracker can record, for instance, that a bald, bearded man in a red sweater and blue jeans entered a department store on a

Saturday at 11:07 A.M., walked directly to a first-floor display of wallets, picked up or otherwise touched a total of twelve of them, checked the price tag on four, then chose one, and moved at 11:16 to a nearby tie rack, stroked seven ties, read the contents tags on all seven, read the price on two, then bought none and went directly to the cashier to pay. Oh, wait, he paused for a moment at a mannequin and examined the price tag on the jacket it wore. We'd mark that down, too, just as we'd note that he (the man, not the mannequin) entered the cashier line at 11:23 and exited the store at 11:30. Depending on the size of the store and the length of the typical shopper's stay, a tracker can study up to fifty shoppers a day. Usually we'll have several trackers at a site, and a single project may involve the simultaneous study of three or four locations. For huge stores like a home improvement center or a mass merchandiser, we may put ten or twelve trackers on the floor.

By the end of a job, an incredible amount of information has been crammed onto those sheets. They come back to the office, where an experienced clerk spends another day or so typing all the information, every single notation on every track sheet, into a computerized database. Over the years, we've spent tens of thousands of dollars and countless frustrating hours with computer programmers, trying to come up with a database that could handle the kind of work we do. The big problem is that while we crunch the same numbers in the same ways from job to job, each project usually requires us to do something a little differently—to collect different kinds of data or to devise new comparisons of facts we just uncovered. We've hired fancy consultants who spend six months at a crack with us, trying to build us a computer system. They ask us to list everything we want our program to do, but every week we add six new things to the list that negate all their work from the previous month. And of course, our turnaround time has to be swift, so there's no time to change the system completely for each job— we may need to do one new comparison for a project today and then not have to perform that function again for seven months.

In the early '90s, Microsoft Excel came along. Where had it been all my life? It was designed as a spreadsheet program, intended for accountants to do the relatively simple calculations they require. But

Excel's beauty was its open architecture—you could get in there under the hood and tinker, soup it up, make it purr. It also had a fairly simple way of writing macros, or lines of code, that allowed you to make the alterations easily. Today, while we still use Excel, we've moved on to other programs like Access and SPSS—but for years, Excel made our work possible. It's as though Microsoft built a very nice bicycle, which we then turned into a data-busting all-terrain vehicle. When Microsoft became a client and we showed them what we'd done with Excel, they were amazed.

When the videotapes come back from the sites, it's someone else's job to screen every bit of footage. Depending on the size of the store, we may have ten cameras running eight hours a day trained on specific areas—a doorway, for example, or a particular shelf of products. The video produces even more hard data. If, for example, a client wants us to determine in part how a particular cash register design affects worker fatigue, we may use the video and a stopwatch to time how long it takes for a clerk to ring up a sale at ten A.M. as compared to four P.M.

The list of particulars we're capable of studying—what we call the "deliverables"—grows with every new project we take on. At last count, we've measured close to a thousand different aspects of shopper-store interaction. As a result of all that, we know quite a few facts about how human beings behave in stores. We can tell you how many males who take jeans into the fitting room will buy them compared to how many females will (65 percent to 25 percent). We can tell you how many people in an IBM employee cafeteria read the nutritional information on a bag of corn chips before buying (18 percent) compared to those lunching at Subway (2 percent). Or how many browsers actually buy computers on a Saturday before noon (4 percent) as opposed to after five P.M. (21 percent). Or how many shoppers in a mall housewares store use shopping baskets (8 percent), and how many of those who take baskets actually buy something (75 percent) compared to those who buy without using baskets (34 percent). And then, of course, we draw on all we've learned in the past to suggest ways of increasing the number of shoppers who take baskets, for the science of shopping is, if it is anything, a highly practical discipline concerned with using research, comparison and analysis to make stores and products more amenable to shoppers.

Because this science is being invented as we go along, it's a living, breathing field of study—meaning we never quite know what we'll find until we find it, and even then, we sometimes have to stop to figure out what it is we're seeing. Yes, for a lot of work now, after more than thirty years we have a good sense of what we are going to find, but what makes the science of shopping interesting is that things change and we still get surprised. I like to think of retail as the dipstick of our evolution. As we change as a species, those changes show up both in how we shop and what we shop for. That said, there are constants that relate to what we are biologically, and much of this book is about those constants.

For example, we discovered a phenomenon that journalists love to report—what's become known as the "butt-brush" effect—completely as the result of a happy accident. As part of a department store study, we trained a video camera on one of the main ground-floor entrances, and the lens just happened also to take in a rack of neckties positioned near the entrance, on a main aisle. While reviewing the tape to study how shoppers negotiated the doorway during busy times, we began to notice something weird about the tie rack. Shoppers would approach it, stop, and shop until they were bumped once or twice by people heading into or out of the store. After a few such jostles, most of the shoppers would move out of the way, abandoning their search for neckwear. We watched this over and over until it seemed clear that shoppers—women especially, though it was also true of men, to a lesser extent—don't like being brushed or touched from behind. They'll even move away from merchandise they're interested in to avoid it. When we checked with our client, we learned that sales from that tie rack were lower than they expected from a fixture located on a main thoroughfare. The butt-brush factor, we surmised, was why that rack was an underperformer.

And in fact, when we delivered our findings to the store's president, he jumped up from his chair, grabbed the phone, and ordered someone to move that tie rack to a spot just off the main aisle. A few weeks later, we heard that sales from the rack had gone up quickly and substantially. Since that day we've found countless similar situations in which shoppers have been spooked by too-close quarters. In every case, a quick adjustment was all that was needed. So the idea of a body bubble gets applied to shopping—and we can push the idea even farther. It isn't that we hate crowds. A teeming cluster of people can be exhilarating. At Yankee Stadium, or even a sale at the local fashion emporium, we show up expecting company, and a lot of it. Sure, we can get claustrophobic and sometimes even scared, but after all, we're the ones who put ourselves there. Where butt-brush kicks in big time is where we get bumped and we don't expect it.

Another such "accident" of patient observation and analysis happened during a supermarket study we performed for a dog food manufacturer. While staking out the pet aisle, we noticed that while adults bought the dog food, the dog treats—liver-flavored biscuits and such— were more often being picked out by children or senior citizens. After giving it some thought, we realized that for the elderly, pets are *like* children, creatures to be spoiled with sweets. And while feeding Fido may not be any child's favorite chore, filling him up with doggie cookies can be loads of fun. Parents indulged their little ones' pleas for treats here just as they did over in the cookie aisle.

Because no one had ever noticed who exactly was buying pet treats, however, they were typically stocked near the top of the supermarket shelves. As a result, our cameras caught children actually climbing the shelving to reach the treats. We witnessed one elderly woman using a box of aluminum foil to knock down her brand of dog biscuits. Move the treats to where kids and little old ladies can reach them, we advised the client. They did so, and sales went up instantly.

Even the plainest truths can get lost in all the details of planning and stocking a store. A phrase I find myself using over and over with clients is this: The obvious isn't always apparent.

While studying the cosmetics section of a drugstore chain, we watched a woman in her sixties approach a wall rack, study it carefully and then kneel before it so she could find the one item she needed:

concealer cream, which, due to its lack of glamour, was kept at the very bottom of the display. Similarly, in a department store we watched an overweight man trying to find his size of underwear at a large aisle display—and saw him stooping dangerously low to reach them, down near the floor. In both cases, logic should have dictated that the displays be tailored to the shoppers who use them, not to the designers who made them. Move the concealer up, we advised, and put something aimed at younger shoppers down near the floor. Young shoppers will find their products wherever they're stocked.

In some studies, we synthesize every bit of information we can possibly collect into a comprehensive portrait of a store or a single department. A major jeans manufacturer wanted to know how its product was sold in department stores, so in one weekend we descended on four sites, two in Massachusetts and two in the Los Angeles area. Each department was similar—the jeans section was a square area that held from eight to twelve tabletop displays and some wall shelving. We started by drawing a detailed map of each, showing the displays and the aisles leading into and out of the sections but also where any signs or other promotional materials were posted. During that weekend we tracked a total of 727 shoppers and observed many more on camera. We paid particular attention to the "doorways," our term for any path leading into or out of an area of a store. Until the client knew which paths were most popular, it was impossible to make informed decisions about where to stock what or where to place the merchandising materials meant to lure shoppers.

By the time our study was completed, we could say what percentage of customers used which paths into each of the sections. Once we knew that, it was clear, for instance, that much of the signage was misplaced—common sense dictated that it be positioned to face the main entrance of the store, when in fact most jeans shoppers came upon the section from a completely different direction. Even the client's big neon logo and a monitor showing rock videos were facing the wrong way if their job was to signal to the greatest number of shoppers. We tracked shoppers from table to table, seeing where they stopped, what signs they read, whether they noticed the video monitors, and how they handled the merchandise, including if they took anything to the dressing rooms. If they seemed to be showing jeans to a companion, we noted that, too. Our interviewers also questioned some of the shoppers captured on video so that their demographic information and their attitudes and opinions could be correlated with their behaviors—to see, for example, whether young shoppers with high school educations who say they depend on brand name when choosing jeans read price tags. After the research is done and the numbers are crunched and analyzed, we see what sense can be made of what we've learned.

For example, if we were to find that a high percentage of male shoppers buys from the first rack of jeans they encounter, and that these shoppers tend to enter the section through the aisle leading from men's accessories rather than from the women's side of the store or from the escalator, then we would advise our client to ask for the display table nearest men's accessories.

Or maybe there's another determining factor—maybe men who are accompanied by females and entering the section from the women's department buy more jeans than men who are alone. In that case, the best table would be nearest the women's merchandise. But no one knows for sure until we collect the data.

In other instances, we're hired to study some small retail interaction in great detail. A premium shampoo maker who wanted to know about the decision-making process of women shoppers who buy generic, or store-brand, beauty products commissioned one such project. The client was interested in the "value equation" women bring to each shopping experience—how does the shopper who buys from the generics section at the supermarket in the morning and then from Bloomingdale's in the afternoon decide which product she'll buy where? Does she judge that her skin deserves the premium brand but her hair can settle for the generic? Once upon a time, only the budget-conscious bought store brands, but now you find them in everyone's shopping basket. What's the secret?

Let's call her shopper number 24, a thirtysomething woman in yellow pants and a white sweater, accompanied by a preschool-age girl, who enters the health and beauty aisle of a supermarket at 10:37 A.M.

on a Wednesday morning. She has a handbasket, not a shopping cart, and has already selected store-brand vitamin C capsules and a large container of Johnson's baby powder. She is also holding a shopping list and a store circular. She goes directly to the shampoo shelves and picks up a bottle of Pantene brand, reads the front label, then picks up a bottle of the store brand and reads the front label, then reads the price tag on the Pantene, then reads the price on the store brand, and then puts the store brand in her basket and exits the section forty-nine seconds after she entered it. In that brief encounter, there was lots of data to collect—what she touched, what she read, and in what order—about twenty-five different data points in all. If, in one day, we track a hundred shoppers in that store's health and beauty aisle, it amounts to twenty-five hundred separate data entries. As the woman exits the section, we interview her, asking twenty questions in all. So each of the twenty-five data points has to be cross-tabulated with each of her twenty answers—a cross-tab challenge, take it from me. Until quite recently no university ever attempted such a study, and so it was left to the world's businesses—its retailers, banks, restaurant chains, manufacturers and designers of displays and packaging—to underwrite the creation of this science, which they did and continue to do by hiring us and sending us out into the field.

I make much of the accidental nature of the science of shopping, and perhaps it's because this all began almost by accident when I was a student and admirer of one of America's most esteemed social scientists, William H. Whyte, author of such highly influential books as *The Organization Man, The Last Landscape, City: Rediscovering the Center* and *The Social Life of Small Urban Spaces.* He was also the founder, in 1974, of the Project for Public Spaces, or PPS, which still exists and is still a magnificent contribution to the preservation and ongoing good health of the urban landscape.

William H. Whyte, or "Holly," as his friends called him, was, in his active days, a quixotic, beloved figure (he died in 1999). He had the white hair and aristocratic mien of a WASP banker, yet he had fallen in love with the streets of New York City and worked hard to learn how people might best use them. Whyte's greatest contribution was his research into how people use public spaces—streets, parks, plazas and so on. Using time-lapse photography, hidden trackers and interviews, he and his associates would stake out some urban plaza or minipark, say, and study it, minute by minute, over the course of several days. By the time they finished, they could tell you everything about every bench, ledge, path, fountain and shrub, and especially how people interacted with them, using them as places to lunch, sun, socialize, people-watch, nap or just happily and peacefully loiter. Whyte and his colleagues would measure everything—the ideal width of a ledge for sitting; how sunlight, shade and wind affect park use; and how a public space's surroundings, the office towers or construction sites or schools or neighborhoods, determined the quality of life there.

Whyte, who started his career as an editor at *Fortune* magazine, was, essentially, a scientist of the street—the first one, which is amazing when you think of how long streets existed before he came along. His work has been used to make public spaces better and more useful to citizens, which in turn made cities better and more useful, too. Whyte's methods were a kind of lens through which a physical environment could be studied and improved, and my work on behalf of shopping owes a great deal to his methods.

Back in 1977, I was a part-time instructor at City University of New York, teaching courses in fieldwork techniques for the environmental psychology department. I was also working in an establishment of which I was part owner, the Ear Inn, a bar in downtown Manhattan. There, I had a customer who had been hired to design a system of signage at Lincoln Center, the performing arts complex that's home to the Metropolitan Opera House, Avery Fisher Hall—about a dozen theaters in all. He told me they needed someone to look into the usage and circulation patterns of the underground concourse that connected the buildings to parking garages and the subway. There was a small, makeshift gift shop down there at the time, but Lincoln Center wanted to see if a larger store might be viable there. First, though, they needed to make sure that a store wouldn't create congestion in the pedestrian walkways. With my customer's help, I got the job.

So I recruited a few of my students to help and we took some cameras, staked out our observation spots and went to work counting and mapping. The crowding question was easy enough to answer—we roped off an area exactly the size of the store they wanted to build, then watched and filmed pedestrians streaming through during the busiest times. We suggested then that with the room available, they should add some benches down there, to make it something of a destination rather than just a corridor. Our client declined to take our advice then, but today the benches are in place. I also strongly recommended that they double the size of the ladies' room, and they declined to take that advice, too. Today, thirty years later, the line at the ladies' room still goes out the door during busy times. Shameful.

As I was compiling the data to write the report and looking at the many hours of film I had shot, I realized that from one of the camera positions I could see inside the gift shop, all the way to the cash register. There, as I watched, two customers lined up to pay. One looked to be a wealthy woman, probably an opera-goer, who had piled a small tower of boxes on the counter. Next to her was a teenage girl whose purchase required just one small brown paper bag. I couldn't see enough to tell exactly what was going on, but I was intrigued.

I visited the shop the next day and talked to the clerk, who told me that the woman was the wife of a Mexican diplomat who had decided to buy some fancy music boxes as gifts to take home with her. The boxes were expensive, and she was buying about a dozen of them, for a total sale of close to $9,000. She needed to pay quickly, before intermission ended, and she had to arrange to have the boxes delivered to her. There was also the matter of having sales tax waived owing to her diplomatic status. A complicated transaction, to say the least.

But this had to wait while the clerk handled the transaction with the teenage girl, who had arrived at the register first bearing her selection— a ballerina pen.

It was clear even to an academic like me that the cash register procedure could stand a little reorganization and clarification. These two transactions should not be competing for the same clerk's attention. And then the lightbulb clicked on. Why not take the tools of urban anthropology and use them to study how people interact with the retail environment?

Years earlier I had witnessed an argument between the esteemed sociologist and author Erving Goffman and Jack Fruin, the chief engineer of the Port Authority of New York and New Jersey, who was at that moment in the midst of a gigantic undertaking, the planning and construction of Newark International Airport. Jack was expressing his emphatic frustration with the world of academia; he had attempted to hire some scholar-experts to guide his engineers and architects in their work, but instead of the clear-cut advice he had hoped to receive, he was getting buried under the academics' typical inability to assert any fact, no matter how small, that hadn't been completely proven by research. Goffman held the intellectual high ground in their argument, but at one point I clearly remember thinking, *I'd have a lot more fun working for Jack than for Erving. Erving's hiding in his ivory tower. Jack is out there* doing *stuff.*

Not long after the Lincoln Center assignment, I was sitting with some friends at a nightclub in Greenwich Village. One of the guys at our table was a young executive with Epic Records, a division of CBS, and I described to him my bright idea of measuring what happens in stores—the thought that there might be something worth learning by turning scientific tools on shopping. And over the course of a few beers my idea must have sounded interesting, because the guy said, "Why don't you send me a proposal?"

Full of ambition the next morning, I rose early, dragged out my manual typewriter and drafted a plan. I sent it over quickly, then waited. For, oh, about a year. Of course I tried writing again and telephoning during that time, but no one ever returned my calls. These were the dark ages of the science of shopping, remember.

And then, out of the blue, I heard from a woman who was in charge of market research for CBS Records. She said that they had found my proposal in a dusty file somewhere and were all quite fascinated by it, and was I still interested in studying a record store?

Sure, I said, inwardly rejoicing that a major American corporation was actually going to underwrite—to the tune, I think, of about $5,000—my research into the habits of the modern shopper. I immediately called a few of my students, assembled some notebooks and time-lapse cameras, and made my way to a record store in a northern New Jersey mall.

Now, nearly decades and close to two million hours of videotape and much personal observation later, that study seems almost charmingly rudimentary. But at the time, it felt as though the discoveries came flying fast and furious.

For instance: In the late '70s, when the study was being done, traditional singles—45 rpm records—were still big sellers. The store, wisely, displayed the *Billboard* magazine chart of bestselling singles near the racks of records, as a stimulus to sales. But our film showed that most buyers of 45s were adolescents—and the chart was hung so high on the wall that the kids had to stand on their toes and crane their necks to see what exactly was at the top of the chart. We suggested to the manager that the chart be lowered, and a week later he called to say that sales of 45s had gone up by 20 percent. Just like that! Lower the chart! It worked!

We spent a lot of time that weekend watching people in line to pay at what the retail industry calls cash/wraps. Regardless of what store designers and merchandise managers think, in many ways the cash/wrap area is the most important part of any store. If the transactions aren't crisp, if the organization isn't clear at a glance, shoppers get frustrated or turned off. Many times they won't even enter a store if the line to pay looks long or chaotic.

At this store, there were several big displays of new releases as soon as you walked in, just a few feet from the cashier. This was fine as long as the store was empty, but if customers were in line, their bodies completely hid the displays. Put up a stanchion and a velvet rope to keep the line off to one side, we suggested, and again, our advice had an instant effect—sales of records from the displays went up immediately.

Doesn't all this sound just the least bit obvious? It does to us, too, especially after we've spent so much time watching and filming and timing and interviewing and so on. Until then, however, these were the kinds of problems that had remained hidden in plain view.

While watching the record store customers, we noticed an odd pattern: The LP section (this was pre-CD, remember) was always more crowded than cassettes, but sales were split evenly between the two formats. Following customers, the reason became clear: Because the LP covers were bigger, it was easier to read the song lists and see the photos, so cassette shoppers would browse in LPs, make up their minds, and then go to the tapes section to find their choices. Our suggestion was to make the aisles wider in LPs so that shoppers wouldn't feel crushed and rushed, a definite sales killer. Also, we thought the store should invest in more durable carpet for the sections that got significantly more traffic.

My final memory from that study comes from a video clip I still show to audiences: a young man shoplifting classical music tapes. Only after watching him take the tapes over and over on the film did I notice that the bag he slipped them into was from a chain that had no location at that mall. I passed this tidbit on to the client's security executive and told him that they should be watchful whenever such "wrong" bags were spotted in their stores (remember, this was before security tagging). I got back a note saying that they had prevented several thousands of dollars in theft using that method of detection.

And thusly, a science was born.

Before the science of shopping existed, there were at least two other ways to measure what took place in a store. The most common way of viewing a store is to simply examine "the tape"—the information that comes from the cash registers, which tells what was bought, when and how much of it. This is how virtually every retail undertaking, from the largest, most sophisticated multinational chain to the corner newsstand, does it. It's a fine way to see how the store as a whole has performed this quarter, or this year, or on any given day, or even time of day, and is, in the end, the measure of a store's overall health and growth (or decline) that counts. But as a diagnostic tool, or as a way of figuring out what happens in the store and how, it is not very useful. Sales research records your victories; what it does not do is look at where you are losing. What hurts is when you get the shopper in the door, down the aisle and in front of the product, and for whatever reason, they don't buy. When businesspeople attempt to infer too much from sales data, it can be downright misleading. Here's a good example, from a chain drugstore in a Massachusetts mall. This was the first mall store owned by this particular company, and so management was eager to see the results. Based solely on total sales, our client was pleased overall, and in particular with how the aspirin section of the store was performing.

But based on all our many previous studies both of drugstores and of the aspirin category, one crucial figure was on the low side. The product conversion rate—the percentage of shoppers who bought—was below what we expected. In other words, plenty of customers stopped at the aspirin section and picked up and read the packages, but too few of them actually bought aspirin. And the conversion rate for aspirin is usually high—it's not the kind of product you idly browse; you tend to go to that aisle only when you're in need. So we spent some time specifically watching the aspirin shelves, and we trained a video camera on them, too.

Over the course of three days, a pattern emerged. The aspirin was displayed on a main aisle of the store, on the path to some refrigerated cases of soft drinks, which tended to draw a great many customers to that part of the store. That might lead one to expect that the aspirin would sell well, but just the opposite happened. The main customers for cold drinks were teenagers, and our observation showed many of them entering and making a beeline for the coolers. In fact, this was a favorite place for the mall's young employees to grab a quick cold soda during breaks.

These young shoppers were supremely uninterested in aspirin. The shoppers, often seniors, who *did* want aspirin stood a little nervously at the shelves, searching for their usual brand or figuring out which was the better deal while also trying to stay clear of the teenagers tearing down the aisle. In fact, a substantial number of aspirin shoppers became so irritated or thrown off balance by the teenagers that they would prematurely break off their browsing and walk away empty-handed. It was a modified version of the butt-brush effect—the shoppers weren't being jostled exactly, just a little rattled. You could see it plainly on the videotape—some customers were practically cringing and hugging the shelves, not the ideal shopping position. And when we timed shoppers, we found that they were spending less time at the shelves than our experience led us to expect.

This is something that comes up in our work all the time: A store has more than one constituency, and it must therefore perform several functions, all from the same premises. Sometimes those functions co-exist in perfect harmony, but other times—especially in stores selling diverse goods, like cold drinks and medicines—those functions clash. We also saw this in a Harley-Davidson dealership, where a roughly three-thousand-square-foot showroom has to make room for well-off male menopause victims looking to recover their virility by buying bikes, blue-collar gearheads who are there for spare parts, and teenage dreamers interested in the Harley-logo fashions. All three groups want nothing to do with one another. When a premises' functions clash, a way must be found to accommodate as many uses as possible. In this drugstore, we advised our client about what we had learned and suggested a counterintuitive move—that the aspirin be relocated to someplace off the main drag. Fewer total customers would come upon it, we knew, but more aspirin would be sold. When they moved the shelves, sales rose by 20 percent.

We performed research for a large bookstore that had recently put a big table of discounted books just inside the entrance, where every customer would see it first thing. And it performed admirably—almost everyone stopped for at least a cursory browse, and the percentage that bought at least one book was high. Which meant that, according to the cash register tape, the table was a resounding success.

Except that as we tracked shoppers, we found that the number who would go to the table and then travel through the rest of the store was lower than it should have been. In a case like this, every hour on the hour a tracker would hurry through the entire store and note how many shoppers were in each section, including the register area, the coffee shop and so on. This is the density check that we perform as part of every store study, and it tells us a great deal: It gives an instant snapshot of the store's population and where people are drawn or not; it suggests when something about the architecture or the layout may be inhibiting shoppers from visiting certain areas; and it shows how shoppers move (or fail to) through the premises. And in fact, taken section by section, the number of shoppers who were penetrating the rest of the store was uniformly down. Also, our track sheet maps of customer travels began showing a telltale shallow loop—shoppers would enter, hit the bargain table, then maybe visit one or two more displays, but they never strayed far from the front of the store before heading to the cashier. This was no coincidence, needless to say—customers were choosing from the discount table, then going directly to the register, paying for their bargains and leaving without even browsing the bestsellers or any of the other books selling at the normal profit margins. Our shopper interviews turned up an unfortunate side effect, too: Thanks to the prominence of the bargain table, the store was gaining a reputation as a discounter rather than as the place to go for the hot new book. The success of the table was causing the failure of the rest of the store.

So much for what can be learned from the register tape.

The second means of learning what goes on in a store, employed by the most famous names in market research (whether political, commercial or any other) is simply to ask people questions about what they just saw, or did, or considered doing. That can happen in person, online, on the phone or in a focus group—it's all about asking people what they think.

Let's take a telephone poll conducted by the Democrats and the Republicans, for instance, or just the shopper interviews that take place as you exit a store or a shopping center. After a long list of questions, some basic demographic information is taken (age, education, income, sex, race and so on). From those two, a big fat binder full of suppositions is assembled: Forty-year-old Caucasian college-educated married mothers of two living in Northeastern suburbs and driving station wagons would prefer Jif even more if it were low-fat, for example. Or men who buy Coke at convenience stores say they would notice their brand less often if it were any color but red. Or one quarter of all college graduates eats pasta once a week. The possibilities for cross-referencing are endless, and there is undoubtedly some marketing wisdom to be gotten from such studies. But they don't really reveal much about what happens in a store, when shoppers and goods finally come together under the same roof. There are surveys that do ask customers for information about what they saw and did inside a store, but the answers are often suspect. Sometimes people just don't remember every little thing they saw or did in a store—they weren't shopping with the thought that they'd have to recall it all later. In a fragrance study we performed, some shoppers interviewed said they had given serious consideration to buying brands that the store didn't carry. In a study of tobacco merchandising in a convenience store, shoppers remembered seeing signs for Marlboro even though no such signs were in that store.

If we went into stores only when we needed to buy something, and if once there we bought only what we needed, the economy would collapse—boom.

Fortunately, the economic party that started the second half of the twentieth century has fostered more shopping than anyone would have predicted, more shopping than has ever taken place anywhere at any time. You almost have to make an effort to avoid shopping today. Stay out of stores and museums and theme restaurants and you still are face-to-face with Internet shopping twenty-four hours a day, seven days a week, along with its low-rent cousin, home shopping on TV. You have to steer clear of your own mailbox, too, if you're going to duck all those catalogs.

As a result, every expert agrees, we are now dangerously over-retailed—too much is for sale, through too many outlets. The economy even at its strongest can't keep up with retailing's growth. Judging from birthrates, we're generating stores a lot faster than we're producing new shoppers.

In 2008, across most of the first world, we are building stores and malls no longer to serve new customers but to steal someone else's. There is no irony that the cutting edge of retail today is no longer found in North America or Western Europe. Moscow, Dubai, Shanghai and Mumbai are the newest retail hot spots—places where money is young, economies are booming and you have a whole lot of pent-up demand.

Still, here in the United States, our focus has been on same-store sales—how can you do more business in the same space or location? That focus on tactics has been another accelerant that has fueled the growth of the science of shopping.

There's another reason that the science of shopping is a force today.

Generations ago, the commercial messages intended for consumers' ears came in highly concentrated, reliable forms. There were three TV networks, AM radio only, a handful of big-circulation national magazines, and each town's daily papers, which all adults read. Big brand-name goods were advertised in those media, and the message got through loud, clear and dependably. Today we have hundreds of TV channels, and remote controls and TiVo to allow us to skip all the ads if we choose to. There's FM and satellite radio now, a plethora of magazines catering to each little special interest, a World Wide Web of infinitely expanding sites we can visit for information and entertainment, and a shrinking base of daily newspaper readers, all of which means that it is harder than ever to reach consumers and convince them of anything at all.

Simultaneously, we are witnessing the decline of the influence of brand names. A generation or two ago, you chose your brands early in life and stuck by them loyally until your last shopping trip. If you were a Buick man, you bought Buicks. If you were a Marlboro woman, you smoked Marlboros. You chose your team—Coke or Pepsi, Kenmore or Whirlpool, Zest or Ivory—and stayed with it. Today, in some ways, every decision is a new one, and nothing can be taken for granted.

What all that means is that fewer buying decisions are being influenced outside the premises of the store. And many more of those decisions are being made in the store itself. It means that shoppers are susceptible to impressions and information they acquire inside stores, rather than relying on brand-name loyalty or advertising or marketing to influence what they buy. The level of impulse purchasing is going through the roof—in supermarkets and everywhere else, too. Even big decisions are being made right there on the selling floor.

As a result, the most important medium for transmitting messages and closing sales is now the store and the aisle. That building, that place, has become a great big three-dimensional advertisement for itself. Signage, shelf position, display space and special fixtures all make it either more or less likely that a shopper will buy a particular item (or any item at all). The science of shopping is meant to tell us how to make use of all those tools: how to design signs that shoppers will actually read and how to make sure each message is in the appropriate place. How to fashion displays that shoppers can examine comfortably and easily. How to ensure that shoppers can reach, and want to reach, every part of a store. It's a very long list—enough to fill a book, in my opinion.

Finally, our studies prove that in general, the longer a shopper remains in a store, the more he or she will buy. And the amount of time a shopper spends in a store depends on how comfortable and enjoyable the experience is. Just as Holly Whyte's labors improved urban parks and plazas, the science of shopping creates better retail environments—ultimately, I would argue we're providing a form of consumer advocacy that benefits our clients as well.

When I started work on this book in 1997, Envirosell was a pioneer in the world of stores and commercial environments. Ten years later, the term "science of shopping" is part of the vocabulary of any merchant or marketer. And a lot of firms now claim to do what we do. After all, observation is a seminal form of how human beings learn, so why not start an observation business? To every company that has copied what we do, I welcome you to the community of people dedicated to making our lives work better. At the same time, there are other interlopers who have truly muddied the waters.

The first? Technology companies that have streamlined data collection. They have software packages that can hook up to a facility's surveillance cameras and count bodies, one after another. How relevant is it to measure the number of people passing a sign or a display? Does that mean they've looked, read or shopped? As I sit at my desk on the corner of Twentieth Street and Broadway in New York City, I have a stream of technology companies coming in to showcase their latest cutting-edge products. How many times have I heard the expression "This is going to transform retail"? Most of it is what I call technology in search of an application. It can do this and gather this piece of information, and there's bound to be someone out there willing to pay for it.

Or I get a call from someone begging me for an hour and I agree to meet them, but before we do there arrives a seventeen-page nondisclosure agreement, or NDA. I have to explain that if someone hires me I'm happy to sign documents left and right, but to call me out of the blue and expect me to review a seventeen-page legal document borders on the obnoxious. Over the years I've come up with a good plan. I'll meet for an hour with anyone who wants to show me something and I'll give that person my honest response—if he, she or the company gives a $750 donation to the charity of my choice. I've raised tens of thousands of dollars for halfway houses for homeless women in New York.

Some of the stuff I get is outright silly, like a software package designed to track tank movements from spy satellites. Put enough cameras with wide-angle lenses into your ceiling and voilà!—instant science of shopping. Quite a few of these companies are backed by serious venture capital money and propelled by slick presentations, expensive Las Vegas dinners at the appropriate conventions and lots and lots of promises. The venture capital firms see them not as research or consulting firms but as software ventures. Once in place, the output is automated; you sign a two-year contract that promises you weekly reports. The only problem is that two months later, you look up from yet another weekly report and ask, what in the world do we do with this? We have a number of clients who defected from us and bought a fancy software package only to return to us two years later. We were happy to have them back.

The other objection I have is with what we around the office call Envirosell Lite, where untrained and inexperienced people are sent into the field to do the same work we do: observe what is seen, what is touched, what is read. Simple as it sounds, these terms have to be defined carefully or what you get out the other side of the process is gobbledygook. We now have a number of competitors who sell a lower-priced version of what we do. You get what you pay for.

———

TWO

What Retailers and Marketers Don't Know

I t might be useful right about now to pause and look at the science of shopping from the perspective not of the scientist but of the practitioner—that is, the retailer and marketer. He or she is certainly part of the equation we're studying, the provider of product services and shopping experiences, as it were. The retailer is also the one who's expected to absorb all our lessons and then apply the principles of what we've learned. The marketer needs to understand how his or her product or category of goods is shopped and bought. And since it's his or her own store we study, it's fair to ask: How much doesn't the retailer already know?

Well, more than you might think. For example, it's a testament to the until-recently uncharted state of the untamed retail environment that an extremely intelligent and able man, a senior executive in a multibillion-dollar chain, could be so very wrong when asked this simple question:

How many of the people who walk into your stores buy something?

You'd know that, wouldn't you, if you were he? You'd think so, and trust me, this fellow is no slouch in the knowing department. He knows quite a bit that goes on in his chain's thousands of stores, and he learns more on a daily basis—genuinely important things like total tickets (the number of transactions *and* their dollar value), and average sale amount, and sales in any given store compared to sales on the same day the year before, and sales within the various regions, and profitability by item and category and store and maybe even phase of the moon.

He knows all that.

When I asked how many of the people who walk into his stores buy something, his answer was: all of them, pretty damn near. And when I say it was his answer, I mean it was also the answer of the huge, PC-networked, data-chewing, number-crunching, cipher-loving organization at his command. Everybody there agreed: What we call the conversion rate—the percentage of shoppers who become buyers—was around 100 percent. After all, this corporation reasoned, their outlets were destination stores, so people didn't go there unless they had some very specific purchase in mind. Hence, they believed, the only time shoppers *didn't* buy was when their selection was out of stock.

In fact, the very concept of conversion rate, implying as it does that shoppers need to be somehow transformed—"converted"—into buyers, was alien to this man and this corporation (as it still is to many other successful companies and executives).

I was asking the question because we had just performed a large-scale study of this chain's stores. And I knew the conversion rate, based on our having spent hundreds of hours counting, among other things, the number of shoppers who entered and the number who made purchases. It was a very good conversion rate for stores of this kind. But it was about half of what this man thought it was. To be precise, 48 percent of shoppers bought something.

The man, because he believes in the value of information, was taken aback but eager to hear more. Some in his organization, though, were incredulous, outraged, insulted, and certain that we had made a terrible miscalculation. So they performed their own homegrown version of our study, standing at the door of a store or two, counting the number of people who went in and the number who emerged holding bags.

Their result was identical to ours. Which, in the end, was very positive news for them. It meant that a good company could change some very specific things and become even better. If you talk to the executive, he'll say that our study brought about "a fundamental change in some of the long-held beliefs and opinions of this company." At any rate, they've begun to do some things differently in store layout, display, merchandising and staffing, and I have no doubt that they'll improve their conversion rate and make more money as a result.

Our findings were also important to that company's big picture. We showed that meaningful growth—which Wall Street demands and everybody else is pretty fond of, too—can be stimulated at the store level, without having to expand the empire, an expensive strategy that always runs out of gas sooner or later. In 2007, same-store sales are the bellwether for a chain's good health.

The marketer was equally in the dark through the end of the twentieth century. Until the past decade, there was sales data or the compilation of register tapes. Today, however, almost all major consumer product companies have shopper- and consumer-insight groups. They often fiercely debate the difference between what happens to people in the store (shoppers) and what happens once they get their products home (consumers). All in all, insight groups have been a positive change. Yet for the marketers sitting in their suburban campuses, there are often some pretty striking disconnects. In 2008, it is easier to collect data than to figure out what it means, much less map out what you can or should do about it. Since the science of shopping was invented, there are now a lot of companies talking about the scale of their databases—we tracked a million shoppers with security cameras and so on—yet, in the end, what does it mean? To me, ten years after I wrote the first edition of this book, the rightful evolution of the science of shopping is for a corporation to look at what they do with this information and, based on whatever measure they use, ask themselves: Did it make or save us money?

Let's go back to the basics. Conversion rates vary wildly depending on what kind of store or product we're talking about. In some sections of the supermarket, the conversion rate probably *is* around 100 percent (I'm thinking of dairy or toilet paper here). In an art gallery or high-end jewelry store full of big-ticket items, maybe one shopper in a hundred will buy something, and that's plenty. Whatever's being sold, though, I think it's impossible to dispute that conversion rate is a critically important measure of performance. Marketing, advertising, promotion and location can bring shoppers in, but then it's the job of the merchandise, the employees and the store itself to turn them into buyers. Conversion rate measures what you make of what you have—it shows how well (or how poorly) the entire enterprise is functioning where it counts most: in the store. Conversion rate is to retail what batting average is to baseball—without knowing it, you can say that somebody had a hundred hits last season, but you don't know whether he had three hundred at-bats or a thousand. Without conversion rate, you don't know if you're Mickey Mantle or Mickey Mouse.

Yet conversion in its simplest form has its limits. In the past ten years a number of companies have rigged up electronic counters on the doorways of stores, then hooked them up to the register. Voilà—instant ongoing conversion rates. Yet the real story is often hiding in the details. What's the difference between men and women? What happens when you add a kid to the process, or an African- or Latino-American? That counter at the door counts bodies, and that's all it counts, never mind the fact that it's unlikely a family of four will walk out of a store lugging four big-screen TVs, one per person. Yes, some of the more upscale ones can calculate body mass and get some gauge on people's gender, but I wouldn't bet the farm on it. We get a lot of calls from companies that installed counting systems, and three months into the daily stream of data, they're still wondering how they can turn that information into an ongoing, proactive, workable tool. For store managers it can be frustrating when the home office fires off numbers, and they respond, "Well, of course we have lower conversion numbers, because we get more casual, time-killing people in the door; as you might notice, we're located next to a kitchenware store and thus attract an entire army of exiled male spouses."

Still, a great many businesspeople don't know from conversion rate. It's not one of the ways of measuring a business that business schools emphasize. It's not about profit margins or return on investment or money supply or any of that. It's all about what happens within the four walls of the store.

I can think of other underutilized ways to measure what happens inside a store. Once I asked a major cosmetics executive how much time women actually spent shopping for makeup per store visit.

"Oh, about ten minutes," he said.

"Hmm," I replied, knowing from the study we had just completed for him that the average shopper spent two minutes in the cosmetics section. The average shopper who bought something spent only thirty seconds more. Putting it into broader context, the average supermarket visit is about twenty-five minutes, including checkout. The average time spent in a hypermarket, or multidepartment store—whether a Wal-Mart Supercenter in the U.S., a European Carrefour, or a Pick n Pay in Cape Town, South Africa—is about thirty minutes. That's stopwatch time. But if you ask someone how long he or she spent in a store, that person will often double that number. In any commercial setting, time comes in three forms. There's real time, there's perceived time and then there's a combination of the two.

Now, the amount of minutes a shopper spends in a store (assuming he or she is shopping, not waiting in a line) is again an important factor in determining how much she or he will buy. Over and over again, our studies have shown a direct relationship between these numbers. If the customer is walking through the entire store (or most of it, at least) and is considering lots of merchandise (meaning he or she is actually looking and touching and thinking), a fair amount of time is required. In an electronics store we studied, nonbuyers spent five minutes and six seconds in the store, compared to nine minutes and twenty-nine seconds for buyers. In a toy store, buyers spent over seventeen minutes, compared to ten for nonbuyers. In some stores buyers spend three or four times as much time as nonbuyers. A great many factors contribute, one way or the other, to the length of a shopping trip, and studying them is most of what we do. The majority of the advice we give to retailers involves ways of getting shoppers to shop longer. But you've got to know how long people spend shopping your store or your product before you can know how to increase it.

The flip side of that measure is what we call the confusion index, or the number of people walking around stores completely at sea. Remember that time is relative, so if the ten minutes you spend at a Target or Wal-Mart is spent walking in circles, it'll feel like you've been in there for a half hour. And in the end, while you may stumble on something good, if you can't find what you came in for, what's the point? One of the major victories we have won in the past ten years has been with office product superstores. In 1997, whenever Staples, OfficeMax or Office Depot opened a new location, they used a warehouse format. Shelving ran twelve to fifteen feet in the air—making it a challenge, to say the least, for customers who didn't shop the store every week to find stuff. In many aisles, a third of the people there weren't shopping for anything in that aisle. They were browsing, or killing time, or, far more often, they were utterly clueless as to where the computer paper was stacked. All too many shoppers found what was on their list and left. Staples was the first superstore to make changes based on our suggestions. They developed what we call an "arena concept," where the aisles in the middle of the store are low and get gradually higher as customers reach the perimeter. The change, I have to say, is pretty remarkable. You walk in . . . and even in a large store you see everything. The full monty. Almost no one walks down a particular aisle who doesn't want to be there. OfficeMax and Office Depot have come up with their own versions of an arena. In some cases, same-store sales are up 20 percent or higher. Do the new stores hold people longer? You bet, and the time customers spend there is considerably happier.

Here's another good way to judge a store: by its interception rate, meaning the percentage of customers who have some contact with an employee. This is especially crucial today, when many businesses are cutting overhead by using fewer workers, fewer full-timers and more minimum-wagers. All our research shows this direct relationship: The more shopper-employee contacts that take place, the greater the average sale. Talking with an employee has a way of drawing a customer in closer.

We studied a large clothing chain where the interception rate was 25 percent, meaning that three quarters of all shoppers never spoke a word to a salesperson. That rate was dangerously low—it meant that in all probability customers were becoming frustrated, wandering the stores lost or confused or just in need of information, trying (and *trying*) to find a clerk with an answer. It also meant that employees couldn't have been spending much time actively selling anything. They were stocking the shelves and ringing up transactions and not finding time to do much in between. This was practically a guarantee that the store was under-performing. It was also a telling clue as to why.

Across the world we, as a species, like to be recognized, but we also value our privacy. One of our clients has a rule that if an employee gets within six feet of a customer, that employee has to say hello. I don't like the rule because it takes the judgment out of the hands of the person working the floor—but I do like the idea behind it.

Here's another measure, a real simple one: waiting time. This, as we discuss elsewhere, is the single most important factor in customer sat-isfaction. But few retailers realize that when shoppers are made to wait too long in line (or anywhere else), their impression of overall service plunges. Busy executives hate to wait for anything, but some don't real-ize that normal people feel the same way. One housewares chain's vice president was startled when we showed him video in which a woman who had just spent twenty-two minutes shopping in his store joined a very long checkout line, stood there until it dawned on her that she was in cashier hell, and abandoned her full cart and exited the place. We weren't surprised—we see this happen all the time. We once did a job for a bank that was about to institute a policy where customers made to wait five minutes or more would receive $5. After studying the teller lines over the course of two days, we informed the client that this policy would cost them about triple what they had set aside. They dropped the plan and went to work on shortening the wait.

One final calculation doesn't involve any particular way to measure a store, but it's a remarkable example of businessperson ignorance: They often don't really know who their shoppers are. I've already discussed the pet treats manufacturer whose product was typically stocked high on shelves, unaware that its main buyers were old people and children. We studied a chain of family-style restaurants whose outlets had too many tables for two and not enough tables for four, which caused head-aches during busy times—all because no one had ever bothered to count the size of dining groups. In another family-style chain we studied, each restaurant devoted roughly 10 percent of its floor space to counter seat-ing. During slow times it went unused because lone diners preferred tables, where they could read newspapers or magazines. During busy times it went unused because parties of two, three or four wanted to sit at tables. The counters were empty even as groups of diners stood in line waiting for tables.

The issue of retailers not knowing who shops in their stores comes up all the time. A newsstand in Greeley Square here in New York wanted to increase sales and planned to do so by expanding the space devoted to magazines. We pointed out that a large percentage of his customers was either Korean—the square borders on a large Korean enclave—or Hispanic. Stock Korean-language magazines (Korean papers already sold well) and soft drinks popular in the Latino market, we advised, and when they did, sales rose immediately.

This related issue comes up all the time in New York, Los Angeles and other big cities: foreign shoppers in need of a break from stores and restaurants. Almost no accommodation is made for Asian shoppers, despite their numbers and tendency to spend a lot of money on luxury goods. But there are no sizing conversion charts, no currency exchange rates posted, not even a little sign or two in Japanese or Korean telling shoppers which credit cards are accepted. Smart retailers would reward employees who learned a little Japanese, German, French or Spanish—even just a handful of phrases would make a difference, as anyone who has shopped in a foreign country would realize. Restaurants should have menus in Japanese and German on hand.

But it doesn't have to involve anything so exotic for retailers to be woefully clueless about who's in their stores. I loved visiting a national chain drugstore's branch in Washington, DC, where there was a large assortment of dye and other hair products for blondes—in a store where over 95 percent of shoppers are African-Americans. I also was amused in a Florida-based drugstore chain's Minneapolis branch, where a full as-sortment of suntan lotion was on prominent display—in October.

II

**Walk Like an Egyptian:
The Mechanics of Shopping**

The first principle behind the science of shopping is the simplest one: There are certain physical and anatomical abilities, tendencies, limitations and needs common to all people, and the retail environment must be tailored to these characteristics. Our technical term for it is "the biological constants."

In other words, stores, banks, restaurants and other such spaces must be friendly to the specifications of the human animal. There are all the obvious differences in shoppers due to gender, age, income and tastes. Going outside North America, we face other issues, too—the relative density of a population, the weather, security considerations, a country's economic well-being and so on. But, that said, there are many, many more similarities. This fact—and the accompanying thought that any built environment (whether it's a hotel, a stadium, an airport, a hospital, even a home or an apartment complex, much less a store or bank) should reflect the nature of the beings who must use it—seems too obvious to bear mentioning, doesn't it? After all, who designs and plans and operates these premises but human beings, most of whom are also at one time or another shoppers or users themselves? You'd think it would be easy to get everything right.

Yet a huge part of what we do is uncover ways in which environments fail to recognize and accommodate how human machines are built and how our anatomical and physiological aspects determine what we do. I'm talking about the absolute basics here, such as the fact that we have only two hands and that at rest they are situated approximately three feet off the floor. Or that our eyes focus on what is directly before us but also take in a periphery whose size is determined in part by environmental factors, and that we'd rather look at people than objects. Or that it is possible to anticipate and even determine how and where people will walk—that we move in predictable paths and speed up, slow down or stop in response to our surroundings.

Whether I'm in Tokyo or Paris, Cape Town or Orange County, California, whether I am two hundred centimeters tall (read six feet, five inches) or five foot four, our basic human measures fall into a completely predictable range. I can be Chinese, Indian or Mexican—it doesn't matter. Everywhere in the world, our eyes work and age in the same way.

The implications of all this are clear: Where people go, what they see and how they respond determine the very nature of their experience. They will either see merchandise and signs clearly or they won't. They will reach objects easily or with difficulty. They will move through areas at a leisurely pace or swiftly—or not at all. And all of these physiological and anatomical factors come into play simultaneously, forming a complex matrix of behaviors that must be understood if any environment is to adapt itself successfully to our animal selves.

The overarching lesson that we've learned from the science of shopping is this: Amenability and profitability are totally and inextricably linked. Take care of the former, in all its guises, and the latter is assured. Build and operate a retail environment that fits the highly particular needs of shoppers and you've created a successful store. In the five chapters that follow, we'll see how the most elemental issues—the holding capacity of the human hand, the limits to what a being in motion can read, even the physical needs of the nonshopper—matter in determining the shopping experience.

Take that same model and you'll notice it applies to every physical environment you interact with.

THREE

The Twilight Zone

Stop.

Stay here with me a minute. Don't ask. Just watch.

I *know* we're standing in the middle of the parking lot. That's the point.

Do you notice how everybody's moving at a pretty brisk clip toward the store? Is it because they're all so darned excited to be going there? Well, maybe, but I've spent a lot of time watching people move through parking lots, and this is how they all do it—fast. A parking lot isn't the place for a leisurely stroll. It's not Fifth Avenue, or even Main Street. It's speeding cars, exhaust fumes and asphalt, with the usual elements on top—rain, wind, cold, heat.

Okay, so let's join everybody rushing for the store. What do you see ahead? Windows. And what's in them? Stuff. Or is it signs? Or is it stuff *and* signs? It's hard to tell, exactly, because of how the sunlight glares off the glass. Or because it's dark out, and the lighting is too low. Most retailers don't change the lighting depending on whether it's day or night, meaning that visibility must be pretty bad during at least one of those periods, if not both.

For the sake of discussion, let's say we actually can tell what's in the windows: some kind of display—mannequins or a still life. Whatever it is, though, the scale is wrong. There are too many small things there that we can't quite see from this distance. Bear in mind, too, that the faster people walk, the narrower their field of peripheral vision becomes. But by the time we get close enough to see the goods or read the signs, we're in no mood to stop and look. We've got that good cardiovascular parking-lot stride going, and it's bringing us right into the entrance. So forget whatever it is those windows are meant to accomplish—when they face a parking lot, if the message in them isn't big and bold and short and simple, it's wasted.

Boom. We hit the doors and we're inside. Still got that momentum going, too. Have you ever seen anybody cross the threshold of a store and then screech to a dead stop the instant they're inside? Neither have I. Good way to cause a pileup. Come over here, stand with me now and watch the doors. What happens once the customers get inside? You can't see it, but they're busily making adjustments—simultaneously they're slowing their pace, adjusting their eyes to the change in light and scale, and craning their necks to begin taking in all there is to see. Meanwhile, their ears and noses and nerve endings are sorting out the rest of the stimuli—analyzing the sounds and smells, judging whether the store is warm or cold. There's a lot going on, in other words, and I can pretty much promise you this: These people are not truly in the store yet. You can see them, but it'll be a few seconds more before they're actually *here*. If you watch long enough you'll be able to predict exactly where most shoppers slow down and make the transition from being outside to being inside. It's at just about the same place for everybody, depending on the layout of the front of the store.

All of which means that whatever's in the zone they cross before making that transition is pretty much lost on them. If there's a display of merchandise, they're not going to take it in. If there's a sign, they'll probably be moving too fast to absorb what it says. If the sales staff hits them with a hearty "Can I help you?" the answer's going to be "No thanks," I guarantee it. Put a pile of fliers or a stack of shopping baskets just inside the door: Shoppers will barely see them and will almost never pick them up. Move them ten feet in and the fliers and baskets will disappear. It's a law of nature—shoppers need a landing strip.

The same thing is true in a hotel lobby. Put a directory too close to the front door, and the people behind the front desk will have to answer stupid questions 24/7. Throughout our work looking at the lobbies of business hotels, the lack of what we call an "information architecture plan" can have a disastrous effect on customer service. If the concierge or bellhop has to tell people coming into your hotel all day, every day where the bathroom is, well, I don't care how much training you give people, *you* try answering the same question five hundred times a week and see if you don't get cranky, too. The windows, the doorways and the landing strip are the start of the consumers' experience, and the same goes for hotel guests.

When I talk to clients, they invariably point to our findings on the transition zone, or what has been termed the "decompression zone," as among our most meaningful and useful work. It is also perhaps the most startling news we deliver. I think that's mostly because our counsel defies the most ingrained human yearnings about the front: We all want to be there, at the front of the pack, the head of the line, the top of the class. To the front-runner go the spoils.

In the retail environment, however, up front is sometimes the last place you want to be. For instance, retailers will charge manufacturers for placing their name on the front door, which sounds like a smart use of the marketing dollar—everybody sees the front door. And then you realize that when shoppers approach a door, all they're looking for is a handle and some sign indicating whether to pull or push. We've yet to see a shopper actually stop his or her progress to read a door. There's only one time when anyone pauses to study what's written there: when the store is closed. Which may be worth something, as marketing tools go, but not a lot.

Today many stores have automatic doors, which make life easier for customers, especially those with packages or baby strollers. But the effortlessness of entering only serves to enlarge the decompression zone—there's nothing to slow you down even a little. Revolving doors are even worse, as they actually thrust you into the store with a fair amount of momentum. Some stores, especially smaller ones, benefit from having the entrance provide more of a threshold experience, not less. Even a small adjustment—a slightly creaky door or a squeaky hinge—does the trick. Special lighting on the doorway also clearly marks the divider between out there and in here. Other stuff works too, like a change in flooring color or texture.

A big store can afford to waste some space up front. A smaller one can't. In either case, store merchandisers can do two sensible things where the decompression zone is concerned: They can keep from trying to accomplish anything important there, and they can take steps to keep that zone as small as possible.

A good lesson in what *not* to do with the entrance and decompression zone comes courtesy of a big, sophisticated company. In the early '80s, Burger King was testing a new salad bar. To introduce it with a bang, they decided that they'd switch the entrances and exits on many of their restaurants. Until then, the door closest to the parking lot was always the entrance. They turned that entrance into an exit and put the salad bar just behind the big window next to it, so you'd walk from your car, go to the old entrance, see the salad bar, and be so tempted by it that when you entered—through the *new* entrance—you'd head straight for the lettuce.

But here's what actually happened: Customers went to the old entrance and tried to find the handle, which had been removed as part of the reconfiguration. They would then back up, scratch their heads and begin searching for a way to get into the place. They weren't looking at the salad bar—they were too busy looking for a door! And once they found it, and burst into the restaurant feeling hungry and frustrated, all they wanted to do was find the counter and order their usual burgers and fries. In that atmosphere, the salad bar never had a chance.

Another bad idea for the decompression zone was invented at an athletic goods chain where management decreed that every incoming shopper had to be greeted by a salesclerk within five seconds of entering the store. Here's how that played in the real world: You'd walk in and come face-to-face with a lineup of eager clerks hovering just inside the entrance like vultures, ready to pounce with a hearty hello. There's an interesting curve here: Greet people too early and you scare them away. Talk to them too late and you get a whole lot of frustrated customers. In our work with Estée Lauder's cosmetic counters, we were able to plot this curve pretty precisely. Leave people alone for at least one minute. Let them play first, and then you go from salesperson to cosmetics coach.

We discovered another misuse of the zone a few years ago, when we tested an interactive computerized information fixture that had been designed for Kmart by a division of IBM. It had a touch screen and a keyboard, and you'd ask it where men's underwear was, for example, and it would give you a map of the store and maybe a coupon for T-shirts or socks. A terrific idea, executed well. It helped customers and spared the store from having to pay someone to stand behind a desk and tell people where boys' sweaters were seventy-two times a day.

It wasn't long, though, before store executives discovered a little glitch: Few shoppers used the fixtures. The problem was that no one admits, six steps into a store, that they don't know where they're going. At that point you haven't even looked around long enough to realize you're lost. Placing the computers too close to the door had turned them into very expensive pieces of electronic sculpture. The store gave up on them right away, but I'm certain they could have worked just fine—maybe a third of the way into the store, at about the point where customers really *do* realize they're lost.

What *can* you do with the decompression zone? You can greet customers—not necessarily to steer them anywhere but to say hello, remind them where they are, start the seduction. Security experts say that the easiest way to discourage shoplifting is to make sure staffers acknowledge the presence of every shopper with a simple hello. Wal-Mart founder Sam Walton's homespun advice to retailers was that if you hire a sweet old lady just to say hello to incoming customers, none of them will dare steal.

You can offer a basket or a map or a coupon. There's a fancy store in Manhattan, Takashimaya, where the uniformed doorman proffers a handsomely printed pocket-size store directory as he ushers you in.

Just to the right of the entrance, within the transition zone, is the store's flower department. As you enter, you see it from the corner of your eye, but you don't usually stop in—instead, you think, "Hmm, flowers, good idea, I'll get them on my way out." Which makes perfect sense, because you wouldn't want to shop the rest of the store carrying a bouquet of damp daisies.

Right inside the door of an H&M, Gap or Wal-Mart, there's what's known as a "power display"—a huge horizontal bank of sweaters, or jeans or cans of Coke, that acts as a barrier to slow shoppers down, kind of like a speed bump. It also functions as a huge billboard. It doesn't say, "Shop me." It says, "Just consider the idea." It serves as a suggestion, plain and simple, and it also gets you in the mood for the rest of the store. You can catch up with the product later, at another time, typically in another section of the floor. Remember that more than 60 percent of what we buy wasn't on our list. And no, this isn't the same as an impulse purchase. It's triggered by something proposing the question "Don't you need this? If not now, then maybe in the near future?" The power display of beverages may remind you of who's coming home from college next Tuesday, the sweater of fall coming or the chilly weather in Maine, where you're planning a getaway weekend—and lo and behold, you leave the store with two six-packs of ginger ale and a new fleece.

Another solution to the decompression zone problem, which I saw at Filene's Basement, is to totally break the rule. Not just break it, but smash it. There, just inside the entrance, they've placed a large bin of merchandise that's been deeply discounted, a deal so good it stops shoppers in their tracks. That teaches us something about rules—you have to either follow them or break them with gusto. Just ignoring a rule, or bending it a little, is usually the worst thing you can do.

I'd love to see someone try this out-of-the-box strategy: Instead of pulling back from the entrance, push the store out beyond it—start the selling space out in the parking lot. After all, football fans make elaborate use of parking lots even in the worst weather, barbecuing and eating and drinking and socializing on asphalt. Drive-in movies everywhere are turned over to flea markets during daylight hours, proof that people will comfortably shop al fresco. Some supermarkets bring seasonal merchandise out into the parking lot during summer; I visited one at a seashore resort that had all barbecue supplies, beach toys, suntan lotion and rubber sandals in a tent outfitted with a clerk and a cash register— allowing beachgoers to pull up, grab a few necessities and drive away, all without having to drag their wet, sandy selves through the food aisles and long checkout lines.

Pushing the store outside also begins to address an interesting situation in America, the fact that so much of the country has been turned into parking lots. Buildings can be put to a variety of uses—a clothing store can sell electronics or groceries or even be converted into office space. But our vast plains of asphalt will require more imaginative thinking. A few years ago, I visited a shopping mall in Johannesburg, South Africa, where they put a drive-in movie on the roof of one of their city's parking garages. Also in Johannesburg, I saw a display of Audis—every model car in every color an Audi can come in, some forty-seven cars in all, lined up in tight rows—and yeah, you bet, it was mobbed with people.

Our finding that being first isn't necessarily best actually extends beyond the decompression zone and into the store proper. In any section of a store, the first product customers see isn't always going to have an advantage. Sometimes just the opposite will happen. Allowing some space between the entrance of a store and a product actually gives it more time in the shopper's eye as he or she approaches it. It builds a little visual anticipation. Someone making a study of, say, the computer printer section of a store is highly unlikely to stop at the very first model and buy it with no further comparisons. By the time he reaches the midpoint of the printer section, though, he may feel confident and informed enough to decide. At trade shows, the booths just inside the door may seem most desirable, but they're pretty bad locations. Visitors zoom past them on their way into the hall, or, even worse, they arrange to meet friends by the entrance, thereby creating the (false) impression that there's a crowd at the first booth and scaring off genuine clients. Besides, just inside the door is usually drafty. It feels as though you're in the vestibule.

Cosmetics and beauty product firms don't usually want to occupy the first counter inside the entrance of a department store's makeup bazaar—they know that women, when reinventing themselves before a mirror, prefer a little privacy. That's not the only reason to wish for a little peace and quiet. If you were one of the two major players in the home hair coloring market, you'd want the best position possible in drugstores. Now, young women tend to buy hair color as a fashion statement— they've decided to go red for prom or they've been dreaming of that little extra glamour that being a platinum blonde creates. Older women, however, buy it as a staple—they've been using a particular color for fifteen years now, and more gray is coming in every day, so it becomes as regular a purchase as soap. As a result of that difference, older shoppers just find their color, grab it and go, while younger ones need to study the rack and the packaging awhile before they buy. In one study we performed for a shampoo maker, we found that older women shop for one third fewer products than their younger counterparts, 2.2 to 3.3. And so in a store where younger shoppers predominate, hair color will do best away from the bustle and the crowding, which usually means away from the front of the store. If most shoppers are older women, however, closer to the entrance is better for hair color—these shoppers won't be browsing for long anyway.

Finally, there's a famous (around our offices) story about a very elaborate and costly supermarket display for chips and pretzels—a handsome fixture featuring the cartoon character Chester Cheetah, who, aided by a motion-detector device, would say, "If you're looking to feed your face, you're in the right place," every time a shopper walked past. Frito-Lay, the fixture's owner, paid a great deal of money to have the displays stationed up front in supermarkets. They were effective—so much so that the greetings ran constantly, which soon maddened the cashiers who had to listen to the drawling voice for eight hours straight. Before long, at least one market's employees solved the problem neatly—they disconnected Chester, rendering him instantly agreeable but forever mute.

————

FOUR

You Need Hands

It's a chilly day and the shopper is a woman. What does that tell us?

It says that at the very least she's carrying a handbag, and that she's wearing a coat, which she'll probably want to remove once she's inside the store, meaning she'll have to carry that, too. God gave her two good hands. But she's shopping with one.

If she selects something, the free hand carries it. Now she's down to no hands. Maybe, if it's small and light, she can tuck the purchase under one arm. Perhaps she'll sling the handbag over a shoulder or forearm. Then she'll have . . . let's call it a hand and a quarter. If she picks one more thing, though, she'll run out of hands. Only an extremely motivated buyer will persevere. Human anatomy has just declared this shopping spree over.

This is a classic moment in the science of shopping. The physical fact (most shoppers have two hands) is fairly well known. But the implications of that fact go unimagined, undetected, unconsidered, unaccommodated, unacknowledged. Ignored.

The hand-allotment issue came up early in the science of shopping.

It was the late '70s, and I got a chance to pitch what I do to Eastern Newsstand, the largest operator of newsstands in North America. Boy—talk about a tough business. Long hours, early morning deliveries, plus a complicated system of returning all the papers and magazines that don't sell. My girlfriend at the time knew the wife of the boss, and I got my loafer inside the door as a cocktail-party favor, if memory serves. They treated me okay, but I remember they started off pretty skeptical, and who can blame them?

I did the work as a freebie. Though I wasn't paid, the experience taught me plenty, and it also set me up with the Newspaper Association of America, or NAA, with whom I've had a rewarding relationship for more than a decade.

The site they assigned me was a newsstand at that great crossroads of humanity, Grand Central Station in New York City. We pointed our cameras at the stand and watched it during the busiest times, the morning and evening rush hours.

The success of the business depended on one crucial task—the newsstand's ability to process large numbers of transactions during the periods when everybody is in a hurry, either rushing from train to job in the morning or from job to train at night. Commuters on the run glance over at the newsstand to see how crowded it is. If it looks as though they can breeze in, buy a paper or magazine or cigarettes or gum and then be on their way, they'll stop. If it looks swamped with customers waiting to pay and nervously checking their watches, they'll keep going. They'll say to themselves, "Too much of a hassle, I'll miss my train, it'll be faster to get it elsewhere."

The other related fact of newsstand life we noticed was that every customer had one hand already occupied, either with a briefcase or a tote bag or a purse or a lunch. Almost no one goes to work empty-handed nowadays. When you think about it, it's a rare moment in the modern American's life when both hands are completely free. Yes, we have backpacks and messenger bags, but those simply allow us to turn ourselves even more into pack animals. Add to the mix a mobile phone, a coffee cup or the occasional ice cream cone, and in most commercial settings, at least half the people you see are moving with only one hand free. I might even venture to say that finding yourself with both hands free is a little disconcerting, as we immediately think we've left something behind.

The second (and kind of seminal) observation we made was painfully simple: Since 90 percent of us are right-handed, we use our left hand for carrying stuff, or our left shoulder for a shoulder bag—which frees up our right hand for grabbing. Pause for a minute. Let's assume you're reading this book while sitting in an airport waiting to board a plane. As you stare at the concourse, take a quick poll of right- versus left-handed luggage or briefcase carriers. It should be about six to one. The reasons why we might carry a bag in our right hand may be based on weight, size or some other environmental factor. Eliminate those, and the ratio might be even bigger. So whether you're selling newspapers, trying to get someone to pick up a brochure or designing the check-in desk at an airport or rental car location, a right-handed bias has significant implications (apologies to all you southpaws out there).

The final factor in our study was the stand itself, which was of typical design—a low shelf where the day's newspapers went, above which were racks for magazines, above which were shelves holding candy and chewing gum and mints, and inside the circular structure, above it all, the cashiers.

Thanks to the videotape, we could break each transaction down into its smallest components. Here's what we saw: Carrying your briefcase, you'd approach the stand, bend and pick up, say, a newspaper. Then you'd straighten up and brandish the paper so the clerk could see your choice. At that point you'd either put your briefcase on the floor or you'd put the paper under your briefcase arm, and, with your free hand, you'd hold out the money. (If you were a last-minute type, you'd have to reach into your pocket, find the money, and hand it over.) You would then stand tilting slightly toward the clerk, waiting with free hand outstretched for your change. The change goes into the pocket and you pick up your briefcase—or the paper goes from the briefcase armpit to the free hand—and then you turn and depart, squeezing through the rest of the throng trying to buy something.

The stand's designer obviously believed that the best possible structure was the one that displayed the most merchandise. Maybe the stand's owner believed that, too. But from the customer's point of view, the design was all wrong. There should have been a shelf at about elbow height—someplace where customers could rest their briefcases or purses or purchases while digging out their money and waiting for change. A counter, in other words.

Instead, the only shelf was at about shin height, which displayed newspapers just fine but turned each transaction into an awkward ballet starring a tilted one-handed commuter. As a result, the typical purchase involved more steps than were needed and so required more time to complete—even split seconds add up—which in turn limited the number of transactions possible during rush hour. Which caused congestion, scared away customers, and ultimately cost the newsstand sales. A better design—one that took human anatomy into consideration—might have displayed less merchandise but accommodated more customers.

Almost thirty years ago, when I presented that study to a bored audience of newsstand executives, I got back the blankest of stares. Sometimes I wonder today whether if I'd taken it several steps further and done a calculation on lost revenue, or did a simple sketch and proposed a test, I would have gotten any more traction. In retrospect, one of the most important things to learn is this: How you present your ideas and information is just as—or more—important as the ideas themselves. Our present-day maps, charts, diagrams and Photoshopped pictures, along with video clips, help frame what we do and what we think our clients can do with this information. I believe passionately in edutainment—whether in front of a business audience, a classroom of students or a crowd of parishioners at church. Laughter and knowledge combined make up one powerful cocktail, and if you can mix in some pictures and images, all the better.

We've done studies on fast-food restaurant drive-thrus and worked out the same equation. The speed of transactions is especially important at drive-thrus because the line of cars is so much more apparent to potential customers than the line inside the restaurant. Particularly in North America, where the steering wheel is on the left, we use our left hand to grab our burger and fries and pay at the payment and pickup window. A ten-second reduction in average transaction time during a busy lunch rush contributes almost immediately to the bottom line.

That woman I began this chapter by describing could have been shopping at a big discount drugstore like Walgreens. It was during a study we did for one such chain that we thought of one simple but very effective solution to the hand shortage.

The eureka moment came on a sultry August night in my office as I listened to the Yankees on the radio and watched videotape of people shopping in the drugstore. I was viewing footage from the camera we had trained on the checkout line, witnessing a shopper trying to juggle several small bottles and boxes without dropping any. That's when it dawned on me: The poor guy needed a basket.

Why hadn't he taken one? The store had plenty of them, placed right inside the door. Maybe people don't associate drugstores with shopping baskets. Perhaps they come in thinking they need just one or two items and only later do they realize they should pick up a few more things. The biggest culprit, of course, was the decompression zone—the baskets were so close to the entrance that incoming shoppers blew right by without even seeing them down there. I immediately began to scan all three days' worth of checkout line video and saw that fewer than 10 percent of customers used baskets, meaning there were quite a few amateur jugglers shopping at the store. And I thought, *If someone gave these people baskets, they'd probably buy more things! They wouldn't buy fewer items, that's certain.* But here we were, allowing the arm and hand capacity of human beings to determine, ultimately, how much money they spent.

We suggested that all drugstore employees be trained to offer baskets to any customer seen holding three or more items. My drugstore client gave it a shot. And because people tend to be gracious when someone tries to help, shoppers almost unanimously accepted the baskets. And as basket use rose instantly, so did sales, just like that.

We've made a direct link over the years between the percentage of shoppers using a basket or a cart and the size of the average transaction. Want people to spend more money? Make sure more of them are using a shopping aid of some kind. For a while the merchant community got the message but didn't quite grasp the subtext. What happened is the carts got bigger. From Wal-Mart and Target to Carrefour and Auchan in Europe, grocery carts swelled in size. In 2006, we noted that all across the world, whether in supermarkets, hypermarkets or mass merchant stores, the number of people using carts and baskets declined. "I'm just running in for a few things," people told themselves. *Not* taking a cart or a basket became a way for the customer to define his or her mission. And if customers were just running in for a few things, they didn't want to drive a Mack truck (read: large cart) up and down the aisles of the store. The problem was that shoppers picked up a few things, then found themselves face-to-face with the wine aisle, and look! there was their favorite pinot grigio on sale, two for one, and . . . now what do they do?

Our answer? Give customers a shopping aid strategy right at the door, when they first come in. Cart or basket? Then place other shopping baskets at strategic locations throughout the store. If no one bites, try another location. (We also recommend getting away from those Little Red Riding Hood plastic baskets. A great basket is one that a customer wants to either buy or steal. In this case, neither applies. Plastic baskets are clumsy and not very attractive, and for guys who don't see themselves making their way to Grandmother's house, they're almost an affront to masculinity. Plain and simple, we just need a better basket.)

Quite a few malls and stores have added carts with definite kiddie clout. You get the basket on top, while your junior Dale Earnhardt gets to sit in a model racing car below.

Earlier this year I was reviewing a new prototype Spar store in a train station in Milan, Italy. Spar is a European convenience store chain, like 7-Eleven in the U.S. You find them throughout Europe and in many emerging markets that were once European colonies. I was there with the president of Spar Italy. It was a good store. All across Europe, food-shopping in commuter train stations has taken a massive turn for the better. While the food offerings at Grand Central Station in New York are impressive and very high-end, and the small farmers' markets that have attached themselves to the BART stations in the East Bay of greater

San Francisco are a step in the right direction, the food offerings at the
Gare du Nord in Paris, Helsinki's Central Railway Station in Finland and
almost any train station in Japan put their North American counterparts
to shame. They're good, affordable and generally fast. In a train station,
however—unlike an airport, where we shop because we're trapped—
speed is critical. As a customer, your train is coming any minute, and
you need to get in and out. But from the merchants' standpoint, what's
important is to build the ticket or transaction. Thus, anyone shopping
without a shopping bag can only buy so much.

The president and I spent about an hour walking through the Milan
Spar. As I say, I liked the place a lot. It had great vegetables, a juicing
operation and a small bakery. Problem was, all of the baskets were clus-
tered by the front door. He asked me what the store could do to increase
performance. "Watch me," I said. I grabbed three baskets and moved
through the store. Each time I found someone with their arms full, I offered them a basket along with a nice smile. No one turned me down.

There are moments in this business when you see the lightbulb flick
on in people's minds. You can kick around simple ideas all you want, but
watching one happen in real time brings it all home. I'd seen the president smile over the course of the hour we'd spent together. But at that
moment, for the first time I saw him *grin*.

As the science of shopping evolves, my number-one worry is that as
we fall further in love with technology—with that sensor on the shopping card, with the software package that hooks up to a store's closed-
circuit cameras—merchants get duped into believing that sitting behind
a desk staring into a computer screen is an acceptable replacement to
getting out on the floor and taking a good look.

In a very successful bookstore near my office, a pile of shopping baskets sits in the usual erroneous place—in a corner just inside the door.
Judging by where the baskets are kept, you'd think that retailers think
that shoppers enter bookstores saying to themselves, "Well, today I plan
on buying four books, a box of arty greeting cards and a magazine, and
so first thing I will take a basket to hold all my purchases." But common
sense tells us that people don't work that way—more likely somebody
walks in thinking about one book, finds it, then stumbles over another

that looks worthwhile. In such moments the very heart of retailing lies. For many stores, add-on and impulse sales mean the difference between black ink and red.

Anyway, when our book shopper stumbles upon a second worthy volume, she then begins wishing she had a basket to make life a little easier. And if at that exact moment a basket suddenly materialized—in plain sight and easy to reach *without stooping*—then she would probably take one, and then, perhaps, go on to buy books number three and four. Maybe even a bookmark.

The lesson seems clear: Baskets should be scattered throughout the store, wherever shoppers might need them. In fact, if all the stacks of baskets in America were simply moved from the front of the store to the rear they would be instantly more effective, since many shoppers don't begin seriously considering merchandise until they've browsed a bit of it. The stack should be no lower than five feet tall, to make sure the baskets are visible to all, yes, but also to ensure that no shopper need bend down to get one, since shoppers hate bending, especially when their hands are full. A good, simple test on placement is that if you have to keep restocking a pile of baskets through the day, it's probably in a good place.

The baskets themselves also need to be rethought. This bookstore uses shallow, hard plastic ones with hinged steel handles, the same as supermarkets and convenience stores offer. They're perfect if you're buying bottles, jars or crushable items but make no sense for books, office supplies or clothes. When the contents grow heavy the handles become uncomfortable in your hand, but you can't sling the basket over your arm or shoulder, as common sense might wish you could. As a result, you don't want to let that basket get too full. How do we usually carry books? In bags, tote bags especially. A rack of canvas or nylon tote bags would be much better here and would have the added advantage itself of being salable merchandise. The clerk could unload the bag, total up the damages, ask if the customer wants to buy the tote and then reload everything and save on plastic to boot.

The cleverest use of baskets I've seen yet is at Old Navy on Seventeenth Street in Manhattan. While the Old Navy chain has had its ups and downs, whoever manages this particular store does a great job.

I take visiting retailers there—it's one of the liveliest, most energetic shopping experiences in the city. As soon as you step inside there's a gregarious, smiling employee greeting you and proffering a black mesh tote bag to carry your purchases. The bags are cheaper, lighter and easier to store than plastic baskets, and they look a whole lot better, too. In fact, when you bring yours to the checkout, the cashier will ask if you want to buy the bag, and a fair number of people say yes, adding one final sale at the last possible moment.

The least clever use of baskets was one I witnessed in a Southern department store during the Christmas season. There was a large rack of mesh totes perfectly positioned just inside the entrance. But some merchandising wizard decided to place in front of it an even larger display of stuffed Santas—rendering the bags totally invisible to entering shoppers. (Exiting shoppers saw them just fine.) I don't know how many Santas were sold, but it couldn't have been enough to offset that bad decision.

When we studied its stores, the dinnerware maker and retailer Pfaltzgraff was already providing baskets as well as shopping carts to its customers. But at the checkout, we noticed that many of the carts were filled to capacity with dishes and bowls and so on. The supersizing of grocery carts was a retail trend Pfaltzgraff hadn't yet acknowledged. The company immediately replaced the carts with new ones that were roughly 40 percent larger. Just as fast, the average sales per customer rose.

One of my favorite stores in the world is Vinçon, a design store in Barcelona, Spain. Every season they redesign their shopping bags. They are often funny, edgy and filled with social commentary. I am convinced that a high percentage of people shop there just to get hold of that season's shopping bag. How many times walking through Chicago or New York City do you see American Girl Place bags? That shopping bag marching happily through a community is a billboard you don't have to pay for.

This all serves as a reminder of one of the most crucial big-picture issues in the world of retailing: You can't know how much shoppers will buy until you've made the shopping experience as comfortable and easy and practical as possible.

There's a rather elaborate way of keeping customers' hands free that I'd love to see some retailer try. This plan would keep shoppers feeling 100 percent unburdened until it is too late—after they've reached the exits.

The idea would be to create a combination coat check/package-call system. Customers could unload all encumbrances as soon as they entered the store. And instead of carrying their selections around with them, they'd instruct sales clerks to dispatch the bags and boxes to the will-call desk near the exit. After a full session of vigorous, hands-free shopping, the customer would head for the door, pick up coat and hat and purchases, and be gone, into a car or taxi or waiting limousine.

In 2006 we started working for the park division of the brewing giant Anheuser-Busch, which operates Busch Gardens and various SeaWorlds across America. In the parks where we worked, the company had a system at every gift store where you could send your purchases up ahead to the main store at the gate. Ride the Flume, get your picture taken (and stamped onto a mug), send it on, then jump aboard the next ride, hands free. Whee! In theory, you could make purchases throughout the park and pick them all up on your way out the door. The problem? Customers typically found out about this service only after they had bought something, and even then it wasn't as clearly explained as it should have been. I wondered how many people moving through the park or browsing the gift stores didn't understand this service—and decided not to buy something, because who wants a personalized beer mug on your lap when you're riding the Tilt-A-Whirl? My point was that Anheuser-Busch needed to spell out this great service right at the park's entrance.

Sometimes even that might not be enough. A souvenir shop that we studied at Disneyland is still working on this problem. There, all day long the store is virtually empty, since visitors wisely don't want to lug their purchases around the park all day. But by 4:30 P.M. it's a madhouse of souvenir lust. A will-call desk was established so that shoppers could buy in the morning, leave the store empty-handed, and then drop by the will-call desk to retrieve their purchases at day's end. The only problem is that a great many shoppers forget to come by for their purchases.

My fullest vision of such a service was one I suggested to Bloomingdale's. In the flagship store in Manhattan, the eighth floor is not terribly well suited to selling, due to its hard-to-reach location. So I suggested that the floor be turned into a kind of semiprivate retreat for better customers, complete with attended restrooms, ATMs, a café, a concierge, and other similar amenities—including, of course, the coat check/will-call desk. If shoppers are just visiting New York, delivery could even be made to their hotels. In fact, I envisioned that membership in this semiprivate club could be sold to hotels, which would then pass along the benefits to their guests. This kind of service would actually be most profitable on an even bigger scale. Someday soon a mall or shopping center developer will institute such a system to serve all tenants, doing his part to drive up sales—and, of course, his or her own take, too.

It's hard to overemphasize the importance of the hand issue to the world of shopping. A store can be the grooviest place ever, offering the finest/cheapest/sexiest goods to be had, but if the shopper can't pick them up, it's all for naught. Later I will explain the crucial matter of touch, trial and other sensory aspects of shopping. If shoppers can't reach out and feel certain goods, they just won't buy. So it's not simply a matter of making sure shoppers can carry what they wish to take. They won't even get close to making that decision if their hands are full. It's why, in many cases, flat tabletop displays are better for showing apparel than hangers on racks: It's a struggle to examine something on a hanger if you've only got one hand free, while you can place your burdens on the tabletop and unfurl that sweater to get a good, close look and feel.

The most amusing manifestation of the hand issue was in a supermarket I visited. Like just about every retailer in America today, this market had decided to put in a coffee bar where shoppers could sit and drink if they wished. This wasn't the first coffee shop I'd seen in a supermarket, but it was the first one to truly understand how the whole thing should work: It had also put in cup holders on the shopping carts, meaning that you could drink and drive. That clever little touch sells coffee, I'll bet.

———

FIVE

How to Read a Sign

W ell," he says to me, "what do you think?"

And with that, the marketing executive unveils the sign that's about to go into five hundred or so stores.

I'm seated in a comfortable chair, in a climate-controlled conference room with perfect lighting. The sign is right in front of my nose, at the ideal viewing distance, beautifully printed on expensive paper, which has been exquisitely matted by professionals. There's a kind of hush all over the room.

"Gee," I answer, "I don't know what I think."

Worried glances all around. They're not worried about me—they're worried *for* me.

"What do you mean you don't know?" the executive asks. "You're *supposed* to know."

And that's when I try to explain.

I start by saying that unless every customer is going to come upon the sign, or more recently a flat-screen television display, under the exact same conditions that I first saw it, it's impossible for me to know if it's the greatest piece of communication ever designed or a tragic waste of time, space and money. I attempt to remind everybody that people in stores or restaurants or banks are almost never still; they're moving from one place to another. And they're not intent on looking at signs or flat screens—in fact, they're usually doing something else entirely, like trying to find socks, or seeing which line is shortest, or deciding whether to have the burger or the chicken. And there's that brand-new piece of communication, somewhere in the distance, off at a sharp angle, partially hidden by a tall man's head, and the lighting isn't so hot and there's a little glare coming into the store, and anyway somebody's talking to the customer and distracting her.

In other words, I end by saying, showing me a sign in a conference room, while ideal from the graphic designer's point of view, is the absolute worst way to see if it's any good.

To say whether a sign or any in-store media works or not, there's only one way to really assess it—in place. On the floor of the store.

Even there it's no picnic. First you've got to measure how many people actually looked at it. Then you've got to be able to say whether they looked long enough to read what it says, because if they're not reading it, even the best sign won't work. Now, the difference between an inadvertent glance at a sign and a thorough reading might be two or three seconds. So you can see what kind of challenge this is for our researchers. They've got to discreetly position themselves just so, behind the sign itself, and then watch a shopper's smallest eye movements while simultaneously keeping track of the stopwatch, just to be able to say with absolute scientific certainty that this man focused on that sign for four seconds, and then his eyes shifted to that poster and looked at it for four seconds. We watch shopper after shopper for hours on end, hundreds of people, thousands of minutes, and then assemble all our findings before we can say whether a sign is any good.

Go try. It ain't easy.

But after thirty years of doing this work, we're pretty confident about shooting from the hip, and most of the time we're right. There are some basic rules about typefaces, colors and layout. And we've learned some things as well about how what we call "on-location communication" interacts with circulation in different environments. But to really measure the success or failure of a sign, we need to put some alphanumeric values to it—17 percent notice the sign; of those, 12 percent bother to read it; and the average viewing time is 2.9 seconds— and the only real way of doing that is to put the thing in place and watch it.

There are companies that will measure sign readability by putting subjects into high-tech helmets that measure the smallest eyeball movements and holding signs before them. But even that won't tell you if you've put the right sign in the wrong place, which happens all the time (and which, by the way, is actually worse than putting a so-so sign in the perfect place). And it surely can't predict whether shoppers will read and respond to a sign on the floor of a store, where distractions abound.

But back to our conference room. The most common mistake in the design and placement of signs and other message media is the thought that they're going into a store. When we're talking signs, it's no longer a store. It's a three-dimensional TV commercial. It's a walk-in container for words and thoughts and messages and ideas.

People step inside this container, and it tells them things. If everything's working right, the things they are told grab their attention and induce them to look and shop and buy and maybe return another day to shop and buy some more. They are told what they might buy, and where it is kept, and why they might buy it. They're told what the merchandise can do for them and when and how it can do it.

A great big three-dimensional walk-in TV commercial.

And just as if scripting and directing a TV commercial, the job is to figure out what to say and when and how to say it.

First you have to get your audience's attention. Once you've done that, you have to present your message in a clear, logical fashion—the beginning, then the middle, then the ending. You have to deliver the information the way people absorb it, a bit at a time, a layer at a time, and in the proper sequence. If you don't get their attention first, nothing that follows will register. If you tell too much too soon, you'll overload them and they'll give up. If you confuse them, they'll ignore the message altogether.

This has always been so. The main reason it's so important today, as I mentioned earlier, is that more and more purchasing decisions are being made on the premises of the store itself. Customers have disposable income to spend and open minds, and they're giving in to their impulses. The impact of brand-name marketing and traditional advertising is diffuse now because we all absorb so much of it. The role of merchandising has never been greater. Products now live or die by what happens on the selling floor. You can't waste a chance to tell shoppers something you want them to know.

And shoppers are more pressed for time than ever. They're not dawdling like they used to. They've grown accustomed to stores where everything for sale is on open display, and they expect all the information they need will be out in the open, too. Nobody wants to wait for a clerk to point him or her in the right direction or explain some new product. Nobody can find a clerk anyway. Once upon a time you went into a coffee shop and the only thing to read was the menu and the *New York Post*. Now you go into even the smallest Starbucks and there are eleven distinct signage positions communicating everything from the availability of nonfat eggnog to the tie-in with Paul McCartney's latest album.

So you can't just look around your store, see where there are empty spots on the walls, and put the signs there. You can't simply clear a space on a counter and dump all your in-store media. Every store is a collection of zones, and you've got to map them out before you can place a single sign. You've got to get up and walk around, asking yourself with every step: What will shoppers be doing *here*? How about *here*? Where will their eyes be focused when they stand *here*? And what will they be thinking about over *there*? In this zone people will be walking fast, so a message has to be short and punchy—arresting. Over there, they'll be browsing around, so you can deliver a little more detail. In this area they'll be thinking about—oh, let's say we're standing near the motor oil shelf, so they'll be thinking about their cars. So maybe it's a good opportunity to tell them something about replacement windshield wipers. Over here by the registers they will be standing still for a minute and a half, a perfect window for a longer message. And then they'll be on their way out of the store, but you can use the exit path to give them a thought for the road.

Each zone is right for one kind of message and wrong for all others. Putting a sign that requires twelve seconds to read in a place where customers spend four seconds is just slightly more effective than putting it in your garage.

I'm forever walking around and adding to my mental list of places shoppers stand around doing nothing, where some message might be appropriate. One struck me the other day: In a shoe department, you tell the clerk what you want and he or she goes off to find your size. At that point you've already examined all the shoes, so what do you do? It's probably a good spot for a sign promoting other merchandise. You'd probably welcome something to read right then and there; maybe something about handbags.

One clever placement I've seen lately is the small signs tacked on the inside of bathroom stalls. It almost guarantees a 100 percent capture rate, and it's a place where you can get really creative with the message.

Here's another good spot for signs currently being neglected: escalators. That struck me as I ascended from the tracks on the Underground in London. There you spend a lot of time rising slowly past what used to be signs and are now flat screens. When someone asks me about a good application of digital signage I ask if they've ever ridden the Tube.

It isn't enough simply to figure out the general vicinity where a sign should go. We once studied shoppers who came upon a banner hanging directly over the cash/wrap area of a store. Good placement, no? No. A very low percentage of shoppers even saw it. Nobody stands around in a store looking straight up in the air. We recommended that the banner be moved four feet away, and the number of people who saw it doubled. When it comes to positioning a sign, the difference between an ideal viewing spot and a terrible one is often just a few feet or a ten-degree angle. For maximum exposure, a sign should interrupt the existing natural sight lines in any given area. So you've got to stand in a spot and determine: Where am I looking? That's where the sign goes. It's no surprise that the number-one thing people look at is other people.

That's why some of the most effective signs in fast-food restaurants are the ones sitting atop the cash registers—more or less at the level of the cashiers' faces. Smart sign placement simply tries to interrupt the shopper's line of vision and intercept her gaze.

Sometimes, though, you've got to get creative with message placement. Lawn mower manufacturing company Toro made an in-store video to promote its automatic-mulching mower. Naturally, they were placing them in home and garden supply stores, but where? In the mower section, where shoppers would see the monitors going but then realize that they'd have to stand still for ten minutes to watch the whole thing, and not only that, but they'd have to stand in the middle of an aisle and quite possibly get mowed down (and mulched) by shoppers on their way to barbecue accessories?

Instead, the video went into repair department waiting areas, where it played before captive audiences grateful for even the slightest distraction. Everyone who visits the repair department of a home and garden supply store is going to buy a new mower *someday*. For some reason, we find that even retailers who pile on the signs elsewhere will fail to appreciate the possibilities for communication in waiting areas, where people tend to be bored to tears. We once studied a car dealership's service area waiting room that offered not one word of reading material—not a single piece of promotional literature. Not an issue of *Car and Driver* or *Road & Track*. Not even an old *Reader's Digest*.

It's no secret that New Yorkers don't like to wait—we want our egg and cheese on a roll almost instantaneously after we order it; if we have to wait any longer than that, we're going to the deli across the street the next time. So I had to appreciate the popular upscale sandwich shop around the corner from my office, which cleverly offers the day's *New York Times* and magazines for varied interests in order to placate the customers, who are often waiting more than five minutes for their made-to-order slow-roasted pork and pickled-pepper relish delicacy.

Nobody studies signs like the fast-food industry. Even if you don't plan on owning a Burger God franchise, it's instructive to see how they do it.

They realize that you can put an effective sign in a window or just inside a doorway, for example, but it has to be something a customer can read in an instant. Just two or three words. We've timed enough people to know that such signs get, on average, less than two seconds of exposure per customer.

I was once asked to evaluate a door sign that had ten words on it.

"How much can you read in a second and a half?" I asked the designer.

"Three or four words, I guess," he admitted.

"Hmmm," I replied.

Fast-food restaurants used to hang all kinds of signs and posters and dangling mobiles in and around doorways to catch customers' attention fast, until studies showed that nobody read them. When you enter a restaurant, you are looking for one of two things: the counter or the bathroom.

There's no point in placing a sign for people on their way to the bathroom to see. They've got more important things on their minds. But a sign facing people as they leave the bathroom works just fine.

As people approach the counter, they're trying to decide what they're going to order. In the fast-food arena, that means they're looking for the big menu board. But they're not going to read every word on it—they're just going to scan until they see what they're looking for. If they're regular customers (as most customers are), they probably already know what they want and aren't even looking at the menu.

If there's a long line, customers will have lots of time to study the menu board and anything else that's visible. After the order is placed, the menu board and counter-area signs still receive prolonged customer attention. McDonald's found that 75 percent of customers read the menu board *after* they order, while they wait for their food—during the "meal prep" period, which averages around a minute and forty seconds. That's a long time, and that's when people will read almost anything— they've already paid and received their change, so they're not preoccupied. That's a perfect window for a longer message, something you want them to know for the next time they come. If we look at the aggregate of all menu board data, from fast food to deli counters in supermarkets,

61 percent of the total time someone spends looking at a menu board is done after they've ordered.

Then they either leave or they go to the condiments. You can place promotional materials over the condiment bar, though it's pointless to advertise burgers there—too late. But it's a good opportunity to tell diners something about dessert. This is a lesson in the logical sequencing of signs and fixtures. There's no point in telling shoppers about something when it's too late for them to act on it. For instance, it's a good idea to position signs for shoppers standing in line to pay, but it's a bad idea if those signs promote merchandise that's kept in the rear of the store.

After the condiment bar, diners go to their tables to eat. A few years ago, there was a move in the fast-food business to banish all dining area clutter—the hanging signs, mobiles, posters and "table tents" (those three-sided cardboard things that keep the salt and pepper company). That was a mistake, it turned out, one that was made because the store planners failed to notice what was going on in their own restaurants, specifically the social composition of the typical fast-food meal.

We tested table tents in two types of restaurants—the "family" restaurant, like Applebee's or Olive Garden, and the fast-food establishment. In the family place, the table tents were read by 2 percent of diners.

At the fast-food joints, 25 percent of diners read them.

The reason for that dramatic difference was simple: At family restaurants, people usually eat in twos, threes or fours (or families!). They're too busy talking to notice the signs. But the typical fast-food customer is eating alone. He's dying for some distraction. Give him a tray liner with lots of print and he'll read that. Give him the first chapter of the forthcoming Stephen King novel, and he'll read *that*. One of our clients, Subway, was printing napkins boasting of how much healthier their sandwiches were than burgers. Go a step further, we advised—print the napkins with a chart comparing grams of fat. In the seating area of a fast-food restaurant you can practically guarantee that customers will read messages that would be ignored anywhere else. There's an obvious role model: the back of the cereal box.

You can see, then, how a fast-food restaurant is zoned: The deeper in you are, the longer the message can be. Two or three words at the door;

a napkin filled with small type at the tables. I passed a fast-food place the other day with a perfect window sign. It bore this eloquent phrase: BIG BURGER. Only when you entered the place did you come upon another sign explaining the details of the teaser. (They were selling . . . big burgers.) That's smart sign design—breaking the message into two or three parts, and communicating it a little at a time, as the customer gets farther into the store. Thinking that every sign must stand on its own and contain an entire message is not only unimaginative, it's ignorant of how human brains operate. It even takes the fun out of signs—I can remember the Burma-Shave (an early shaving cream brand) billboards on the way to my grandfather's farm. It was the sequencing of the billboards that made them such icons of American humor.

This Shave
Is Like
A Parachute
There Isn't
Any Substitute
Burma-Shave

Another lesson in sign language comes courtesy of the United States Postal Service, for which we performed a huge study to help design the post office of today, complete with a self-service postal store and easy-to-use weighing and packaging stations.

In one of the prototype stores we studied, hanging behind the cashiers were large banners promoting various services. Fourteen percent of customers read those banners, our researchers found, for an average of 5.4 seconds each. There were also posters pushing stamp collecting hung on the walls to either side of the cashiers. Fourteen percent of customers read those, too, for an average of 4.4 seconds each.

Which is pretty good in the sign world. And not unexpected, because when you're in line at the post office, what else is there to do? The area behind or to the side of the cashiers is almost always the hottest signage real estate.

The post office also hung signs and installed electronic menu boards meant to be seen by customers using the writing tables. Those signs were read by just 4 percent of customers, for an average of 1.5 seconds each. Mobiles hanging over the weighing stations were read by just 1 percent of customers, for an average of 3.3 seconds each. Which was no surprise—when you're writing or weighing, you're not reading. Those signs were as good as nonexistent.

Banks also expend a lot of energy trying to figure out which signs work and which don't. Banks, fast-food restaurants and the post office have this in common: lots of customers standing still and facing the same direction—ideal opportunities for communication. The difference is that banks are some of the worst offenders in the art and science of sign placement. I can take you to branches of the world's biggest and most sophisticated financial institutions where placement of merchandising and informational materials is laughably inept. There are church bake sales and kiddie lemonade stands that exhibit better signage sense than some banks I can name. Five minutes from my office is a branch of Citibank where you can find this merchandising innovation: a cheap card table covered by the cheapest blue plastic tablecloth you've ever seen, atop which someone tossed some brochures for car loans and mortgages, joined by a TV monitor, once intended perhaps for showing in-branch videos but now unused and completely covered by a blanket of dust. The table is jammed into a corner in the front of the bank, just a few feet from the customer service desk. It's so bad that it's funny. A lot of bank signage can claim that distinction.

A California bank client decided—correctly—that it would be smart to promote its new free checking policy by hanging outdoor banners visible from the heavily traveled road beyond its door. And then it decided—incorrectly—that the banners should say PLEASE COME IN AND ASK A FRIENDLY BANKER TO EXPLAIN OUR WONDERFUL NEW FREE CHECKING POLICY or something to that effect. Drivers would have had to pull over to read the sign, it was so verbose. On a highway, two words—maybe something catchy, like FREE CHECKING—must be made to suffice.

We did a study for a Canadian bank that had just installed some very sophisticated backlit displays on the customer writing tables. These exhibits detailed the various services and investments the bank offered.

They were quite beautiful. Nobody read them.

Again, when you're filling out a deposit slip or endorsing checks, you're concentrating too hard to think about anything else. And once you've filled out the paperwork, you race to get into line.

We delivered our sad findings, and the bank's president said, "God, you just saved us from wasting about a million bucks on those damn things." He still spent the million bucks on in-branch media, of course— but on things that would make a difference.

It was also at a bank that we discovered one of our easiest and most effective fixes ever. We were hired to study all aspects of a bank branch, including the large rack that held brochures describing the money market funds, certificates of deposit, car loans and other services and investments offered. The rack was hung on the wall to the left of the entrance, so you'd pass it on your way in.

Everyone passed within inches of it. No one touched it.

Again, the reason seems obvious: You enter a bank because you have an important task to perform. Nobody goes into a bank to browse. And until you perform that task, you're not interested in reading or hearing about anything else. The fact that the rack was to the left side of the doorway, when most people walk to the right, only made it worse.

We took that rack and moved it inside, so that customers would pass it as they exited rather than entered, and we had a tracker stand there and watch. With no other change, the number of people who actually saw the rack increased fourfold, and the number of brochures taken increased dramatically.

Banks aren't the only places where task-oriented behavior must be reckoned with. We enter a drugstore intent on seeing the pharmacist and turning over our prescription, and we don't notice a single sign or display we pass until that mission is accomplished. Then we've got some time to kill, only we're in the rear of the store, and all the signs and fixtures are positioned to face shoppers approaching from the front. Or we've gone to the post office for a roll of stamps, and we're not slowing down until we've secured our position in line. Or we're at the convenience store, hot on the trail of barbecue starter fluid, and until we're sure they have it, we won't be distracted by anything else. In all those instances, it's futile to try to tell shoppers anything until after they've completed their tasks. So in that drugstore, for instance, two separate signage strategies must be mapped out—one for shoppers walking front to back, and the other for shoppers walking back to front, from the pharmacist to the front.

At a bank client's branch we studied there was a standing rack of brochures located in the general vicinity of the teller lines. But it was positioned a little too far away—customers standing behind the ropes could barely read the brochure titles, let alone grab them.

"Whose job is it to set up the ropes and stanchions and the brochure rack?" we asked the branch manager.

"Well," he said, "the cleaning woman mops up every night, and when she's through she puts all that stuff back on the floor." And sure enough, that cleaning crew didn't know squat about signage.

There's one arena of American life where sign design and placement isn't just a somewhat important issue, it's a matter of life or death. I'm speaking about our roads, especially our interstate highway system. There, signs are almost as important as surface and lighting to maintaining safe, well-ordered conditions. As a result, engineers make sure to get the signage right. The principles seem simple enough: no extra words; the right sign at the right place; enough signs so that drivers don't feel ignored or underinformed; not so many signs that there's clutter or confusion. The fact that you can be driving in a place you've never been and know for sure that you're heading in the right direction—without stopping for directions or even slowing down to read a message—is a testament to the power of a smart system of signs. Having driven all over the world, I can say that the American highway sign system is one of the best. The only one that might be a little better is the Swiss one. At least the Swiss do a better job of trimming the brush on the highway so you can read what's up there.

Look at the most common road signs in the United States: STOP and ONE WAY. A big red octagon with bold white capital letters—what else could it mean? If you couldn't read it, you'd still stop. ONE WAY is a perfect marriage of words and symbol—you catch it from the corner of your eye and you know what it means. The arrow keeps you going in the right direction without forcing you to slow down or even pause to read it. On the road we use a vocabulary of icons, the universal language that tells us what we need to know without words. When you see a sign with a gas pump, or a fork and spoon, or a wheelchair, you understand at a glance. That's the best way to deliver information to people in motion. Also on road signs, the technical aspects are usually perfect—the color combination provides enough contrast, the lettering is large, the lighting is good, and the positioning is just so.

Back in my urban geographer days I took part in a study of the directional signs in the underground concourse at Rockefeller Plaza in New York City. Down there you have no bearings except for what the signs provide, so they're very important. On film, we saw how people moved along until they began to worry that they were getting lost, or until they saw a fork up ahead where they'd have to choose a direction. Then you'd see their heads begin to swivel and their pace begin to slow. Just before that spot, then, was the logical place for a directional sign— something to head off their confusion and worry.

We also saw that their main concern was not to bump into other people while walking. So if they had to really scour the area for a sign, or if the type was so small that they had to get really close to read it, or the sign was small or badly placed, walkers would be torn between looking at the sign and watching where they were going. Any time pedestrians had to slow down or stop, we concluded, it was because the signs had failed to do their job. That's what really taught me the similarity between people walking and drivers driving—the best sign in either case is one you can read fast and is positioned so you can read it while moving. And the only way to achieve that, in most instances, is to break the information down into pieces and lay them out one at a time, in a logical, orderly sequence.

Of course, the only way we discovered all that was by watching lots and lots of pedestrians move through the space. Otherwise, all the signage decisions would have been made by the concourse planners themselves—the only people in the world who *didn't* need signs to find their way around down there.

I'm still trapped in this conference room.

So if I can't get out, I'll make life for this sign as difficult as possible. I'll put it on the floor, leaning against the wall, then I'll take ten paces away and see how it looks. I'll stand practically alongside it and see if it catches my eye. I'll stride by it at my normal pace and see if it registers. I'll turn down the lights. If the sign doesn't work in an imperfect world, it doesn't work. Believe me, real life is even tougher on signs than I am.

We're now arriving at a state of communication overload, and most of the problem is due to commercial messages. Little advertising stickers stuck to your apples and pears are either the cleverest thing ever or the most obnoxious defacement of God's bounty, depending on your point of view. There are too many words telling us too many things, and people are getting mad as hell and they're not going to read it anymore. Even as some opportunities for communication are being missed, many are being cluttered with so many messages that none stands out. One display or sign too many and you've created a black hole where no communication manages to get through.

Here's a personal example. I spend a lot of time waiting for planes in airports, and like most road warriors I work while I wait. Lately, though, my concentration is always being broken by Airport Network—the CNN-produced programming for air travelers. Try as I might, I can't find a way to have it turned off (a few years ago, I saw advertised online something that its maker claimed would allow you to turn off any public TV set, but every time I tried to log on to the site, it was down). Even when I'm the only person in the lounge, it must remain on. And so I quietly burn and vow never to watch CNN again. But there is a place in airports where even the busiest traveler stands around dumbly waiting rather than working: Near the baggage carousel, praying for luggage. There, before the suitcases begin to roll, we're all grateful to get a little Wolf Blitzer.

In general, the state of commercial messages is haphazard. Half of all signs that are shipped to stores, banks and restaurants never even make it onto the floor, according to one study. All over America, retail managers end long, tiring days by sitting in storage rooms, unloading huge cartons of signs and other point-of-purchase materials sent by a merchandising manager who may never even have seen their particular store. Believe me, those tired, overworked store managers aren't agonizing for too long over which sign goes where.

Once I went to a sales meeting of one of the world's largest manufacturers of carbonated beverages at which they ran a competition between different display manufacturers: How fast could they set up their point-of-purchase display designed for the front aisle of a supermarket? It was pretty comical. The teams were a bunch of twentysomethings clad in Ralph Lauren chinos and oxford shirts with the name of the company embroidered across their chests. The fastest time clocked was about three minutes. When asked for my commentary, I suggested they run the same competition at midnight, when the same teams had been working for twelve hours straight—oh, and it had to happen in a crowded back room under the lousiest possible lighting.

Conversely, once some signs make it onto the floor, it's hell getting rid of them. Every February I make a game of seeing how many liquor store windows still bear holiday-themed displays and signs. It's always quite a few. We once studied a major New York bank branch where bits and pieces of twenty-seven different promotions were all still evident. In a car dealership's window, we once found a sign announcing the arrival of new cars—the *previous year's* new cars.

Some signs are perfectly fine, except they're in places they were never intended to go. You'll pass a drugstore display window and see a stack of cough syrup boxes with a tiny sign showing the sale price, a sign that was obviously meant to go on the shelves, where shoppers are a foot or so away, not in a window facing a busy street. Often, retailers simply ask too much of a sign—more than any sign can deliver. A fast-food chain tested a sign system explaining one version of its "meal deals," then tried to make the signs clearer, then tested them again and fixed them again until they realized that it wasn't the signs that were bad—the meal deals were just too complicated to be explained. The deals were changed and the signs worked just fine. We did a study for a department store in the South that blanketed the place with signs announcing big discounts. The only problem was that you practically had to be a mathematician to figure out what you'd save. Even the sales clerks had trouble keeping all the percentages straight. That store didn't need signs to explain the discounts, it needed university textbooks.

The world of signs today is actually enjoying something of a renaissance. Just look at what's happened to billboards. Thirty years ago, Lady Bird Johnson was going to outlaw them as part of her American beautification scheme. Today, even in postliterate America, they're our most visually exciting, inventive and clever form of commercial expression. They're more stylish than print ads, hipper than TV commercials and more fluent in the language of imagery and graphics than anything you'll find on the web. Both the iPod and the Mini Cooper have used the billboard to their advantage. Billboards are to print ads what YouTube is to the Internet—the edge of the envelope, the lab for experimenting with new ideas in communication. Technology has given us three-part shifting billboards, video JumboTrons, rotating sports arena message boards and digital menu boards featuring flying french fries. At a fast-food restaurant we studied, a moving digital menu board panel was read by 48 percent of customers, compared to 17 percent for the same menu board—a nonmoving version—tested earlier. Those numbers have held up over many tests we've done comparing moving and nonmoving signs. But there's an underside to this data: While an "activated" sign attracts more than twice the number of eyeballs as a static sign, the amount of time people look at the thing stays the same.

But a sign need not be on the cutting edge of technology to leave an impression. Not long ago I entered the elevator of a hotel in the financial district in New York. On the wall was a mirror, below which were these words: YOU LOOK FAMISHED. And below that were the names and brief descriptions of the hotel's restaurants. I guarantee that sign gets close to 100 percent exposure and that everyone who sees it smiles, then checks in with their stomachs to see if they really *are* famished. A good sign.

SIX

Shoppers Move Like People

Anatomically speaking, the most crucial aspect of shopping is the one that looks the simplest—the matter of how exactly human beings move. Mainly, how we walk.

Now, people move pretty much as their bodies allow them to move, as is most natural and comfortable. This gets tricky only when you realize that a good store is by definition one that exposes the greatest portion of its goods to the greatest number of its shoppers for the longest period of time—the store, in other words, that puts its merchandise in our path and our field of vision in a way that invites consideration. It's fairly simple to measure whether a store accomplishes this or not: We simply chart the paths of shoppers and then determine which parts of the store are going undervisited. We routinely perform an hourly "plot" of a store—on the hour, a tracker quickly breezes through every part of the store, counting how many shoppers are in each. If a store's flow is good, if it offers no obstacles or blind spots, then people will find their way to every nook and cranny. If there's a problem with flow, some flaw in the design or the layout, then we'll find some lonesome corners.

The smart store, then, is designed in accordance with how we walk and where we look. It understands our habits of movement and takes advantage of them, rather than ignoring them or, even worse, trying to change them.

Here's a simple example: People slow down when they see reflective surfaces. And they speed up when they see banks.

The reasons are understandable: Bank windows are boring, and nobody much likes visiting a bank anyway, so let's get past it quickly; mirrors, on the other hand, are never dull. Armed with this information, what do you do? Well, never open a store next to a financial institution, for when pedestrians reach you they'll still be moving at a speedy clip—too fast for window-shopping. Or, if you can't help being next to a bank, you can make sure to have a mirror or two on your facade or in your windows, to slow shoppers down.

Here's another fact about how people move (in retail environments but also everywhere else): They invariably walk toward the right. You don't notice this unless you're looking for it, but it's true—when people enter a store they head rightward. Not a sharp turn, mind you; more like a drift.

One of the questions I'm asked a lot when I travel is, how much of this right-hand bias is based on how we drive? Do people in Japan, Britain and Australia, much less India, have this same drift-to-the-right tendency? Yes, there's a local effect. Go to the Tate Britain art gallery in London. The people circulating clockwise are locals and the people circulating counterclockwise are visitors. Say what you will about the English love of order, but to my eye an English store such as Selfridges or Harrods functions more schizophrenically than any store in New York City, where walking manners are important. All the bad ethnic jokes point to Brits having a history of crimes against nature. However, my British colleagues who teach environmental psychology tell me that if you yell "Fire!" in a dark movie theater, in Britain people will head automatically toward the door on the right. Generally, in retail, the traffic patterns in England mimic how they drive.

Japan? A case unto itself. People from Osaka walk differently than people from Tokyo. In Osaka people waft toward the right, in Tokyo they waft toward the left. My friend Kaz Toyota, who comes from Nara, a suburb of Osaka, explains the difference this way: In Tokyo people are overcivilized, while the folks in his hometown are more natural and free.

This right-leaning bias is a profound truth about how most humans make their way through the world, and it has applications everywhere, in all walks of life. It took us a while to see this pattern, and ever since we've collected data that bears it out (though not in Japan, apparently). But how can a retail environment respond?

We performed a study for a department store where just to the right of the entrance was the menswear department. And by our count, the overwhelming majority of shoppers in the store was female. Having menswear there meant that women shoppers would simply sail through the section, barely looking at the merchandise, determined to get to their main destination—ladies' clothing—first. In fact, because the front door was in the center of the store rather than to one side, our trackers charted lots of women who walked in, stepped right, looked around and saw that they were in menswear, then veered off sharply to the women's apparel sections on the left side of the store—never again to return to the right side, even to the right rear, where the children's clothing was displayed. Not coincidentally, our track sheets showed that children's clothing was the least-visited section in the entire store; fully half of the main floor was going undervisited due to this error in planning—because female customers never even saw it! An obvious solution to this adjacency mix-up would be to place the children's clothing section at the rear of the women's apparel section, rather than beside the neckties and men's bathrobes.

A similar situation held at an electronics store we studied. There, the cash/wrap was against the left-hand wall, near the front of the store. Shoppers would enter and head right, but then see the register and the clerks and turn sharply left so they could examine the merchandise there or ask where to find what they had come for. In some cases, those shoppers headed toward the rear to browse the displays there, but few of them ever made it back to the right half of the store. They were moving in a kind of question-mark track. To alter that, the register was moved to the right-hand wall and farther back, about halfway into the store. That then became the main hub of activity. A second area of high shopper interest, a telephone display, was installed on the right wall but closer to the front. The hope was that shoppers would enter, walk right toward the cash register area, and then visit the phone displays. Those adjustments shifted the store around to a configuration more natural to how people move, and instantly, the circulation patterns improved—more people saw more store. Because American shoppers automatically move to the right, the front-right of any store is its prime real estate. That's where the most important goods should go, the make-or-break merchandise that needs 100 percent shopper exposure. That's one way to take advantage of how people move.

Shoppers not only walk right, they reach right, too, most of them being right-handed. Imagine standing at a shelf, facing it—it's easiest to grab items to the right of where you stand, rather than reaching your arm across your body to the left. In fact, as you reach, your hand may inadvertently brush a product to the right of the one you're reaching for. So if a store wishes to place something into the hand of a shopper, it should be displayed just slightly to the right of where he or she will be standing. Planograms, the maps of which products are stocked where on a shelf, are determined with this in mind: If you're stocking cookies, for instance, the most popular brand goes dead center—at the bull's-eye—and the brand you're trying to build goes just to the right of it. (Again, in Britain and Australia, the drive-left-reach-right rule creates conflicts in design that we do not have in North America.)

An even simpler aspect of how people move is the one that raises the greatest number of logistical issues for stores. In fact, this particular peculiarity of human ambulation can be said to render nearly every retail space seriously ill-suited to its purpose. It's this: People face and walk forward.

The implications of this are enormous, only because the normal retail environment is actually designed for those nonexistent beings who walk sideways—sidling like the figures drawn in ancient Egyptian hieroglyphs—rather than place one foot in front of the other. Picture it: If you're walking straight down a store aisle, you're looking ahead. It requires an effort to turn your head to one side or the other to see the shelves or racks as you pass them. That effort even makes you vaguely uncomfortable, because it requires you to train your eyes somewhere other than where you're walking. If it's a familiar environment (say, your favorite supermarket) and the setting feels safe (wide aisles, no boxes or other obstacles on the floor to trip you up), then maybe you'll turn your head as you walk and take in the merchandise. In a less familiar setting, you'll see less—subconsciously, you've got your peripheral vision on the lookout so you don't trip over a box or a small child and fall on your nose. If, as you walk, a display gets your attention, you may stop in your tracks and look upon it as it was meant to be seen, straight in the eye, as it were. But only then.

This issue is not limited to a store's shelves. On the street, how do you approach a display window? In almost every instance, from an angle—as you're walking toward the store from the left or the right. But most display windows are designed as though every viewer is just standing there staring into them head-on. Which is almost never the case. This comes up regarding outdoor signs, too. Near my office there's a new restaurant that spent a lot of money on a very handsome hanging sign, but instead of positioning it perpendicular to the building, so it is visible to pedestrians approaching from either side, it hangs parallel to it, so it can be read only from directly across the street. Which is how maybe 5 or 10 percent of possible customers approach the facade.

Obviously, that sign could be rehung in an hour and the problem would be solved. Windows can easily accommodate how people approach them: Displays must simply be canted to one side, so they can be more easily seen from an angle. And because we walk as we drive—to the right—window displays should usually be tilted to the left. Such a move instantly increases the number of people who truly see them.

But how can our insistence on walking and looking forward be accommodated inside the typical store? One method is used in almost every store already. Endcaps, the displays of merchandise on the end of virtually every American store aisle, are tremendously effective at exposing goods to the shopper's eye. Almost every kind of store makes use of them—in record stores you'll see one particular artist's CDs or some discounted new release; in supermarkets there's a stack of specially priced soft drinks or a wall of breakfast cereal. An endcap can boost an item's sales simply because as we stroll through a store's aisles we approach it head-on, seeing it plainly and fully. Endcaps are also effective because you pass them on your way into an aisle, so if you see, say, a mountain of Oreos on the endcap, you'll stock up before coming upon the rest of the cookie display ten feet down the aisle.

Of course, there's a built-in limitation to the use of endcaps: There are only two of them per aisle, one at each end. But there's another effective way to display goods so they'll be seen. It's called chevroning—placing shelves or racks on an angle, like a sergeant's stripes, so more of what they hold is exposed to the vision of a strolling shopper. Instead of aisles being positioned at a ninety-degree angle to the back wall of the store, they're at forty-five degrees. A huge difference, and an elegant solution, too. There's only one catch: Chevroning shelves takes up about one fifth more floor space than the usual configuration, so a store can show only 80 percent as much merchandise as it can the traditional way. The big question is, will chevroning more than make up for that loss with increased sales? Can a store that shows less sell more, if the display system is superior? I can't answer that. We've suggested chevroning schemes to a number of clients, but no one wants to take the total plunge. It's certain, however, that especially for products that benefit from long browsing time, chevroning works.

How we walk determines to a great degree what we'll see, but so too does where our eyes naturally go. If you can only see a tabletop full of sweaters when you're standing right in front of it, then its effectiveness is limited. If you don't see a display from a distance—say, ten or twenty feet—then you won't approach it except by accident. That's why architects have to design stores with sight lines in mind—they must ensure that shoppers will be able to see what's in front of them but also be able to look around and see what's elsewhere. It's also why printed display fixtures, such as a sign reading FIVE PRE-WASHED T-SHIRTS FOR $20.99, should bear their message on every surface, so no shopper confronts a blank side.

Once sight lines are taken into consideration, retailers must take care not to place merchandise so that it cuts them off. This happens all the time: A freestanding display is placed in front of wall shelves, blocking whatever's there from the shopper's vision. Or a sign obscures the goods it's meant to describe. Ideally, a shopper should be able to examine goods but then look up and notice that over there, fifteen feet away, there's something just as appealing. It's a pinball effect—the felicitous dispersal of merchandise bounces shoppers throughout the entire store. In that way, the merchandise itself is a tool to keep shoppers flowing. That's how good stores operate: You feel almost helplessly pulled in by what you see up ahead or over there to the right.

We have studied how much of what is on display in supermarkets is actually seen by shoppers—the so-called capture rate. About one fifth of all shoppers actually see the average product on a supermarket shelf. There's a reliable zone in which shoppers will probably see merchandise. It goes from slightly above eye level down to about knee level. Much above that or below and they probably won't see it unless they happen to be looking intently. This, too, is a function of our defensive walking mechanism, for if you're looking up you can't see what's in your path.

This means that a huge amount of retail selling space is, if not quite wasted, seriously challenged. If a store can avoid displaying goods outside that zone, fine. But most stores don't have that luxury. One thing stores can try is to display only large items above or below the zone. It's easier to spy the economy-size Pampers down by your ankles than it is the Tylenol caplets. If the bottom shelf tilts up slightly, that helps visibility, too. Packaging designers can also effectively address this issue. Every label, every box, every container should be designed as though it will be seen from a disadvantageous perspective—either above the shopper's head or below her knees. Packaging should also be made to work when seen from a sharp angle rather than just head-on. We'd see a lot more large, clear type in high-contrast colors if that happened. This also has implications in stores where merchandise is stored on the selling floor instead of in stockrooms. I'm thinking here of computers, telephones, personal stereos and other consumer electronics that are sometimes stacked from the floor to over one's head. The boxes haven't been designed to be on display, but that's exactly how they end up. That alone should make no-frills packaging—brown kraft paper, no images, little description of the contents—obsolete. Boxes should be thought of as signs or as posters for a product—same as a box of cereal. Typically, package designers will place the manufacturer's name at the top of a label, thereby satisfying corporate egotism, and the product ID on the bottom; but this is exactly the wrong decision if the box is ever stored down near the floor. When it's down there, shoppers will see the brand name easily but not the description of what is in the box. And since no designer has control over where or how a box is stored, the product ID should *always* be on top, and the label should always look a little like a billboard—clean, high contrast, with a visible image and large-enough type.

Unfortunately, the managers of most companies fail to understand the importance of well-designed packaging. I've battled with young management consultants who can't wave their Wharton MBAs fast enough. They have the spreadsheets, they've crunched all the numbers, but they haven't taken a single look. Among the many pieces missing from business education is an understanding of the fundamentals of packaging and how that affects the brand. In business school, you can take courses in global brand strategy, Internet marketing, category management and so on, but to my knowledge there's no major business school in the world that teaches a course in twenty-first-century printing. Not IMD in Lausanne, not the IESE in Barcelona, not the London Business School—and certainly not Wharton. What we can do with printing presses in 2008 makes what we could do ten years ago seem quaint. Split runs and 360-degree color for starters. Today's technology makes it possible to customize packages for individual stores in different parts of the country. But a digitally-controlled printing press is only as sophisticated as the person making the order. While the graphic designers and the printers themselves know the score, that young gung-ho MBA commissioning the work usually doesn't.

Getting back to the floor, another matter of concern is something we call the boomerang rate. This is the measure of how many times shoppers fail to walk completely through an aisle, from one end to the other. It looks at how many times a shopper starts down an aisle, selects something, and then, instead of proceeding, turns around and retraces her or his steps. We'll call it a half boomerang, say, when the shopper makes it halfway down an aisle before turning back. Typically, he or she heads down the aisle in search of one or two things, finds them, and then heads back without even looking around (or, if she looks, she doesn't see anything worth stopping for). What do you do about that? The obvious answer for retailers is to position the most popular goods halfway down the aisle. Manufacturers should attempt to do just the opposite—to keep their products as near to the end of the aisle as possible.

But there are also ways to try to keep shoppers interested. One of the newest and most effective of these requires the presence of kids, which is why it's been used so well in the cereal aisles, where Mom and Dad typically want to grab and run. There, we've seen a floor graphic of a hopscotch game work extremely well to nail shoppers down for a while. In one store we studied, the average time kids played on the hopscotch graphic was almost fourteen seconds—a long time to be standing in front of cereal without buying some.

There's one aspect of how shoppers move that most people are familiar with: the quest to get us all the way to the back of a store. Everyone knows why supermarket dairy cases are usually against the back wall: Because almost every shopper needs milk, and so they'll pass through (and shop) much more of the store on the way to and from the rear. That is pretty effective, too, or at least it was, but it also created a terrific opportunity for a competitor. In fact, the convenience store industry exists because of its ability to put milk and other staples into shoppers' hands quickly, so they can run in, grab and go. Lots of new supermarkets now feature a "shallow loop"—a dairy case up near the front of the store, so shoppers can grab and go there, too.

Large chain drugstores use the pharmacy in the same way—that section is almost always on the back wall, so customers will be forced to visit the rest of the store, too. But a special accommodation must be made for those customers, lest the strategy backfire. When shoppers are headed for the pharmacy, they typically have a serious task at hand, and so they're not interested in browsing the shelves of the store on their way back. Therefore, drugstores must be merchandised from the rear as well as from the front—at least some signs, displays and fixtures must be positioned so they are visible to shoppers walking from the back of the store to the front. It's almost like planning two different stores on the same site, but it must be done because the pharmacy is so effective at pulling shoppers through the store.

In the opening chapter, I mentioned a drugstore that was the location of choice for young mall employees who needed a quick soda during their breaks. To take advantage, the store placed the coolers in the rear, which forced the kids to race in, hurry to the sodas and race back out so they could enjoy their fifteen minutes off. And in fact, those teenagers were never going to buy shampoo or alarm clocks or talcum on their soda runs. So the store humanely decided to move the coolers up front, as a favor to loyal soda drinkers who might have found another, more convenient place to fuel up on breaks.

Still, getting shoppers to the back wall of any store is usually a challenge. The Gap, Aéropostale and Anthropologie—all apparel store chains—put their discount sale products in the back left-hand corner of the store. They've trained their most veteran shoppers to visit the remotest corner of the store. Once they've gotten them to the back, their challenge is to make sure the pathway back to the front of the store is well merchandised and that at least some of the signage is facing the customer going back-to-front.

Wisely, most retailers don't sell their bread-and-butter merchandise from the back wall. Still, every square foot of selling space is equally expensive to rent, heat and light. A store that flows interestingly and smoothly from one section to another will automatically draw shoppers to the farthest reaches. If, from the front of the store, shoppers perceive that something interesting is going on in back, they'll make their way there at least once. A simple solution is to have what amounts to a mandala (like the statue at the far end of a Buddhist temple, meant to entice you further in) hanging on the rear wall, a large graphic, for instance, or better yet, something back there that makes some visual noise, that gives shoppers the sense that something interesting is going on. They may not head there the second they enter, but they'll drift that way, as if drawn by a magnet. Anything is better than the sense you get in most large stores—that the rear wall is the dead zone.

The front of a store has utmost importance in determining who enters. When RadioShack decided to increase the percentage of women shoppers, it did so in great part by devoting itself to the telephone business. But it made sure to display those phones near the front of its stores, in order to lure those women in most effectively. In fact, we advise some clients to change the front-of-store merchandising several times in the course of a day, to attract the different shoppers passing by. At a mall bookstore, for instance, we realized that in the morning most shoppers were stay-at-home mothers with baby strollers. So we told our client to position books on child care, fitness and family up front. (We also advised that there be enough room for all those strollers to maneuver.) In the afternoon, kids getting out of school ran wild in the mall, so there should be books on sports, pop music, TV and other adolescent subjects. After five P.M. was when the work crowd streamed through, so there should be books on business and computers. And because the mall was used very early in the morning by senior citizens getting their walking exercise, we told our client that before the store closed for the night its windows should be stocked with books on retirement, finance and travel. In fact, the store bought large, cylindrical display fixtures that could be turned around depending on the time of day and which books needed to be shown. Supermarkets are jam-packed up front from Friday to Sunday, and so the space is designed to handle the crush. On Monday and Tuesday, though, it's mellow up there. We've advised clients to turn the area just before the registers into a new selling zone, kind of a small bazaar of impulse items rather than just the usual rack or two.

How often shoppers move through your store is also something to be accommodated. If the average customer comes every two weeks, then your windows and displays need to be changed that often, so they'll always seem fresh and interesting. Here's another example of how design and merchandising must work hand in hand: If windows are made so they are easy for employees to get into, the displays will be changed more often than if it's a pain in the neck. If something about the design makes carrying merchandise into the window a burden, or if display racks block access to the windows, they'll suffer from a lack of attention, I guarantee.

Some facts of shopper movement can't be turned into universal principles, but they certainly have had their impact in specific environments we've studied. We did a study of a branch of a major family restaurant chain with a location on Sunset Boulevard in Los Angeles. By day the fact that its restrooms were just inside the front door seemed to be perfectly sensible. By night, however, when the street outside came alive with, among other things, the trade of some friendly neighborhood streetwalkers, the ladies' room location was a definite liability. It became a kind of hookers' lounge, a place they could wash, put their feet up and chat a spell between engagements. Not the greatest thing for the rest of the diners.

Some Hallmark card stores feature custom-printed stationery departments, places where brides-to-be can go for invitations and so on. The design of the department, a writing table with shelves for the large stationery sample books, was perfectly adequate. But in one busy New Jersey mall, the station was located in the front of the store, just beyond the cash register, perhaps the noisiest, most populated part of the room. The sole person using it was filling out a job application.

SEVEN

Dynamic

Stand over here. *Behind* the underwear.

What do you see? A couple? How old? Sixties? Anything special? Just your average slightly tubby mom and pop out on the town, at Target or some such place, about to splurge on new briefs for the old guy, am I right?

Hold on—what's he saying?

"Now, where's my size?"

What's she saying?

"Over here."

Now what's he saying?

"I guess I'll just get this three-pack."

Fascinating. What did she just say?

"No, get the six . . . I can wear 'em, too."

Whoa. What kind of weirdness is going on here? I can't even bear to picture it, the two of them rolling around in only their—

Hey, stop that. You just missed an invaluable lesson in the true dynamic nature of shopping and buying. You don't even have to be a scientist of shopping to figure out what just happened, though if you're a woman it might help, especially an overweight woman, especially an overweight woman whose choices in underwear are limited to styles with thin, biting elastic bands at the waist and the leg holes—an uncomfortable prospect, I can only imagine (reluctantly).

In 2004 I worked on underwear issues across the world—in North America, Europe and Japan. That summer I gave a keynote speech at a gathering of lingerie executives in Winston-Salem, North Carolina. I opened my lecture by saying that as a man who lives with a New England woman, I know much more about lingerie professionally than I do personally. A central global issue in this industry is the difference between underwear designed for sex and that designed for comfort. Most women do not parade around as if they were on this month's cover of the Victoria's Secret catalog. While some underwear for some women are items they put on so they get help taking them off, underwear for most people most of the time is about how good it feels and whether or not it complements what they're wearing on top of what they're wearing underneath. Underwear if you are eighteen is a fashion accessory, not unlike hair color. But comfort and fit are seminal drivers for most post-forty women, especially those carrying a few extra pounds.

Since that event, which happened a few years back, women's underwear styles have come to resemble men's, with their wide, flat (nonconstricting) elastic and soft cotton fabrics, thereby solving our woman's particular problem and keeping her out of her husband's drawers.

As of 2008, Victoria's Secret still sells the pink frilly stuff, but relative newcomer Gap Body carries the more athletic and comfortable stuff, or what some in the industry cynically call the butch lines. What we're still missing, however, is a powerhouse merchant who's willing to focus on the needs of the mature woman.

On the other side of the fence is an interesting boom in what's called male lingerie. It used to be boxers or briefs. Now any self-respecting underwear section has at least three more styles—boxer-briefs, slips (or the male version of a bikini) and midrise (which sit a couple of inches higher than a bikini). In my dotage I am still your basic briefs guy, but back to our story.

Shoppers make the ultimate determination of how they use the retail environment and the products that are sold in it. Product designers, manufacturers, packagers, architects, merchandisers and retailers make all the big decisions about what people will buy and where and how they will buy it. But then the shoppers themselves enter the equation and turn nice, neat theories and game plans into confetti.

In this particular case, was the general unsuitability of most underwear for ladies of size known to the designers and makers of said garments? Maybe not. Maybe they knew it but didn't know what to do with that information. Maybe they assumed that women wouldn't wear briefs that looked like men's underwear, although, clearly, the general drift in women's clothes has been toward a more masculine ideal. If some underwear executive had been standing in that aisle next to our researcher, maybe he would have realized that this woman was teaching him something extremely important about his own product. Perhaps the revolution in women's underwear would have started earlier than it did.

Then again, maybe not.

Here's another example of shoppers forcing the retail environment to bend to their will. It involves what is perhaps *the* major issue in the design and furnishing of public spaces: seating.

I love seating. I could talk about it all day. If you're discussing anything having to do with the needs of human beings, you *have* to address seating. Air, food, water, shelter, seating—in that order. Before money. Before love. Seating.

In the majority of stores throughout the world, sales would instantly be increased by the addition of one chair. I would remove a display if it meant creating space for a chair. I'd rip out a fixture. I'd kill a mannequin. A chair says: We care.

Given the chance, people will buy from people who care.

This happened in a large, well-known women's lingerie store. One that was providing insufficient seating for the men who wait for the ladies who shop. How do we know it was insufficient? Because the husbands and boyfriends were led to improvise, which human beings will always do when a need is going unmet. Whenever you encounter shopper improvisation in the retail environment, you have found poignant evidence of one person's failure to understand what another person requires.

If I may digress for a good illustration: In the casino-hotels of Atlantic City, where kindness is, shall we say, not excessively idealized, you see lots of people who have wagered and lost but must linger until their tour buses depart. The casinos, for obvious reasons, wish these people would wait in the gaming area, parked in front of a slot machine or a dealer. To encourage that, there are no chairs in the hotel lobbies. How do the visitors respond? They sit glumly on the floors, dozens and dozens of sour-faced losers in a row, not a sight that evokes the opulent gaming ambience of Monte Carlo for the incoming suckers. These people need chairs!

In lingerie stores, too, the need is plain. While women shop, men wait, and when men (or women) wait, they prefer to sit. Is any truth truer? Is any nose on any face plainer than that fact? Still, designers of commercial spaces screw up royally when it comes to seating. In my days as a scholar of parks and plazas with the Project for Public Spaces, we spent a great deal of our time thinking about how to improve outdoor benches—where they should go, how wide they should be, whether they should be in shade or sunlight, how close they should be to the main thoroughfares, whether they should be wood or stone (stone gets awfully chilly in winter). A bench, we realized, might actually double the distance an older pedestrian could cover—someone might walk a while, tire slightly, and consider turning back, but then there'd be an inviting bench in the shade. Once restored, the pedestrian would continue forth. In the retail environment, a chair's main purpose is slightly different: When people go shopping in twos or threes, with spouses or children or friends along for the trip, seating is what keeps the nonshopping party comfortable and contented and cared for and off the shopper's back.

In that lingerie store, the womenfolk were shopping but the menfolk were not—they were waiting for the womenfolk. They'd have loved a place to sit, but this store chose not to provide it. Why not? Maybe there wasn't enough space for chairs. Maybe there was a chair and it broke.

Maybe somebody decided that a bunch of guys hanging around would spoil the decor.

Did that mean the men would stand, or lean? Of course not—it meant they'd invent seating. In this case, they gravitated toward a large window that had a broad sill at roughly the height where a bench would be. And the sill became a bench.

And where exactly was this ad-hoc bench? Through no one's fault or design, it was immediately adjacent to a large and attractive display of the Wonderbra, the architectural marvel that gave life such a lift. It seems easy in hindsight to predict what happened next: Women approached the display, began to study the goods, and then noticed that they were being studied by the guys on the windowsill. On the day we visited the store, there were two elderly gents loitering there, unabashedly discussing the need for Wonderbras of every woman who was brave enough to stop and shop.

Did I mention that no Wonderbra was purchased while those two codgers sat there?

Now, everyone knows that adjacencies are of huge importance to every product, especially something like the Wonderbra, which requires a little examination and consideration and then a try-on. Great retail minds churn themselves into mush trying to unravel the mysteries of which products should be sold near one another for maximum spark and synergy. And here, completely without intention, a very bad adjacency was created (bad for the shoppers, bad for the store, not so bad for the guys) by human beings who were forced by a retailer to improvise.

We've tried to organize the seating idea by calling it short-, medium- and long-term parking. Short-term parking is outside a dressing room. It's designed for the bored wallet carrier, surrogate security guard or two-legged dog to be parked for three minutes. Medium-term parking is the chair at the doorway or bench immediately outside the door, where the guy, the guard and the dog can be left for ten minutes. Ideally, medium-term parking is designed as a perch for people-watching, not too close, though, so that muttered comments can't be overheard. We find long-term parking in a shopping mall. It's quiet and restful. Sometimes it has a whiff of Zen to it—the noise of falling water or a fountain. It is a comfortable place to be for twenty minutes or longer, whether that's to read a newspaper, fiddle with a BlackBerry or feed a child.

Here's another instance where shoppers rightly confounded the narrow-minded agenda of retailers.

There's an ongoing struggle afoot between the makers of cosmetics and the users. Women want to try on certain cosmetics, lipstick especially, before buying, which is understandable considering how expensive makeup is and how it differs in appearance depending on the skin of the wearer. Cosmetics makers, on the other hand, wish that women would not sample their products quite so liberally, since even slightly used lipsticks are rarely purchased. There are many plans and systems that provide testers to shoppers, but none of these has been so flawlessly successful that it has become the industry standard. And so the game goes on.

Some years ago, a makeup maker thought it had devised a foolproof lipstick—one that couldn't be twisted open without breaking a tape seal. This, the maker thought, would allow women to peer into the tube to see the color but not actually touch the lipstick itself. The boys in packaging were certain that this was going to save the company millions. We were hired to observe how women interacted with the prototype. We watched shoppers remove the cap, look inside, and unsuccessfully attempt to twist it open—at which point they lowered their pinky fingernails into the tube and gouged out a dab to have a look. The experts were foiled again. Their mistake was in even trying to stop women from testing lipstick. The more progressive cosmetics makers recognize that testing leads to buying, and so they encourage it by making it possible without turning women into outlaws. To my mind, the best solution would be one that came with a profit motive—simply package small samples of each season's new colors of lipstick, blush and face powder, enough for two or three applications of each, and charge a dollar or two.

In Japan in 2002, I found that exact idea outside Shibuya Station in Tokyo. The store is called Three-Minute Happiness. The sign reads MIS-CELLANEOUS GOODS THAT MAKE OUR LIFE HAPPY AND EASY. Could anything be simpler? Just three minutes—that's all it takes. A fleeting, serene shopping experience. Even better, it leaves you feeling happy, just as advertised. The store sells samples—of lipstick, nail polish, other beauty products and a few household items—and is organized by price: one hundred yen, two hundred yen, three hundred yen, roughly translating into one dollar, two dollars, three dollars. Off to the side is a coffee and ice cream bar where you put your money into a vending machine with a picture menu board, and out spits a coupon that you then present to the server who makes your coffee or scoops your ice cream—no fumbling with cash. I call it a three-minute retail vacation.

Not every form of improvisation requires remediation. In the heyday of the video retail boom before Netflix (remember the dark ages?), many American families made the weekend pilgrimage to Blockbuster and Hollywood Video mostly in search of new-release movies. The video-rental business made pennies on renting the latest releases but scored big time when it could get you to rent the old stuff—classics like *North by Northwest* or *The Great Escape*. Their ongoing dilemma was how to get what they called "basic inventory" out the door.

We noticed that quite a few of the truly expert searchers among their clientele headed not for the new releases section but for the returns cart, the trolley where incoming videos go before they are filed. There's no reason to attempt to alter that behavior—it actually saves some clerk a little labor, which is a good thing. We suggested spiking that return cart with a few classic films, particularly ones that had some connection to a new release. It worked.

Here's a final example of customers using stores in ways other than those intended, this time to the complete benefit of the business. More than half of all fast food in the United States is purchased at the drive-thru window, and we (along with everyone else) assumed that those diners either ate as they drove off or took the food back to their offices or elsewhere and downed it there. During a series of recent studies, though, we noticed something odd: Around 10 or more percent of drive-thru customers would get their food and then park right there in the lot and eat in their cars. Curiously, the drivers who did this tended to be in newer cars than the restaurants' average customers.

Were they elitist burger-lovers who were simply embarrassed to be seen in a humble grease pit? Or did they enjoy the luxury of eating in an environment where they could talk freely on their cell phones, listen to their own music, and sit in their own seats? Either way, it's a segment of fast-food diners that's worth accommodating—after all, these customers bring their own chairs and clean up after themselves. As a result, we now advise fast-food restaurants to make sure their parking lots are visible from the street, so that drivers can see that there's space for them. We also emphasize the importance of maintaining pleasant conditions—shade, with a view of something other than the Dumpster— for cars as well as people. (In one restaurant we studied, all the best parking spots were taken by employees, whose cars would remain in place for eight hours at a pop, a very dumb practice.) Finally, our finding affirms the overall trend among fast-food restaurants to shrink the size of the building and increase the size of the drive-thru and the parking lot, thereby allowing customers to have it their way—which, in nearly every case, is as it should be.

A final note: What I don't understand is why the fast-food business has not invented and provided a car bib. Something that allows you to eat that burger without spilling pickles and ketchup on that new tie of yours or dropping that stray french fry in between the seats. Something for one of those business-school guys to ponder.

III

Men Are from Home Depot,
Women Are from Bloomingdale's:
The Demographics of Shopping

As we've seen, the simplest aspects of humanity—our physical abilities and limitations—have quite a bit of say in how we shop. But nothing as interesting as shopping is ever quite so simple. We all move through the same environments, but no two of us respond to them exactly alike. This sign may be tastefully rendered, perfectly legible, exquisitely positioned, but you read the sign and I do not. The store flows beautifully, and all the merchandise is easily within my grasp, except that I hate buying clothing and would rather be fishing. No shopping baskets were ever more conveniently located, only you're strapped for cash right now, or you're just constitutionally incapable of buying more than two books at a time.

Certainly we're all aware of how shopping means different things to different people at different times. We use shopping as therapy, reward, bribery, pastime, an excuse to get out of the house, a way to troll for potential loved ones, entertainment, a form of education or even worship, a way to kill time. There are compulsive shoppers doing serious damage to their bank accounts and credit ratings who use shopping as a cry for help. (Then they shop around for twelve-step programs.) And how many disreputable public figures end up arrested for shoplifting small, inexpensive items? It seems we get two or three a year, always in Florida.

In the '80s, Eastern European émigrés who came to America were awestruck by the abundance on display in a typical suburban supermarket. The stores symbolized how free-market democracy comes down to simple freedom of choice—lots and lots of choices. It was in a supermarket that I, too, had an emotionally cathartic shopping experience. This was maybe twenty years ago, a time when it began to seem as though Envirosell might succeed as an ongoing concern. Up until that point, though, it was an open question—I was borderline broke all the time, working like a dog but plowing every nickel I had back into the company. Things were tight: If I had a meeting in Florida, for instance, I would take the last flight of the day down there to get the cheapest ticket, arriving in the middle of the night. Then I'd pick up my cheap rental car, drive to my destination, curl up my six-foot-four-inch frame as best I could, doze lightly in the car, shave and brush my teeth in a gas station bathroom, and go to my appointment trying my best to impersonate a successful research firm founder. *Tight.* Anyway, on the day in question it became clear that I and my company were going to be all right. And on that day I just happened to visit the Pathmark supermarket near South Street Seaport in New York. Standing in the imported goods aisle, it suddenly hit me that I could afford to buy anything there I wanted. If, say, I wished to try some of the English ginger preserves I remembered from my youth, I could just pick up a jar and pay for it, heedless of the fact that it cost maybe *four or five bucks.* No more cheap Welch's grape jelly. At age thirty-five, I no longer had to sweat over my food budget, I realized, and at that moment, I—a six-foot-four, 220-pound, bald, bearded guy—began to cry. Right there in front of all those imported jellies, jams and preserves, I wept with relief and happiness, emotions that had come forth thanks to a supermarket. From that day on, my breakfast of choice at least 150 mornings a year consisted of obscenely expensive ginger preserves and organic peanut butter spread on an English muffin and downed with a cup of strong coffee.

But doesn't *everybody* cry in supermarkets? Much of our work at Envirosell has to do with identifying differences in shoppers, trying to come up with types and generalizations that might be useful to the retailers and others who control our shopping spaces. Not surprisingly, in a world where "men are from Mars, women are from Venus" is a commonplace, we pay close attention to how men and women behave differently in stores. Some of the distinctions are what you'd expect— women are better at it, men are loose cannons. But as men and women (and relations between them) change, their shopping behaviors do, too, which will have huge implications for American business.

The other great distinction we study has to do with the age of the shopper. Once upon a time, children in stores were seen but not heard. Those days are long gone, and now even the smallest among them must be considered and accommodated in the retail equation. At the other extreme, older shoppers are also more important than ever, if only because there are more of them, and they have a lot of money to spend and time to spend it. Their presence will transform how products are sold in the twenty-first century. Enormous cultural and demographic shifts are coming into play; in the four chapters that follow, we'll see how shoppers differ, and how those differences are reflected in the world of shopping.

EIGHT

Shop Like a Man

Men and women differ in just about every other way, so why shouldn't they shop differently, too? The conventional wisdom on male shoppers is that they don't especially like to do it, which is why they don't do much of it. It's a struggle just to get them to be patient company for a woman while she shops. As a result, the entire shopping experience—from packaging design to advertising to merchandising to store design and fixturing—is geared toward the female shopper.

Or so the traditional world of retail maintains. Baloney. Although women are increasingly reaching high-level business positions, we live in a world that is owned by men, designed by men and managed by men, yet somehow they expect women to participate. That they don't get women is a given; that they don't do so well with the guys either is pathetic. Here are the two basic building blocks: Guys are genetically disposed to be hunters, so they walk to the woods and are unsuccessful unless they can kill something reasonably quickly and drag it back home and through the mudroom. Women are gatherers who get immense pleasure out of the act of looking. Thus, two women can spend the day at the mall, buy nothing and have a wonderful time.

Women do have a greater affinity for what we think of as "shopping"—walking at a relaxed pace through stores, examining merchandise, comparing products and values, interacting with sales staff, asking questions, trying things on and ultimately making purchases. Most acquisitioning traditionally falls to women, and they usually do it willingly—even when shopping for the mundane necessities, even when the experience brings no particular pleasure, women tend to do it in dependable, agreeable fashion. Historically, women were the culture's everyday purchasing agents and took pride in their ability to shop prudently and well. In a study we ran of baby products, women interviewed insisted that they knew the price of products by heart, without even having to look. (Upon further inquiry, we discovered that they were mostly wrong.) As women's roles change, so does their shopping behavior—they're becoming a lot more like men in that regard—but they're still the primary buyers in the American marketplace.

Men, in comparison, are more reckless, less poetical. We've timed enough shoppers to know that men always move faster than women through a store's aisles. Men spend less time looking, too. In many settings it's hard to get them to look at anything they hadn't intended to buy. They usually don't like asking where things are, or any other questions, for that matter. (They shop the way they drive.) If a man can't find the section he's looking for, he'll wheel about once or twice, then give up and leave the store without ever asking for help. You can see him just shut down.

You'll see a man move impatiently through a store to the section he wants, pick something up, and then, almost abruptly, he's ready to buy, having taken little apparent joy in the process of finding. A classic example was watching some older guys shopping for Dockers—the Levi Strauss line of basic khakis and chinos. The image of the guy racing to the Dockers wall, finding a pair that matched his specs—thirty-four-inch waist and thirty-two-inch inseam—and turning and almost running to the register is pretty commonplace. It's as if the sheer fact of being in the store is a threat to his masculinity. It's funny that stores like Ca-bela's, REI and even the bricks-and-mortar versions of L.L.Bean make it much easier for older guys to shop for belts, pants and underwear, since they're surrounded by the trappings of fishing, hunting and outdoor exercise. Another example is the Harley-Davidson dealer, where not only do middle-aged guys shop for clothes, but you can sell them stuff for their kids, too.

But when a typical guy is shopping, you've practically got to get out of his way because otherwise he'll flatten you. When a man takes cloth-ing into a dressing room, the only thing that stops him from buying it is if it doesn't fit. Women, on the other hand, try things on only as part of the consideration process, and garments that fit just fine may still be re-jected on other grounds. In one study, we found that 65 percent of male shoppers who tried something on bought it, as opposed to 25 percent of female shoppers. This is a good argument for positioning fitting rooms nearer the men's department than the women's, if they are shared ac-commodations. If they are not, men's dressing rooms should be near the entrance and very clearly marked, because if he has to search for it, he may just decide it's not worth the trouble.

Here's another statistical comparison: Eighty-six percent of women look at price tags when they shop. Only 72 percent of men do. For a man, ignoring the price tag is almost a measure of his virility. As a re-sult, men are far more easily upgraded than are women shoppers. They are also far more suggestible than women—men seem so anxious to get out of the store that they'll say yes to almost anything.

Now, a shopper such as that could be seen as more trouble than he's worth. But he could also be seen as a potential source of profits, espe-cially given his lack of discipline. Either way, men now do more pur-chasing than ever before. And that figure will continue to grow. As they stay single longer than ever, they learn to shop for things their fathers never had to buy. And because many marry women who work as long and hard as they do, they will be forced to shoulder more of the burden of shopping. The manufacturers and retailers and display designers who pay attention to male ways, and are willing to adapt the shopping expe-rience to them, will have an edge in the coming decades.

The great traditional arena for male shopping behavior has always been the supermarket. It's here, with thousands of products all within easy reach, that you can witness the carefree abandon and restless lack of discipline for which the gender is known.

In one supermarket study, we counted how many shoppers came armed with lists. Almost all of the women had them. Less than a quarter of the men did. Any wife who's watching the family budget knows better than to send her inexperienced husband to the supermarket unchaperoned. Giving him a vehicle to commandeer, even if it is just a shopping cart, only emphasizes the potential for guyness in the experience. Throw a couple of kids in with Dad and you've got a lethal combination; he's notoriously bad at saying no when there's grocery acquisitioning to be done. Part of being Daddy is being the provider, after all. It goes to the heart of a man's self-image.

I've spent hundreds of hours of my life watching men moving through supermarkets. One of my favorite video moments starred a dad carrying his little daughter on his shoulders. In the snacks aisle, the girl gestures toward the animal crackers display. Dad grabs a box off the shelf, opens it, and hands it up—without even a thought to the fact that his head and shoulders are about to be dusted with cookie crumbs. It's hard to imagine Mom in such a wanton scenario. Another great lesson in male shopping came about watching a man and his two small sons pass through the cereal aisle. When the boys plead for their favorite brand, he pulls down a box and instead of carefully opening it along the reclosable tab, he just rips the top, knowing full well that once the boys start in, there won't be any need to reclose it.

Supermarkets are places of high-impulse buying for both sexes—fully 60 to 70 percent of purchases there were unplanned, grocery industry studies have shown us. But men are particularly suggestible to the entreaties of children as well as eye-catching displays.

There's another profligate male behavior that invariably shows itself at supermarkets, something we see over and over on video we shoot at the registers: The man almost always pays. Especially when a man and woman are shopping together, he insists on whipping out his wad and forking it over, lest the cashier mistakenly think it's the

woman of the house who's bringing home the bacon. No wonder that
retailers commonly call men wallet carriers, or that the conventional
wisdom is sell to the woman, close to the man. Because while the man
may not love the experience of shopping, he gets a definite thrill from
the experience of paying. It allows him to feel in charge even when
he isn't. Stores that sell prom gowns depend on this. Generally, when
Dad's along, the girl will get a pricier frock than if just Mom were
there with her.

One of my favorite stores is American Girl Place, which has to be
one of the best engines ever invented to take money out of Daddy's
pocket. For anyone who doesn't know what American Girl Place is, it's
a doll store, where dolls are themed to moments in American history,
with skin tone and hair color to match, as well as an era-appropriate
name, like Addy or Felicity, plus a brief bio. You can buy matching outfits for both the doll and your nine-year-old. The store also features a
beauty parlor where you can get your doll's hair done, a doll hospital,
a café with a special seat where your doll can join you for tea, and even
a theater where the story behind each doll is dramatized. Add on books
and magazines, and the average visitor has dropped a couple of hundred
bucks. The café has five seatings a day and most weekends are booked
out six months in advance. It's the dream birthday present for many
American eight- or nine-year-old girls to convince their parents to take
them to American Girl Place for the weekend. There are now three
stores—the original in Chicago, followed by New York and Los Angeles. The only improvement I can think of would be an American Girl
Place Hotel, or maybe an American Girl Place Floor at a nearby hotel
complete with doll beds and nightgowns. I love taking foreign visitors
there. The question we debate is whether a French Girl Place or a Japanese Girl Place would be as successful a way of getting money out of
Daddy's pocket as its U.S. counterpart.

In certain categories, men shoppers put women to shame. We ran
a study for a store where 17 percent of the male customers we interviewed said they visited the place more than once a week! Almost one
quarter of the men there said they had left the house that day with no
intention of visiting the store—they just found themselves wandering

in out of curiosity. The fact that it was a computer store may have had something to do with it, of course. Computer hardware and software have taken the place of cars and stereo equipment as the focus of male love of technology and gadgetry. Clearly, most of the visits to the store were information-gathering forays. On the videotape, we watched the men reading intently the software packaging and any other literature or signage available. The store was where men bought software, but it was also where they did most of their learning about it. This underscores another male shopping trait: Just as they hate to ask directions from sales staff, they like to get their information firsthand, preferably from written materials, instructional videos or computer screens.

A few years back we ran a study for a wireless phone provider that was developing a prototype retail store. And we found that men and women used the place in very different ways. Women would invariably walk right up to the sales desk and ask staffers questions about the phones and the various deals being offered. Men, however, went directly to the phone displays and the signs that explained the agreements. They then took brochures and application forms and left the store—all without ever speaking to an employee. When these men returned to the store, it was to sign up. The women, though, on average required a third visit to the store, and more consultation, before they were ready to close.

Women's and men's roles, of course, are changing. In 2008, the overwhelming majority of students attending institutions of higher learning was female. And it's not just undergraduate education, law school and medical school; women now dominate almost every graduate program except engineering and math. While income disparity is still biased toward men and the glass ceiling is still an obstacle in most professions, never have women had more money of their own than they do right now.

But for the most part, men are still the ones who take the lead when shopping for cars (though women have a big say in most new-car purchases), and men and women perform the division of labor you'd expect when buying for the home: She buys anything that goes inside, and he buys everything that goes outside—mower and other gardening and lawn-care equipment, barbecue grill, water hose and so on.

But let's put those historic roles into some sort of demographic perspective. In the 2002 U.S. Census, only 24 percent of American households had a mother, a father and dependent children. Roughly 15 percent of households consisted of a single parent raising his or her kids. That leaves a huge 60 percent of American households with no kids (some childless, some empty nesters), and the rest nontraditional: roommates, adult kids living with their parents, singles and so on. The basic idea of what we sell to whom is still valid, but paying attention to the nontraditional buyers of everything has never been more important. Roughly half the cars on the road in North America are driven by women. Yet the car dealership remains one of the most hated destinations for women shoppers.

One of the most telling disconnects is in housing, where almost all new homes built in the past ten years have been based around the concept of the nuclear family: one master bedroom and a couple of smaller kiddie rooms. If you have a home that's configured for a nontraditional living unit—for example, with two master bedroom suites—it will sell faster and at a premium.

All across the world it takes two incomes to live a middle-class life. In 1965 when my father bought a home in Chevy Chase, Maryland, that home cost approximately his annual salary. He made forty thousand dollars a year and the house cost the same. Today if anyone lives in a house that's equal to his or her annual income, I don't know whether to be envious or sympathetic. That said, the decision-making process of where we spend our money is in flux.

Even when men aren't shopping, they figure prominently into the experience. As I mentioned earlier, we know that across the board, how much customers buy is a direct result of how much time they spend in a store. And our research has shown over and over that when a woman is in a store with a man, she'll spend less time there than when she's alone or with another woman, or even with children. Here's the actual breakdown of average shopping time from a study we performed at one branch of a national housewares chain:

Woman shopping with a female companion: 8 minutes, 15 seconds
Woman with children: 7 minutes, 19 seconds
Woman alone: 5 minutes, 2 seconds
Woman with man: 4 minutes, 41 seconds

In each case, what's happening seems clear: When two women shop together, they talk, advise, suggest and consult to their hearts' content, hence the long time in the store; with the kids, she's partly consumed with herding them along and keeping them entertained; alone, she makes efficient use of her time. But with him—well, he makes it plain that he's bored and antsy and liable at any moment to go off and sit in the car and listen to the radio or stand outside and watch girls. So the woman's comfort level plummets when he's by her side; she spends the entire trip feeling anxious and rushed. If he can somehow be occupied, though, she'll be a happier, more relaxed shopper. And she'll spend more, both time and money. There are two main strategies for coping with the presence of men in places where serious shopping is being done.

The first one is passive restraint, which is not to say handcuffs. Stores that sell mainly to women should all be figuring out some way to engage the interest of men. If I owned Chico's or Victoria's Secret, I'd have a place where a woman could check her husband like a coat. There already exists a traditional space where men have always felt comfortable waiting around—it's called the barbershop. Instead of some ratty old chairs and back issues of *Playboy* and *Boxing Illustrated,* maybe there could be comfortable seats facing a big-screen TV tuned to ESPN, or the cable channel that runs the bass-fishing program. Even something that simple would go a long way toward relieving wifely anxiety, but it's possible to imagine more: *Sports Illustrated* in-store programming, for instance—a documentary on the making of the swimsuit issue, perhaps—or highlights of last weekend's NFL action.

If I were opening a brand-new store where women could shop comfortably, I'd find a location right next to an emporium devoted to male desire—a computer store, for instance, or a car-parts supply house, somewhere he could happily kill half an hour. Likewise, if I were opening a computer software store, I'd put it next to a women's clothing shop and guarantee myself hordes of grateful male browsers.

But you could also try to sell to your captive audience. A women's clothing store could prepare a video catalog designed especially for men buying gifts—items like scarves or robes rather than shoes or trousers. Gift certificates would sell easily there; he already knows that she likes the store. Victoria's Secret could really go to town with a video catalog for men. They could even stage a little fashion show.

The only precaution you'd need to take is in where to place such a section. You want customers to be able to find it easily, but you don't want it so near the entrance that the gaze of window shoppers falls on six lumpy guys in windbreakers slumped in Barcaloungers watching TV.

The second, and ultimately more satisfying, strategy would be to find a way to actually get the man involved in shopping. Not the easiest thing to do in certain categories, but not impossible either.

We were doing a study for Pfaltzgraff, the dinnerware maker and retailer. Their typical customer will fall in love with one particular pattern and collect the entire set—many, many pieces, everything from dinner plates and coffee cups to a mustard pot, serving platter and napkin rings. It is very time-consuming to shop the store, especially when you figure in how long it takes to ring the items up and wrap them so that they don't break. Just the kind of situation designed to drive most men nuts. But the typical sale at Pfaltzgraff outlet stores can run into the hundreds of dollars, all the more reason to find a way to get men involved.

As we watched the videotape, we noticed that for some unknown reason men were tending to wander over toward the glassware section of the store. They were steering clear of the gravy boats and the spoon rests and drifting among the tumblers and wineglasses. At one point we saw two guys meander over to the beer glasses, where one of them picked one up and with the other hand grabbed an imaginary beer tap, pulled it and tilted the glass as if to fill it. And I thought, well, of course—when company's over for dinner and the woman's cooking in the kitchen, what does the man do? He makes drinks. That's his socially acceptable role. And so he's interested in all the accoutrements, all the tools of the bartending trade—every different type of glass and what it's for, and the corkscrew and ice tongs and knives and shakers. They're being guys about it.

My first thought was that the stores should put in fake beer taps, like props, for men to play with. We ended up advising them to pull together all the glassware into a barware section and to put up on the wall some big graphic, like a photo of a man pulling a beer or making some martinis in a nice chrome shaker. Something so that men would walk in and see that there was a section meant for them, somewhere they could shop. All the bottle openers in the different patterns, say, would be stocked there, too. And because men prefer to get their information from reading, the store could put up a chart showing what type of glass is used for what—the big balloons and the long stems and the flutes and the rocks glasses and steins.

And by doing all that, you could take the man—who had been seen as a drag on business and an inconvenience to the primary shopper—and turn him into a customer himself. Or at least an interested bystander.

We did a study for Thomasville, the furniture maker, and thought that there, too, getting the man more involved would make it easier to sell such big-ticket items. The solution was simple: Create graphic devices, like displays and posters, showing the steps that go into making the furniture, and use visuals, like cross-sections and exploded views, to prove that in addition to looking good, the pieces were well made. Emphasizing construction would do a lot toward overcoming male resistance to the cost of new furniture, but the graphics would also give men something to study while their wives examined upholstery and styling.

One product for which men consistently outshop women is beer. And that's in every type of setting—supermarket or convenience store, men buy the beer. (They also buy the junk food, the chips and pretzels and nuts and other entertainment food.) So we advised a supermarket client to hold a beer-tasting every Saturday at three P.M., right there in the beer aisle. They could feature some microbrew or a new beer from one of the major brewers, it didn't matter. The tastings would probably help sell beer, but even that wasn't the point. It would be worth it just because it would bring more men into the store. And it would help transform the supermarket into a more male-oriented place.

But an experiment run by Envirosell Brazil for Brahma, the country's leading beer brand, teaches a different lesson. In the experiment, they focused on making the beer section more female-friendly on the premise that women buy beer for someone other than just themselves. They took out all the buxom babe stand-ups (what's the exact connection between suds and cleavage anyway?) and put up graphics of a family meal with adult men and women drinking beer. Sales went up 20 percent overnight. Here in the USA, women make up a tiny segment of beer-buying patronage, but when they do buy it, they tend to buy beer in larger quantities. Thus, while the guy is more likely to buy a six-pack, the woman is more likely to buy the twelve. Conclusion: She's buying for the party, the guy is buying for the party of one.

Smart retailers should pay attention. All aspects of business are going to have to anticipate how men's and women's social roles are changing, and the future is going to belong to whoever gets there first. A good general rule: Take any category where women now predominate and figure out how to make it appealing to men without alienating women.

Look, for instance, at what's happened to the American kitchen over the past decade or so. Once upon a time Mom did all the grocery shopping and all the cooking. Now Mom probably works as much as Dad. As a result, men also have to know how to cook, clean and do laundry—it's gone from being cute to being necessary.

Is it a coincidence that as that change took place, kitchen appliances have become so butch? Once upon a time you chose from avocado and golden harvest when selecting a refrigerator or a stove. Now the trendiest stoves are industrial-strength six-burner numbers with open gas grills, and the refrigerators are huge, featureless boxes of stainless steel, aluminum and glass. If you go into a fancy kitchenware store like Williams-Sonoma you'll see that a popular gadget is the little blowtorch used for crystallizing the top of crème brûlée. Have Americans just now fallen in love with preparing elaborate, fatty French desserts? Or does cooking just seem more appealing to men when it involves firing up your own personal flamethrower?

(Similarly, as women stay single longer and sometimes become single more than once, the old-fashioned, boys-only hardware store is being killed off. Our Ace Hardware and True Value hardware clients have done a great job transforming their businesses to become places where female homeowners can become tool-happy do-it-yourselfers in a nurturing, non-gender-specific environment. One of the simpler ways that transformation happens is by hiring more female staff.)

Look at how microwave ovens are sold—the most prominent feature on the description sheet is the wattage. Likewise, when we interviewed men shopping for vacuum cleaners and asked which feature was most important, their (predictable) answer was: "Suck." Read: *power.* As a result, vacuum makers now boast amperage. In both cases, home appliances have gotten more macho as men have gotten less so. They seem determined to meet somewhere in the middle.

Even washday miracles and other household products are being re-imagined with men in mind. I can't say for sure how Georgia-Pacific and Procter & Gamble came to their decisions, but why else would paper towels be called Brawny or laundry detergent be called Bold, except to make themselves respectable items for men to bring to the checkout? How many women wish they had Hefty bags? Now: how many men? The manliest monikers used to go on cars; now they go on suds. The most successful soap introduction of the '90s wasn't anything frilly or lavender. It was Lever 2000, a name that would also sound right on a computer or a new line of power tools. I'd drive a Lever 2000 any day.

Look beyond shopping to the most elemental expressions of contemporary male desire—just think of the difference between Marilyn Monroe and Angelina Jolie. Angie's biceps are probably bigger than Frank Sinatra's and Bobby Kennedy's combined. She's downright muscle-bound and hipless compared to the pinups of three decades ago.

Men have always bought their own suits and shoes, but women, traditionally, shopped for everything in between, especially men's socks and underwear. Now, though, that's changing—men are more involved in their clothing, and women have enough to do without

buying boxer shorts. In Target's menswear department, you'll still sometimes find a female-male ratio of 2:1 or even 3:1. But in expensive apparel stores, among more affluent men, males shopping for menswear
now—finally—outnumber females. We caught a signal moment in the
life of the modern American male on videotape. A man was browsing thoughtfully at an underwear display when he suddenly reached
around, grabbed a handful of his waistband, pulled it out and craned
his neck so he could learn—finally!—what size shorts he wears. Try to
imagine a woman who doesn't know her underwear size. Impossible.
Someday soon, we can all hope, every man will know his.

(Conversely, I am told that women frequently won't buy lingerie
without trying it on—over their own, I am assured. I don't know if I'll
live long enough to ever see a man take a package of Fruit of the Looms
into a fitting room.)

As women stop buying men's underwear, will men begin buying
women's? I met a jeweler who told me, "A lot of my business is with
men trying to buy their way back inside the house." Many a husband or
beau would choose fancy lingerie or jewelry at gift times, but the stores
that sell it, and the merchandise itself, make it daunting. If he can't remember his own size, how can he remember hers, especially when she
has bra and underpants to think about, not to mention robe, nightgown
etc. And how can he be sure he's buying the ring or necklace she wants,
in a color that suits her? We frequently see men tentatively enter these
lairs of femininity, cast anxious glances around, maybe study an item
or two, and then flee in fear and uncertainty. Sales clerks have to be
trained to lure these men in like the skittish beasts they are. Making a
personal shopper available for heavy-duty hand-holding isn't a bad idea,
especially considering the costliness of jewelry or even lingerie.

There also must be a way to simplify apparel sizes to make such
cross-buying possible. Perhaps the easiest solution would be for women
to register their sizes at clothing stores of their liking, then just point
their men in the right direction. The first store that tries this is going to
benefit from lots of latent desire among men to buy frilly underthings.
Then again, maybe they don't want to be seen walking out the door
with a pink shopping bag.

Another gender-related problem that clothing retailers have to solve is this: How do you subtly tell shoppers where the men's and women's apparel is in a store that sells both? Not so long ago, it was unthinkable that men's and women's clothing would be sold side by side, from the same site. That wall was knocked down in the '60s, but some of the bugs still need to be worked out. The cuing now being used, for instance, even in dual-gender pioneers such as the Gap and J.Crew, isn't really working, as you can tell when you suddenly realize that you spent ten minutes browsing through shoes, sweaters or jeans meant for the other sex.

Go into any woman's closet and you'll find something that was made for a man. A jean jacket, a baggy sweater, a T-shirt—my significant other raids my closet and drawers freely. No threat whatsoever to her sexuality. I can't say the same for myself.

Speaking of which, where does the gay shopper fit into this increasingly blurry retail environment? And what differences might there be between what a gay guy or lesbian woman is after versus his or her straight-world counterpart?

Needless to say, most generalizations about homosexual culture are just that—generalizations. There are gay women who feel at home in flannel button-down shirts and khakis, and lesbian princesses who like nothing more than glamming it up on Saturday night. There are gay guys who ego-idealize Brando in *The Wild One,* gay guys who are slobs and gay guys who assemble their wardrobe every morning with the kind of care and attention you don't see outside a West Point plebe barracks. This same wide spectrum shows up in the straight world.

The difference is the gay community has always been a cultural weathervane, with the foresight and instincts and taste to tell us what's in and what's out, what's hot and what's yesterday's news. Where gay culture leads, the rest of us generally follow, as any chiseled, Prada-clad metrosexual would be the first to admit.

At the same time many members of the heterosexual world don't really like to acknowledge this. Straight guys shopping the underwear section come up against a series of crotch-hugging pictorials on the boxes that make them feel as though they have to sneak their new boxer-briefs over to cash/wrap inside a brown paper bag. They feel embarrassed, but their embarrassment just may spring from the fact these sultry male gym pictures have found their target. Gay or straight, show me a teenage boy who hasn't wanted a six-pack or an aging Generation X guy who hasn't looked in the mirror at his tired-looking eyes, swelling flanks and loss of muscle mass, and I'll show you a retail world that hasn't taken into account the fact that a lot of heteros want to look as sharp and pulled together as a lot of their gay-world counterparts. Thing is, few of them want to admit it or show that they give a damn. It goes against the typical male's self-image to admit he cares.

In general, the retailing environment hasn't made allowances for this schizoid sensibility. Lesbians face the same confusion in the marketplace, except unlike their gay male counterparts, a lot of them have to cross over to the other gender's section to find what they want. The retail world generally creates less leeway for most gay women than it does for gay men. A lesbian of my acquaintance who describes herself as butch has a hard time finding even the most rudimentary clothing items and accessories. It's probably why she hates shopping and does most of it online. Most of what's on display is just too girly—coltish and pointy and designed to seduce. Pants are another big issue. There's rack after rack of low-riders, which aren't her style. Shoes? Another dead end. What she typically ends up doing is drifting over to the men's department in search of basic men's loafers—any style, so long as they're utilitarian and don't make her look like Glinda the Good Witch. Her wardrobe is mostly made up of classic casual clothes—baggy khakis, clothes created for women but designed to look like what your older brother might wear. At work, she'll suck it up by wearing one of the two black Eileen Fisher suits she owns, but if she could spend her days attired in baggy pants and a T-shirt she'd be the happiest person on earth. What I hear through her words is that even though she came out in her early twenties, when she's shopping she still finds herself living a double life.

It's worth noting that a lot of gay women can be pretty square, especially lesbian couples with kids. They're conservative, not politically but socially. Many of them don't like to make a fuss over shopping or the latest gowns dripping from store mannequins. Like guys, they just want to get the ordeal over with.

Gay men and women already came out once, which was brave. Retailers shouldn't make them have to dive back into the closet a second time. The gay market is real—and the people who pay attention to it will reap the rewards.

But back to the traditional family guy. Remember when the only men who saw babies being born were obstetricians? Today the presence of Dad in the delivery room is almost as mandatory as Mom's. Men are going to have to be accommodated as they redefine their roles as fathers. It's a seismic change that's being felt on the shopping floor just like everywhere else.

For example, almost no man of my father's generation had the habit of loading Junior, a bottle or two and some diapers into the stroller and going out for a Saturday-morning jaunt. Today it's almost a cliché. That's why progressive men's rooms now feature baby-changing stations, and it's why McDonald's commercials invariably show Dad and the kids piling in—sans Mom, who's probably spending Saturday at the office. (Mom won't let them order Big Macs anyway.) This isn't just an American phenomenon, either—my informal Saturday observation of Milan's most fashionable districts detected that roughly half of all baby strollers were being pushed by Papa. Papa likes to drive.

We tested a prototype Levi's section at a department store in Boston, part of an effort to improve the store's appeal to men in their twenties and thirties. We caught video of a young man walking down the aisle toward the section, accompanied by his wife and baby, whose stroller he pushed. They reached the Levi's, and he clearly wanted to shop the shelves of jeans on the wall. But there were racks of clothing standing between him and the jeans, positioned so close together that he couldn't nudge the stroller past. You can see him thinking through his choice—do I leave my wife and child in the aisle just to buy jeans? He did what most people would do in that situation: He skipped the pants. You'd be amazed at how much of America's aggregate selling floor is still off-limits to anyone pushing a stroller. This is the equivalent of barring a large percentage of all shoppers in their twenties and thirties.

Two decades ago it was the rare father who ever bought clothing for the little ones; today, it's more common to see men shopping the toddler section. Clothing manufacturers haven't caught up with this yet, however, as evidenced by the fact that children's sizes are the most confusing in all of apparel—guaranteed to frustrate all but the most parental of shoppers. The day that size corresponds directly to the age of the child is when men will be able to pull even more of the weight for outfitting the kids. It'll be Dad who springs for the outrageous indulgences here, too—the velvet smoking jacket for his son or the miniature prom gown for his daughter.

And when Saturday morning rolls around and Pop goes to pack the bottles and Cheerios and Goldfish and diapers and baby powder and ointment and wipes and all the rest of that stuff, what does he put it in? Not the big pink nylon bag his wife lugs. In fact, he's probably disposed against any of the available options—even a plain black diaper bag, says Mommy. But what if he could choose a Swiss Army diaper bag? How about a nylon Nike one that looks just like his gym bag? Even better, what if he could push a studly Harley-Davidson-brand baby stroller that came with a built-in black leather diaper bag? The whole baby category needs to be reinvented.

Other traditional female strongholds can also accommodate men, but it's got to be on masculine terms. You've got to be aware of the wimp factor. There are many stores where the floors and the walls and everything hanging on them whisper loudly to the foolhardy male trespasser, "Get the hell out of here—you don't belong!" Near my office there's a store that sells dishes and glasses and such, and it's remarkable because I can actually walk in and not feel like a bull in a china shop. Whereas in Bloomingdale's Royal Doulton section, I feel as though I'm back in my grandmother's dining room—and it's the grandmother who scared me.

There are other such places that men would gladly shop—actually want and even need to shop—if only they felt just a little bit wanted. For example, there are more health and grooming products for men than ever. But if you look at how they're sold, you'll see that most men will never become avid buyers.

In the chain drugstores and supermarket sections where these products are sold, the atmosphere is overwhelmingly feminine. Shampoo, soap and other products that can be used by either sex are invariably packaged and named under the assumption that women will be doing all the buying. It becomes a self-fulfilling prophecy. The products made especially for men, like shaving cream and hair ointments and deodorant, are stocked in a dinky little section sandwiched in among all the fragrant female goods. No man's land, in other words, so how's a guy to shop it?

The traditional beauty business has always prospered by moving upmarket. Estée Lauder and L'Oreal have persuaded women that dropping a small fortune on a night cream is a worthwhile investment. Not the best approach when you're dealing with the male market. The way for male skin-care products to succeed is through better positioning and carefully chosen words and packaging. There's a huge, untapped market for moisturizing creams and sunblock among men who work outdoors—police, construction workers, cable TV and telephone line installers, road crews. But these guys aren't going to traipse through the blushers and concealers to find them. And they're not going to buy a product that presents itself as intended for women and children. If you went through your typical health and beauty section, you'd think that men don't have skin. But they do, and it needs help.

A good solution might be found, say, at a Harley-Davidson dealer. The company could call its skin-care line whatever they wanted—sun shield, windburn care or human leather conditioner. The important thing is that they give it open-road, fuss-free value, plus a name that sounds like burly shorthand. Like Goop, which gets the grease off your hands, or Lava soap, which takes care of pine sap, it should be marketed as killer guy stuff. If Harley leads, John Deere and Caterpillar might follow, and a real step toward preventing skin cancer will have been made.

Clinique makes a complete line of shaving and skin products for men. But at the very sophisticated Bergdorf Goodman department store in New York City, a man has to visit the all-female cosmetics bazaar on the ground floor to find the stuff. It's not even available at the men's store across Fifth Avenue. Who would guess that the shaving cream is right next to the lipstick? I've no doubt that many women buy shaving products for their men, but that's the old-fashioned approach, not the way of the future. Gillette makes shaving creams for a variety of skin types, and there's no doubt that it's for men. But how is a man supposed to know which type of skin he has? A simple wall chart display would do the trick, but I've yet to see one. I recently visited a national chain's drugstore in Manhattan's Chelsea section, the epicenter of gay life here. Even this store shortchanges men—their section (which consisted only of deodorant, a few hair-grooming products, some Old Spice, a tube of Brylcreem) was jammed into a corner shelf between the film-processing booth and the disposable razors. This store would be a perfect place to create a prototype men's section. Instead, it was the same old dreariness.

Giving men their own products, and a place to buy them, would be a good start. But that still smacks of the health, beauty and cosmetics section designed for women. Someone needs to start from scratch in designing a "men's health" department, where you'd find skin products, grooming aids, shaving equipment, shampoo and conditioner, fragrance, condoms, muscle-pain treatments, over-the-counter drugs and the vitamins, supplements and herbal remedies for ailments that afflict men as well as women. There might also be some athletic wear, like socks, T-shirts, supporters, elastic bandages and so on. There should also be a display of books and magazines on health, fitness and appearance. The section itself would have a masculine feeling, from the fixtures to the package designs. And it would be merchandised with men in mind—the signs would be big and prominent, and everything would be easy to find. The number-one magazine success story of the past decade has been the amazing growth of a periodical called *Men's Health,* which sells over 1.5 million copies a month, more than *GQ, Esquire, Men's Journal* and all the others. If the magazine can thrive, why not the store section, too?

NINE

What Women Want

Before this chapter begins, may I take a moment to mark the passing of a great American institution and one of the last true bastions (if not actual hideouts) of postwar masculinity?

I'm speaking, of course, of Joe's Hardware. Or was it Jim's? Doesn't matter—you know the place. Creaky planks on the floor. Weird smell of rubber and four-in-one oil in the air. Big wooden bin of ten-penny nails. Twine. Elbow joints. Mystic tape. Spools of copper wire. Drums of waterproof sealant. Brads. *Brads?* Hell, brads, tacks, staples, washers, nuts, bolts (molly and otherwise), pins, sleeves, brackets, housings, flanges, hinges, gaskets, shims, wood screws, sheet metal screws, a calendar featuring Miss Snap-on Tools in a belly shirt brandishing killer cleavage and a power router, and over there—atop the rickety ladder, chewing a bad cheroot, rummaging blindly in an ancient box of two-prong plugs, cursing genially under his stogie breath—Joe himself. I mean Jim.

Whatever happened to him? Dead. How about his store? Dead.

Who killed them? Who do you think?

Oh, those . . . women! Too fancy to shop at Joe's, am I right? Poor guy stocked everything you could want, but it just wasn't enough. Not the right *color*. Not enough *styles*. The place stinks like *cheap cigars*.

Bye, Joe.

It's no surprise that women are capable of causing such tectonic shifts in the world of shopping. Shopping is still and always will be meant mostly for females. Shopping *is* female. When men shop, they are engaging in what is inherently a female activity. (When a man shops he's practically in drag.) And so, women are capable of consigning entire species of retailer or product to Darwin's dustbin, if that retailer or product is unable to adapt to what women need and want. It's like watching dinosaurs die out.

Need more evidence? Two words: sewing machine.

In the '50s, I am told, 75 percent of American households owned sewing machines. Today, it's under 5 percent. So roll over, Joe—here comes Mr. Singer. (In fact, the sewing machine giant has gone into the military weaponry business.) Women once made entire wardrobes for themselves and their families, and kept repairing garments until they had truly earned their rest. Then the past three decades of socioeconomic upheaval happened and women stopped sewing anything more ambitious than a loose button.

One last illustration?

Paper grocery store coupons.

Gone. Whoosh! In 2007, less than 3 percent of all manufacturers' coupons distributed via newspapers, magazines or in the mail were ever redeemed (in response, the coupon industry is making a valiant attempt to move the coupon distribution business online). Women's lives have changed, and the thought of sitting hunched over the kitchen table scissoring away at the *Daily Bugle* suddenly seems as cost-effective as churning your own butter. Oh, there are some pockets of coupon-clipping resistance—senior citizens, the highly budget-conscious and motivated, mostly women who aren't working at jobs all day. But otherwise— outtahere!

Of course, we're all familiar with how men have become better, more caring, more sensitive shoppers, willing to shoulder some of the burden even of mundane household acquisitioning and provisioning. But let's not forget that this reformation came about in large part because of gentle prompting (if not actual violent pushing and shoving) by women. And let's keep in mind also that while the future of retailing will undoubtedly show the effects of more male energy in the marketplace, for the most part the big shifts will continue to reflect changes in the lives and tastes of women.

But what, as marketing genius Sigmund Freud was moved to ask, do women want from shopping? We speak a great deal of the distinct differences between how men and women behave in stores, but rather than dish out generalizations, let me start with a good example. It's from a study we did for an Italian supermarket chain, and it comes directly from a video camera we trained on the meat counter.

There, we watched a middle-aged woman approach and begin picking up and examining packages of ground meat. She did so methodically, carefully, one by one. As she shopped a man strode up and, with his hands behind his back, stood gazing over the selection. After a brief moment he chose a package, dropped it into his cart, and sped away. The woman continued going through meat. Then came a couple with a baby. The wife hung back by the stroller while her husband picked up a package, gave it a quick once-over, and brought it back to their cart. His wife inspected it and shook her head. He returned it, chose another, and brought it back to their cart. His wife inspected it and shook her head. He chose again. She shook again. Exasperated, she left him by the stroller and got the meat herself. As they walked off, the first woman was making her way through the final package of meat on display. Satisfied with her research, she took the first one she had examined, placed it in her cart, and moved on. My sister complains that her husband goes out of his way to buy tired vegetables. "He doesn't get it. We want to eat fresh ones, not adopt the sad ones."

What makes women such heroic shoppers? The nature-over-nurture types posit that the prehistoric role of women as homebound gatherers of roots, nuts and berries rather than roaming hunters of woolly mammoths proves a biological inclination toward skillful shopping. The nurture-over-nature fans argue that for centuries, the all-powerful patriarchy kept women in the house and out of the world of commerce, except as consumers at the retail level.

This much is certain: Shopping was what got the housewife out of the house. Under the old division of labor, the job of acquisitioning fell mainly to women, who did it willingly, ably, systematically. It was (and in many parts of the world, remains) women's main realm of public life. If, as individuals, they had little influence in the world of business, in the marketplace they collectively called the shots. Shopping gave women a good excuse to sally forth, sometimes even in blissful solitude, beyond the clutches of family. It afforded an activity that lent itself to socializing with other adults, clerks and store owners and fellow shoppers.

As women's lives change, though, their relationship to shopping must evolve. Today, most American women hold jobs, and so they get all the impersonal, businesslike contact with other adults they want (and then some). They also get plenty of time away from the comforts of home. And so the routine shopping trip is no longer the great escape. It's now something that must be crammed into the tight spaces between job and commute and home life and sleep. It's something to be rushed through over a lunch hour, or on the way home, or at night. The convenience store industry is a direct beneficiary of how women's lives have changed—instead of a highly organized weekly trip to the supermarket, with detailed list in hand, women now discover at nine P.M. that they're out of milk or bread for tomorrow's lunches, prompting a moonlit run to the 7-Eleven. Catalogs, TV shopping channels and web shopping all have flourished thanks mainly to the changes in women's responsibilities. And the less time women spend in stores, the less they buy there, plain and simple. As they hand over some of their traditional duties (cooking, cleaning, laundry, child care) to men, they also relinquish control over the shopping for food, soap and kiddie clothes. Women may even become more male in their shopping habits—hurried hit-and-run artists instead of dedicated browsers and searchers. Right off the bat, the advantages of the postfeminist world to retailers (women have more money) are offset by some disadvantages (women have less time and inclination to spend it in stores).

The use of shopping as a social activity seems unchanged, however.

Women still like to shop with friends, egging each other on and rescuing each other from ill-advised purchases. I don't think we'll ever see two men set off on a day of hunting for the perfect bathing suit. All our studies show that when two women shop together, they spend more time and money than women alone. They certainly outshop and outspend women saddled with male companions. Two women in a store is a shopping machine, and wise retailers do whatever they can to encourage this behavior—promotions such as "bring a friend, get a discount," or seating areas just outside the dressing room to allow for more relaxed try-ons and assessments. Stores with cafés on the premises allow women to shop, then take a break, without ever leaving sight of the selling floor.

When you've observed as many shoppers as I have, you realize that for many women there are psychological and emotional aspects to shopping that are just plain absent in most men. Women can go into a kind of reverie when they shop—they become absorbed in the ritual of seeking and comparing, of imagining and envisioning merchandise in use. They then coolly tally up the pros and cons of this purchase over that, and once they've found what they want at the proper price, they buy it. Women generally care that they do well in even the smallest act of purchasing and take pride in their ability to select the perfect thing, whether it's a cantaloupe or a house or a husband. In fact, watch men and women in the produce section—the man breezes through, picks up the head of lettuce on top of the pile and wheels away, failing to notice the brown spots and limpid leaves, while the woman palpates, examines and sniffs her way past the garbage, looking for lettuce perfection. He'll even fail to notice how much the lettuce costs, something almost unthinkable among women. Men do take pride in their proficiency with certain durable goods—cars, tools, boats, barbecue grills, computers. Women, though, have traditionally understood the importance of the impermanent world—cooking a meal, decorating a cake, fixing hair and makeup.

Not that there's anything superficial about the female relationship with consumption. In fact, it's women, not men, who plumb the metaphysics of shopping—they illuminate how we human beings go through life searching, examining, questioning and acquiring and assuming and absorbing the best of what we see. At that exalted level, shopping is a transforming experience, a method of becoming a newer, perhaps even slightly improved person. The products you buy turn you into that other, idealized version of yourself: That dress makes you beautiful, this lipstick makes you kissable, that lamp turns your house into an elegant showplace.

In practical terms, this all means one patently obvious, overarching thing: Women demand more of shopping environments than men do. Males just want places that allow them to find what they need with a minimum of looking and then get out *fast*. If a male is made to wander and seek—in other words, to *shop*—he's likely to give up in frustration and exit. Men take less pleasure in the journey. Women are more patient and inquisitive, completely at ease in a space that gradually reveals itself. Therefore, they need environments where they can spend time and move about comfortably at their own speed in what sometimes resembles a semitrance state. Our most famous discovery, the "butt-brush factor," indicates to us that women have an actual aversion to examining anything much below waist level, for fear of being jostled from the rear. This takes in quite a bit of American retailing's selling space. You can't ask a woman (or a man) to bend over and expect that she's going to feel comfortable for more than a moment or two. You can't crowd a woman and think that she's going to linger. Watch shoppers' faces in busy aisles—once they've been bumped a few times they begin to look annoyed. And irritated shoppers do not tarry; in fact, they frequently leave before buying what they came for. Retailers must keep all this in mind when deciding where to sell what.

It's equally true that women can and will steel themselves for a sale they know will be crowded. They'll shop at Filene's Basement in Boston and the Barneys Warehouse Sale, and their hunger for bargains will overcome whatever issues they have with strangers piercing their body bubbles. What we've noted over the years is that a woman's butt-brush radar is also calibrated to respond differently to other females than unfamiliar males. In most of the crowded places where women wade fearlessly, they're jostled, pulled and yanked not by men but by other women.

For instance, department store cosmetics sections require women to sit or stand in one spot while makeup is demonstrated, which can be a problem during busy times. Over and over, our research has shown that women standing at the corner of a counter, where they can wrap themselves around the angle and nestle in a little bit, actually buy at a higher rate than women standing a few feet away along the main stretch of the counter. Some cosmetics departments use counters to create cul-de-sacs, recessed areas that allow shoppers to stand clear of passing foot traffic and browse without fear—we call them catchment basins, and they are successful at inducing women to shop a little longer. As discussed earlier, drugstores sometimes stock unglamorous products such as concealer cream at the very bottom of a wall display—meaning that older women, the shoppers least likely to appreciate having to stoop, are forced to bend low and stick their butts out where they'd rather not go. As a result, less concealer will be sold than if it was positioned higher.

Women's spatial requirements can be seen everywhere in retailing. Airport gift shops, for instance, are typically divided into the "grab and go" zone—near the register, where you dart in for a paper or gum, pay and run—and the "dwell" zone, farther into the store, where gift items are usually displayed. Our research shows that women in these stores gravitate away from the hubbub around the counter and toward the dwell zone, where they feel protected from foot traffic. Many of these stores' architecture features little nooks and crannies created by shelving and racks—perfect cul-de-sacs for uninterrupted shopping. That's how women prefer to shop: within view of the main flow of traffic, but sheltered in sectioned-off areas.

The butt sensitivity of women also establishes a relationship between store design and typeface: The narrower the quarters, the less time a woman will spend there, so the clearer and more direct signs and other merchandising materials must be. All print must be big and high contrast; designers of shampoo bottles, for instance, or any products sold in the close quarters of a chain drugstore, have to heed this reality. We've studied many drugstore health and beauty departments and the result is always the same—women like to study products before they buy, especially if the product is new on the market. In one study, we saw that 91 percent of all drugstore buyers read the front of a package, 42 percent read the back and 8 percent read the sides. Sixty-three percent of women who bought something read at least one product package. So there's a clear connection between reading and buying. And reading takes time. And time requires space. Here's the breakdown from our compiled database; times are for how long women who made purchases read the packaging first:

Facial cleaners: 13 seconds
Moisturizers: 16 seconds
Hand and body soap: 11 seconds
Shower gel: 5 seconds
Sun care: 11 seconds
Acne medications: 13 seconds

But if women don't feel comfortable, they won't pause for two seconds, and they certainly won't buy any of the products that require a little study. Retailers should walk every foot of selling space asking this question: Can I stand here and shop without being jostled from behind? Any place where the answer is no is no place for merchandise requiring a careful look.

Even in fast-food restaurants, males and females have different spatial requirements. Without much consideration, men choose tables up front, where they have a good view of the busiest part of the room. Women will take a moment or two to shop for where they'll down their Big Macs, and then they gravitate toward the rear, to tables that afford a little privacy. In fact, women aren't all that crazy about going into fast-food restaurants alone. They make up a large percentage of fast-food diners who go through the drive-thru and eat in their cars in the restaurant parking lot.

You can really see the female shopping reverie in stores where women dominate—for instance, at the greeting card shop. There, women aren't merely fulfilling obligations, they're searching for authentic emotional expression. Women will devote quite a bit of time to studying card after card to find the one that speaks their hearts. Card stores should therefore feel like places where the emotional life reigns. A few years ago Hallmark hired an architect with a lot of experience designing department stores to redo its retail spaces. She created a very stylish look, using lots of marble and other expensive materials, but the overall feeling was colder and more elegant than Hallmark customers had been used to. They must have missed their familiar warm and fuzzy environments; in response to the redesign, shopping time dropped.

Card stores must be designed to allow quiet, unhurried contemplation, meaning that aisles should be wide enough to allow room for readers and for those just passing by. Aisles must also be wide enough for baby strollers. Adjacencies should be planned rather than accidental: You don't want to be trying to find the perfect message of condolence and have your concentration broken by the woman next to you laughing at the dirty fortieth-birthday cards. Other important display issues also come to the fore in card stores. Women buy cards only after picking up, opening and reading a great many of them. But the merchandise is fragile—easily folded, torn or soiled. It amazes me that there is still no widely used display system that would allow shoppers to read sample cards but not actually touch the merchandise. Also, in card stores the displays usually start at about a foot or so off the floor and rise to about six feet high. There are two problems with that: One, the low cards are too far down to be seen without stooping; and two, the low cards are too easily touched by grubby-fingered small children accompanying their mothers. If the whole display were raised by a foot, the problems would be solved. Even if the highest cards were seven feet off the floor, they would be within reach of anyone taller than five feet.

The other great arena where female shopping behaviors are on display is in cosmetics. Whether it's in a department store's impossibly glamorous cosmetics bazaar or a chain drugstore's wall display of lipsticks and eye shadow, this is where a woman in jeans and a sweater can be transformed into a princess just by testing a few items and pouting into a mirror. This is as public as a private art form ever gets. There's a good reason cosmetics are usually stocked along a wall or in their own sheltered area—this is where women let their hair down, literally and figuratively. They need a little privacy if they're going to cut loose.

Typically, women start as adolescents buying the cheaper brands down at the drugstore. Then they'll trade up to the fancy, high-priced stuff sold in department stores by the glam representatives of the various manufacturers—the dolls in the officious white lab coats (but Saturday-night-out makeup) brandishing brushes loaded with rouge and base and the rest. This is the high-pressure school of cosmetics selling. You sit on the stool, she turns you into a slightly toned-down version of herself, and you buy what she urged on you (in theory, at least). The prices are intentionally obscure, figuring that you'll be too intimidated to ask.

That's still the standard setup, but it's quickly changing now thanks to the "open sell" concept finally having come to the cosmetics counter. It's a form of women's liberation: The makeup is being freed from the clutches of the demonstrator-saleswoman and is out on its own for shoppers to test, ponder, try and then buy—or not. Some of the old game of let's pretend is gone, but so are some of the old high-pressure tactics. This open sell also allows women to check the price of makeup without having to endure the humiliation of asking that imperious clerk. By lessening the sticker shock, stores should end up selling more cosmetics.

These are the immutables of how women shop, the fundamentals that still (and may always) apply. Which is all well and good and necessary if anyone is going to sell anything. But it's not where the action is today.

We've seen what gender revolt means where male shoppers are concerned: All the contemporary effort lies in taking stores and products intended mainly for women and making them safe for guys. For women, it's just the opposite—the challenge is in making traditionally "male" products and environments appealing to female shoppers.

For example, the old-fashioned emporium of nuts and bolts still lingers here and there, but for the most part, one category killer has done away with it. How did Home Depot and Lowe's manage that? Mainly by reflecting the socioeconomic reality that women no longer depend on men in the old-fashioned way. What does that have to do with wing nuts and duct tape? Well, were the females who spent all day at the barricades of social and political enlightenment going to come home at night and beg hubby (for the fifteenth time) to paint the window trim or install the dimmers? Unlikely. Not to mention the rise over the past three decades of the single female homeowner—women with the money and the desire to feather their own nests. Can we have female cops and firefighters and CEOs and cyber-entrepreneurs and presidential candidates and not have confident, ambitious, fully empowered handywomen, too? I don't think so.

And where would these women go to begin their careers as tool guys? To Joe's Hardware? No—the typical hardware store was exclusively, unapologetically masculine, and maybe even a little unfriendly to female ways. It was a tree house with a cash register. So something had to give. Enter the do-it-yourself chains. (And, from the other end of the retailing spectrum, the hardware boutiques.) They stripped hardware of its arcane side, rendering it unintimidating, even friendly, to the greenest tyro. Doing that required a major shift in mission as well as merchandising: Stores that sold nuts and bolts gave way to stores that sold lifestyles. Under that vast umbrella, nuts and bolts and lumber and sheetrock could be sold alongside lighting fixtures and kitchen cabinets and Jacuzzis and frilly (and nonfrilly) curtains and everything else. These stores sold not hardware but homes. The retail hardware industry has gone from an Erector Set mentality to a "let's play house" approach, from boys-only to boys and girls playing together.

This has also been done by hiring salesclerks who are knowledgeable and able to instruct and inspire confidence in female customers. The new wave of home stores hires women for sales and managerial jobs traditionally held only by guys named Joe (or Jim). There are many Home Depot TV spots in which only females appear. The stores also make enthusiastic use of any opportunity for education, whether with how-to videos or free in-store handyman lessons. These stores realize that the woman who is taught to hang a picture today will spackle tomorrow and install crown molding next month. Who do you think is watching *Extreme Makeover: Home Edition* and HGTV and all the other fix-it shows on TV? The manly men are watching the bass-fishing channel, while the women are watching handymen like Ty Pennington, who resemble nothing more than hunky soap opera stars in toolbelts.

This infusion of female energy changes even how the stores display their goods. No longer can lighting fixtures simply be hung on a rack or stood on a shelf. Retailers have to show exactly how the lights will look in a room. Instead of displaying a box of bathroom faucets, stores now show the whole tub, complete with shower curtain and towels. Here's the indisputable proof of how Home Depot and Lowe's vanquished the old-fashioned nuts-and-bolts emporium: Before, you went to a hardware store only when you needed something. Now, you go just to browse, to see what's new and what's on display. You can now actually shop hardware—which means, by definition, that women have won and Joe (or Jim) has lost.

It's no accident that the most successful recent paint launches sell under the names of lifestyle gurus Martha Stewart and Ralph Lauren. Paint has gone from being hardware to being fashion, all because women got involved. Men don't paint until the walls are peeling and cracking; women do it when they (the women, not the walls) need a change. Of course, painting has always been within the abilities of your average man or woman. But only now has paint itself—the way it is packaged and marketed and sold—gone unisex.

There's another beneficiary of how hardware has changed—all we baby boomer men who somehow made it to adulthood without ever learning how to be handy around the house. As women became more handy, men became less so; we, too, had begun to feel a little intimidated by the old-fashioned hardware store. But even this has come at some cost to men: In the days since feminism's rise, we've seen the decline not only of hardware stores but also of the guys-only barbershop, the shoeshine stand and the men's clothing and shoe store. First the barriers to female admission to universities, the military, private clubs and all the rest fell. Then unisex hair salons and stores like the Gap, Banana Republic and J.Crew came along to desegregate clothing stores and even styles. The overall thrust of the second half of the century has been to flush men out of their dens, and for better or worse, or maybe both, it's worked. (Is the pendulum ready to swing back? Have you been to a cigar bar lately?)

A second great arena for gender upheaval is the computer store and other places where consumer electronics are sold. Stereotypically, we think of males as being the ones at the personal technology frontier, actually knowing what gigabytes mean or shelling out five-figure sums for speakers. More recently, personal computers and cell phones all began life as toys for boys. But the fact is that often, women are the earliest adopters of new technology. When businesses began using computers, the female office workers had to learn first about operating systems and software. Those same women, crunched for time on their lunch breaks, were the earliest enthusiasts of the automated teller machine.

How did we not notice? Because men and women use technology in very different ways. Men are in love with the technology itself, with the gee-whiz factor, with the horsepower and the bang for the buck. Back before cars had computerized innards, the commonest sight in America was three or four guys assembled around the raised hood of a car, watching its owner adjust a carburetor or install a generator and offering copious advice on how it could be done better. Today, those same men are gathered around the barbecue comparing the size of their hard drives and the speed of their BlackBerries. As they say, it's a dude thing.

Women take a completely different approach to the world of high tech. They take technologies and turn them into appliances. They strip even the fanciest gizmo of all that is mysterious and jargony in order to determine its usefulness. Women look at technology and see its purpose, its reason—what it can *do*. The promise of technology is always that it will make our lives easier and more efficient. Women are the ones who demand that it fulfill its promise.

From the vantage point of 2009, we know that the female consumer is key to the health of the consumer electronics industry. RadioShack has gone out of its way to hire female store managers. Best Buy has made the correlation between the success of an individual store and the number of female employees it has out on the selling floor.

What will all this lead to? Well, someday there will be a computer company with a highly visible woman at (or very near) the helm, somebody to hold forth on the business page of the *Times* and on CNBC— kind of like a female Bill Gates (but with a better haircut). Its products will emphasize not the size of the RAM or the speed of the microprocessor but rather ease of use, versatility and convenience. It will focus on results, not process. Its computers will be sold like refrigerators instead of like scientific instruments. The most heavily promoted feature will be a toll-free number for plainspoken technical help when a program freezes or a printer malfunctions. Then some agency will begin using images of women in its TV and print ads, maybe even in a campaign that lampoons how men relate to technology. Finally, designers will provide ergonomically improved keyboards. Computers will be easy to clean (they're almost impossible now). Most will even come in colors other than putty or black! And you'll be able to buy a Coach laptop case in a matching or complementary color.

Need evidence that men and women see technology differently? At a computer software store we studied, the shoppers were largely male, but the conversion rate, the percentage of shoppers who bought something, was highest among women. That's because they were in the store with some practical mission to carry out, not just to daydream over a new Zip drive or a scanner.

The car industry, perhaps the most backward and antishopper business in America, has realized for a few years now that women buy cars. Considering what a male-dominated world car sales has always been, dealers should be hiring lots of women to sell and service cars. But fewer than 10 percent of all car salespeople are female. Hiring women to sell cars isn't just political correctness, either—most women surveyed say they'd feel more comfortable buying cars from other females. They're not male-haters so much as they are feeling a little condescended to and maybe even ripped off by male car salesmen.

Car salesmen live by the conventional wisdom that the male half of a couple makes the decision, not realizing that in many cases the woman is the one who's pushing for the new wheels or that her objections are what must be overcome. So the pitch is directed at the male while the woman silently burns. After the sale is closed, the buyers will usually be brought back to the service department to meet the manager. Back there it's usually 100 percent guy-land, starting even with the choice of magazines in the waiting area (*Car and Driver* and *Sports Illustrated* but not *Vanity Fair* or *People*). Someday soon we may see Ms. Goodwrench or the Pep Girls—Mary, Jo and Jill—but they're not here yet. Women report a distinct distaste for all their dealings with auto dealers, mechanics and car parts stores. They feel patronized, scorned and ripped off, but they also realize there's not much of a choice so far. They deserve better.

Again, the smart first move would be to hire females to fix cars and sell parts. Using actresses in TV spots also goes a long way toward repositioning this all-male world. A few years ago we did a study for a mass merchandiser's auto parts department. Ninety percent of the shoppers were male, but 25 percent of those who used the computerized information fixtures were female. Clearly, those women had questions and wanted answers that they weren't getting from the salesclerks. Maybe the clerks didn't know the answers, or maybe the women just didn't enjoy asking those guys. Either way, it shows that women are eager to learn how to handle the basic maintenance and easy repairs for their cars.

If I bought a gas station tomorrow, the first thing I'd do is put up a huge sign saying CLEAN BATHROOMS. Gas stations persist in displaying most prominently the price per gallon, down to the tenth of a cent, as though we even think that small. Gas is gas, and prices are fairly uniform, too. But clean bathrooms would draw female drivers, who make more use of facilities and so have more bitter complaints about horrible, filthy conditions. The fact is that while gas has become a self-serve item, we need assistance on the road now more than ever. We're going greater distances and so need directions, decent places to eat and drink, and clean bathrooms. Maybe even someplace with a clean baby-changing table and a working sink and a trash can that isn't spilling all over the floor. No woman is going to sweat a few pennies in gas price if she is cared for otherwise. Don't male gas station owners realize that? Mostly they don't—why would they? But if there were more women involved in the car business, from dealerships to parts and repair to gasoline, the whole industry would look different. It would look like—hardware! Which may mean that even the car business isn't quite hopeless.

TEN

If You Can Read This
You're Too Young

No doubt you already know this statistic: By 2025, nearly one fifth of all American people will be 65 or older. If you live in Japan, Italy, Germany, France or China, the percentage gets bigger. You also realize what that means: old baby boomers. A lot of old baby boomers.

But what will *that* mean? Well, right off the bat, it means it'll be good to be old. How could it be otherwise? When boomers were young, youth was good. When they were middle-aged, a certain seasoned maturity was good. And old people of the twenty-first century won't be like the current sober crop of senior citizens. Future oldsters didn't grow up in the Depression or slog through World War II; they came of age during the fat, self-indulgent '50s, '60s and '70s. They weren't force-fed the virtues of sacrifice, self-denial and delayed gratification, nor did they absorb the quaint notion that to be old is to accept infirmity and inability stoically, as one's lot in life. The little old lady of 2025 won't have a spotless Ford Fairlane (that she drives once a week, to church) sitting in her garage. She'll be buzzing around town in an Alfa Romeo (standard equipment including seats with hydraulic lifts), dressed head to toe in the Nike "Silver" line, parking in the plentiful spaces reserved for people who are old but not impaired (as mandated by the 2012 Spunky Aging Americans Act). Thanks to improved health care, nutrition, fitness and cosmetic surgery, at seventy she'll look and feel like her mother did at fifty. The kids will be grown and gone, working like ants to keep Social Security afloat, while we geezers squander the fruits of our 401(k)s along with what we inherited from our departed parents, whose demise is even now beginning to trigger the largest transfer of wealth in the history of money.

For the world of shopping, it's going to be a party! That's obvious. All of retailing—stores, restaurants and banks—is going to have to cater to us, because we'll have the numbers and the dollars. But we're going to need a whole new world. This one's not going to work. And we're not gonna take it!

What's wrong with this world? For starters, all the words are too damn small. See this sentence? How could you? Too damn small. How about the morning paper? Forget it. Too damn small. The directions on your jar of organic herbal laxative? Too. Damn. Small. And you're not even going to try squinting. (It causes wrinkles.) If you can't read it, by gum, you just won't buy it. And if *you* don't buy organic herbal laxative, nobody will. And if nobody buys it . . . well, you see where this is going.

Human eyes begin to falter at about age forty, and even healthy ones are usually impaired by their sixties. With age, three main ocular events take place: The lens becomes more rigid and the muscles holding it weaken, meaning you can't focus on small type; the cornea yellows, which changes how you perceive color; and less light reaches your retina, meaning the world looks a little dimmer than it once did. The issue of visual acuity, already a major one in the marketplace, will become even more critical—not just in some far-off future, but from this moment on.

For example, every current study done of newspaper readership comes back with the same result: Readers want bigger text. Most papers now use body text of roughly nine-point type. (This book is set in 11.75-point type.) Readers want twelve-point or larger. And newspapers are just starting to get it. *The Miami Herald,* I think, was the first major daily to upsize, then the London *Times* went from a broadsheet to a tabloid format, with larger headlines and chubbier font, and in 2007 the *New York Times* actually shrunk the paper size and reduced the number of columns, making the print easier to read, but still uses 8.7-point type. We still have a long way to go, but why did it take this long for them to see us waving at them?

But typeface problems aren't limited to the publishing business. The main market today for drugstores is older people, and that dependence will only increase. Certainly, of all the words we are required to read in the course of our lives, few are more important than the labels, directions and warnings on drugs, both prescription and over the counter. For instance, we have found that 91 percent of all skin care customers buy only after they've read the front label of the box, bottle or jar. Forty-two percent of buyers also read the back of the package. Clearly, reading is crucial to selling skin care and other health and beauty items.

Our studies of drugstore packaging also reveal some interesting comparisons. For instance, the directions, ingredients and/or warning information is ten-point or larger on the packaging for famous brands of hair dye, skin cream, acne medicine and toothpaste. But it's between six-point and nine-point on aspirin and a host of other common analgesics. It is also between six-point and nine-point on cold capsules and other sneezy-stuffy-drippy products, as well as on vitamins. In other words, packaging designers make it much easier for teenagers to read their pimple cream than for seniors to read their headache or cold remedies. The only concession to age we found was on a box of Polident, which uses eleven-point type for directions and eight-point for ingredients.

This is obviously a failing on the part of the wizards in drug companies' packaging divisions. But when you realize that most graphic designers, including those who create labels, are in their twenties, it's easy to see why there has been such a gargantuan miscalculation. The people who make the packaging have no idea how it looks to the people who must read it. Take a gander at publications intended for youthful readers—I mean magazines like *Wired* or *Spin.* In all, the type is tiny and frequently printed on backgrounds that provide little contrast. The message is clear: This magazine is meant for the young and will make no concessions to decrepitude. It's equivalent to when Mick Jagger, a well-born college graduate, slurred and swallowed his lyrics, rendering his music inaccessible to ears that had grown up on Bing Crosby and Patti Page. In the next century, the disparity of age between designers of drugstore products and their most frequent readers will only broaden.

At some drugstores in Florida, magnifying glasses on chains have been attached to the shelves. This is a clever makeshift solution, but it's not going to be enough. Drugstores report that overall, about one shopper in five seeks employee assistance, but almost double that percentage of senior citizen customers ask for help. Invariably, what they require is the aid of younger eyes to find a product or read a label. You can go through *any* kind of store and find commercial type that's a challenge for aging eyes to read. The nutritional information on the side of a cereal box. The laundering instructions on a silk shirt. The directions on hair dye, a self-test for cholesterol, the manual for a camera or software or a DVD player. The specifications on a computer printer ink-jet cartridge. The song titles on a CD. The size on a pair of golf shoes. The price on a paperback. And how are future customers going to find your business— by reading the telephone book or online directory? I can't read it *now*. And let's not forget restaurant menus, train schedules, government forms, birthday cards, postage stamps, thermometers, speedometers, odometers, the radio dial, the buttons on your washer and dryer and air conditioner and refrigerator, your humidifier, your hot-water heater . . . Did I mention those little stickers that tell you the pear you just bought is, in fact, *a pear*? How will you ever know? In every instance, the object makes itself forbidding and even hostile to older shoppers by dint of typeface size alone. Today's senior citizens endure this minor form of discrimination without complaint, as their lot in life. But old boomers, accustomed to having existence itself tailored to their specifications, surely will rebel. By 2025, anything smaller than thirteen-point type will be a form of commercial suicide. Even today, as our vision begins to blur, using nine-point type qualifies as a self-destructive tendency.

But did you notice the dilemma here? The better educated (and therefore better off) the shopper, the more he or she makes decisions based on what's written on labels, boxes and jars. In fact, all retailing depends on the written word now more than ever before. That would seem to call for putting as much information on products, packaging and merchandising materials as possible. But when designers are told to squeeze in more type, they usually do so by making it smaller. Maybe bigger packages are a solution (although that would cause its own difficulties when it's time to allocate shelf space, not to mention the waste of more good trees). Maybe labels should make greater use of graphic images. Maybe it's time for bigger and better signs or talking display fixtures. It might come in the form of a prompt sent to our cell phones or BlackBerries. Or better yet, a completely re-thought-out union of package and instructions—environmentally friendly, with recyclable containers and instructions printed on renewable hemp paper. Maybe we should try all of the above, because we're going to need a culture-wide jump in type size before long.

And size isn't the only optical consideration. The yellowing of the aging cornea means that certain subtle gradations of color will become invisible to a large part of the population. So, for instance, more people than ever will trip up (or fall down) stairs as the clear distinction between step and riser disappears. The difference between blue and green will become more difficult for many shoppers to perceive, and yellow will be become much trickier for designers to use—*everything* will look a little yellow. As a result, packaging, signs and advertising will have to be designed for maximum contrast, not just for the nuanced interplay of colors. We're going to have to see a lot more black, white and red and a lot less of any other hue.

For instance, we tested merchandising materials for a large California savings bank, and while interviewing departing customers, we found that a large poster on the wall behind the tellers had low recall among older patrons. The poster, which promoted the bank's Visa Gold card, showed an oversized credit card sitting atop a gold brick. To us, the image was clear. To older eyes, though, the distinction between the card and the gold was invisible, so it looked like a single large, mysterious yellow shape—a meaningless poster, to many people over sixty-five. We studied signage at a major New York hotel and realized that the color scheme for the room numbers, gold lettering on an off-white back-ground, was making the place difficult to navigate for old eyes.

Finally, the typical fifty-year-old's retinas receive about one quarter less light than the average twenty-year-old's. That means lots of stores, restaurants and banks should be brighter than they are now. There can't be pockets of dim light, not if shoppers are going to see what they're shopping or even where they're walking. Illumination must be bright, especially during those times of day when older shoppers tend to arrive. And again, all print will have to be bold and high contrast—dark colors on white (or light) backgrounds.

Why is it that winemakers have begun thinking of their labels as art projects? From Kroger to Trader Joe's, we've documented a kazil-lion people struggling to read labels. It's even worse at your local liquor store, where the lighting tends to be dimmer than in the big chains and the shelves can be downright gloomy. I'm not suggesting that a label can't be pretty or have a kangaroo on it, just that a bottle has to be picked up and glanced at before it gets bought. This is particularly important for small and up-and-coming vintners. Type of wine, country of origin, year, vineyard and a marketing plug—this is all stuff custom-ers are looking for. Proven snotty French brands can do what they want, but all those superb newcomers to the global wine market from Chile, Argentina, South Africa, Australia and New Zealand need to pay atten-tion.

One of our fast-food clients realized that diners over fifty-five were their fastest-growing demographic, despite the fact that the menu boards used type that was almost impossible for older people to see well. The company redesigned the menus using large photos of the food, and even though it meant listing fewer items, sales rose.

Changing the visual world to accommodate aging eyes will be easy compared to the structural alterations that are going to be required. Even in the twenty-first century, old people will be creaky. And keep in mind that senior citizenship is going to last longer than anyone ever imagined—we'll be old for decades, many of us, longer in some cases than we were young. The same world will have to be navigable by robust sixty-five-year-olds and rickety eighty-five-year-olds. Twenty years ago many of the newly retired bought retirement condos in seaside areas, and some of those apartments were two- or three-story walkups with ocean-view porches—perfect aeries to while away your golden years, it seemed. Now, however, two decades later, many of those springy-gaited sixtysomethings are wheelchair-bound or otherwise unable to climb, rendering those getaways obsolete. How will our stores and streets and malls fare when today's swarms of baby carriages are replaced by motorized wheelchairs? Doorways, elevators, aisles, cash register areas, restaurant tables, bathrooms, airplanes, trains, buses and private cars will all have to be considerably wider than they are now. Ramps will be required by commercial considerations if not by government fiat. Stairs will be relics. Escalators and moving sidewalks will have to be redesigned and in some cases slowed down. Think of all the multilevel malls that by 2025 will seem inconvenient, if not downright impossible, to one fifth of the population. Remember, older shoppers will be everywhere then, at the drugstore but also at the Gap and Ralph Lauren and Toys"R"Us and Starbucks and Borders, the brand names on which tomorrow's codgers—we—came of age. Once manufacturers start making stylish, sporty motorized wheelchairs (they'll be more like street-ready one-person golf carts) and sleek, European-styled walkers, we'll really see the difference. We'll need cops to direct pedestrian traffic.

It won't just be for the immobile that the retail landscape will have to change, either. Even ambulatory older shoppers can't bend or stretch like they used to. And they don't really want to—bending and stretching make them feel their age, which is the last thing they want to feel. At RadioShack, the slowest-selling batteries were for use in hearing aids, so the conventional wisdom dictated they should be stocked at the bottom of the freestanding "spinner" fixtures. Of course, who buys hearing aid batteries but old people, the shoppers least able to stoop? When the batteries were moved higher on the spinners, sales went up, and sales of the batteries that were moved to the bottom didn't drop at all. We looked at the women's couture floor of a New York department store and found a similar issue. Not surprisingly, many of the women who can afford these clothes are older and therefore tend to be of generous proportions. The designers, however, in order to keep up their image, stock sizes 4 and 6 on the racks and keep sizes 14 and 16 in a back room somewhere, forcing the humiliated shopper to ask one of the painfully thin salesclerks to go and fetch her something a little roomier. Elsewhere in apparel a similar situation pertains: Racks and shelves of underwear or trousers are organized in size order, the smallest up top and the largest way down at the bottom—forcing the fattest and oldest customers to strain themselves, while making it easy on the young and the supple.

(Personally, I'd like to lead a revolt of tall shoppers, those of us who are forced to bend low at every ATM and water fountain in existence. We're getting taller as a populace, and older, too, meaning that bending will truly hurt in two or three decades.)

In supermarkets, products stocked too low or too high are virtually off-limits to the older shopper; it's just not worth the trouble, they sigh. I'll find it elsewhere. This is especially so with heavy items like cases of soft drinks or large boxes of detergent—if you can't just slide it off the shelf and into your cart, you won't buy it there. (In fact, for the sake of shoppers of all ages, bulky packages should be shelved at shopping-cart-top height.) Remember our pet treats example from chapter 1? Making life easy on older shoppers not only sells goods, it engenders warm feelings among a group that is often badly served by retailers. The geezer who comes in for hearing-aid batteries and doesn't have to exert himself to get them will probably return when he needs to buy a cell phone or a computer.

Japan is one country that has made great strides in accommodating its aging population. In Japan, land is precious and the malls tend to go up rather than sprawl. In some malls, the escalators move very slowly, not to annoy the sprinting teenagers in the crowd, but in deference to Japan's aging customer base. Japan's largest mobile service provider, DoCoMo, has a senior-friendly phone with big buttons and oversized numerals. It bears asking again: Are we as remotely prepared in the U.S., or in Italy or Russia (two other countries with rapidly aging populations), for the same graying consumers? Our over-fifty population is increasingly unable to endure spatial uncertainty. Which is a fancy way of saying that in stores that cover more than thirty thousand square feet, most graying consumers don't get a kick out of getting lost. Merchants would like their customers to get deliciously lost, not addled-and-simmering-and-ready-to-blow-their-tops lost.

Waiting areas are, or should be, another key concern for merchants and landlords. If your average senior knows she can walk a certain distance and find a place where she can sit, she's more likely to do just that. HEB, the Texas grocery store chain, recognizes that many Latino families enjoy shopping in multigenerational clusters. Having benches scattered through the store is both an act of kindness and guerilla marketing. Plus, any waiting area is a fantastic selling and communications point. Your audience is captive, ready to read any and all information you give them. You'll also score especially big points with elderly customers if you make your chairs easy to get into and out of. Those of us in our presenior years who are in positions of moderate influence have a fairly vested interest in preparing the universe for our own dotage. Now isn't too soon to take a hard look at older shoppers. Before Calvin Klein comes out with a line of designer adult diapers, we need to make our world a lot more senior-friendly.

One of the ongoing challenges in contemporary banking is getting older customers to use ATMs. The automated tellers can be intimidating if you're not already comfortable with interactive touch-screens and machine-speak. Senior citizens can be taught, but it shouldn't be by youngsters or officious junior VP wannabes; older customers prefer to be instructed by their contemporaries, all our surveys say—one older bank employee stationed by the teller lines can escort multitudes of senior customers to ATMs. It also helps to have ATMs within sight of the teller lines; if seniors can watch people use the machines, they lose some of their fearsomeness. Due to failing eyes and arthritic fingers, those ATMs will have to adapt, too—the buttons will have to become larger, as will the screens *and* the words on them. If the gains in economy made by self-serve are to be maintained, lots of machines will have to be redesigned for older hands and vision. The written directions and buttons on the stamp vending machines and do-it-yourself scales at the post office, for instance, are too small for the aged to manage easily. The same is true of the credit card reader and pump at the self-service gas station line, the commuter train ticket machine and the check-in kiosk at the airport.

Tiny buttons and hooks on clothing—especially the inconvenient back closures on women's garments—will have to be replaced with simpler fasteners, like Velcro. Cell phone makers currently compete to see who can go smallest, but at some point the phone with the largest buttons and liquid crystal display will be most desirable, at least among older users. (That'll be at about the same time that cell phones go from being yuppie toys to senior citizen lifelines.) Remote controls for TV, cable box and CD player, the buttons on the camcorder, the notebook computer keyboard—at the current rate, all will essentially miniaturize themselves out of the running for senior citizen dollars. I keep speaking as though all this is going to take place in the future, but that's wrong: It's already begun to happen. The world of retailing is having an interesting response.

Where are all the energy and innovation and capital expenditure in retail environments going today? To serve the coming tsunami of ancient shoppers, of course, am I right? No, I'm wrong—they're all devoted to stores aimed at youthful dollars, like Abercrombie, American Eagle, Roxy and Torrid. The new interactive fixtures and displays coming out of design labs are dazzling—you're never sure if you're in a store or a theme park, which is the whole point, I guess. It must be a lot of fun to dream up such gizmos and the stores that contain them. And so it's no wonder that's where all the action is.

Unfortunately, these stores are catering to a market that's already on the decline. Based on U.S. census data, the number of Americans over sixty-five will more than double by the year 2035—as I said, it's by far the fastest-growing segment of our population. There's plenty of work ahead in making the world of retail better serve senior citizens. For our own sake, let's hope some of that labor, too, is carried out with imagination and verve.

In fact, the time to begin that work is now. Let's start small—by demanding better elevator music! I want to make my supermarket sojourns to the sounds of the Doors themselves, not 1001 Syrupy Strings' version of "Light My Fire." In fact, I can't wait to join a senior citizen social center, where we'll all prop ourselves up on our walkers and careen around the dance floor as the DJ spins the special fiftieth-anniversary edition of the *Saturday Night Fever* soundtrack.

The aging eye is beginning to be felt in marketing. Mass merchandisers have built a pretty good franchise with older consumers in a few categories, including small appliances, hardware, automotive items and seasonal products. They've been much less successful in books, apparel, health-and-beauty aids and over-the-counter drugs. It's not because older people don't care about the written word or about wanting to look good. It's certainly not because they don't need pain relief or the occasional cough drop for an itchy throat. It might have something to do with the products themselves. The fashion world doesn't seem to have grasped the fact that older people want stylish yet suitable clothing that fits.

At the same time, if you're a guy like me, I'll bet you don't need any more stuff. The fifty-and-over crowd is generally downsizing, adjusting for empty nests and aging parents. Right now I own every shirt, tie, pair of shoes and piece of jewelry I foresee needing for the rest of my life. The only things I require are fruit, vegetables, pasta, wine, olive oil, meat and fish weekly, and annual doses of fresh socks and underwear. Everything else is discretionary (although my longtime live-in—who I call Dreamboat, because she is one—did surprise me two Christmases ago with a new gadget called a Slingbox, which hooks up to my cable TV and home Internet service, so now when I'm stranded in a hotel room in Singapore at two A.M., I can watch Yankees games on my laptop from my TV at home—pure heaven). Like most fifty-somethings, and with the notable exception of that Slingbox, which you're not taking away from me, I'll pick experiences over things any day. Plus a few pairs of socks.

I mentioned the brave new world of wheelchairs earlier, virgin territory that no one, to my knowledge, has staked out yet. These personal vehicles will surely receive a makeover, including souped-up engines, cruise control, lots of upholstery choices (will black leather be too hot in summer?), big tires like we had on our Jeeps back in the '90s, cell phone chargers, cup holders, CD players and the appropriate bumper stickers (IF THIS WHEELCHAIR'S A-ROCKIN' DON'T COME A-KNOCKIN'). There will be plenty of licensing opportunities, bringing brand names like Harley, BMW and John Deere (or Louis Vuitton, Chanel and Prada) to the marketplace. They won't even be called wheelchairs—and in fact they'll more closely resemble tractor mowers or three-wheeled motorcycles. These babies won't even necessarily connote a handicap. They'll just be cool conveniences, something for the geezer who has everything.

At the other end of the spectrum, it's no secret that next to kids, old people are the biggest market for sneakers. Who else has a lifestyle that doesn't ever require serious grown-up footwear? In fact, athletic gear—soft, rubber-soled shoes, baggy, open-necked shirts, loose pants with elastic waistbands—is tailor-made for the needs of aging fashion plates. Senior citizens have a lot more money to spend on sneakers than kids do and would gladly pay for features designed to bring extra comfort. Still, no self-respecting teenager wants to wear the same athletic shoes as Grandmom, which is probably why all those ads for Nike and Reebok feature youngsters rather than oldsters. Is there no way for a major athleticwear maker to target aged customers? I bet we'll see it before long—it'll just be too lucrative to miss. (Maybe the commercials will star the sixty-five-year-old Michael Jordan playing one-on-one with the twenty-first century's premiere eight-foot center.)

There's a similar question brewing over how *the* baby boomer fashion staple will age: Will kids buy the brand of jeans preferred by their grandparents? I'm assuming that we boomers will wear blue denim right up to the tomb (and why stop there?). But if it's the uniform of the senility set, will anybody else dare touch it? Or will jeans go the way of fedoras?

The world of health and beauty aids now doesn't pay enough attention to the older consumer, but it will have to in the future. There should be entire brands devoted to the needs of people over sixty-five, including special formulations of products for hair, skin, teeth, male grooming and cosmetics. Somebody is also going to have to figure out how to sell incontinence products to aging boomers. The current category—a few low-key brands of adult diapers sold sheepishly in the feminine hygiene aisle—isn't going to cut it. Will it be Hanes, Calvin Klein, or Estée Lauder? Or will they be sold next to the extra-hold sports bras and athletic supporters?

The mattress store of the future will do well to specialize in selling to seniors. They'll shop long and hard for bedding that's ergonomically sound, and they'll pay for it, too. From Tempur-Pedic to Sleep Number, mattresses will become more quasimedical products than home furnishings. The sleep category is booming. Even hotels are using their beds as a marketing engine for the aging, aching traveler.

When there aren't so many kids afoot in America, the fast-food trade will have to redouble its efforts to keep senior citizen diners interested. They already make up a large part of the fast-food audience, without even being acknowledged beneath the golden arches. Someday it won't be the latest Disney animation flick that gets the Burger King tie-in; it'll be *Rambo: The Nursing Home Insurgency.* And instead of a Beanie Baby, the Happy Meal will come with a Hummel figurine.

When parents shop for clothing, toys, books and videos for their children, they usually know what size to get, or which favored plaything, or at what level the little one is reading. Thirty years from now, though, today's parents will be buying for their grandchildren, and they'll need a little guidance. Will clothing makers have wised up by then and created a sensible, standardized system of sizes? It's chaos out there now, as anyone who shops for kiddie clothes knows. If such a system isn't in place, stores will have to do whatever's necessary—big, easy-to-read size charts, mannequins of different heights, lots of attentive salesclerks, all of the above—to ensure that grandparents can buy clothing with confidence.

If they can't buy clothing, they'll opt for toys or books or DVDs instead. But again, manufacturers and retailers have to make it easier than it is now. The appropriate reader's age should be marked prominently on all kiddie and adolescent books. Same for videos and video games, too. Grandmom doesn't want to accidentally buy Grand Theft Auto for her dear little five-year-old grandson, and she needs a hand to make sure she doesn't.

Of course, we boomers are born technocrats, but who knows what new marvels will exist to intimidate us three decades from now? New technologies usually bring benefits that are perfectly suited to the older shopper: Internet shopping and e-mail make it easy if you can't get around like you used to, and the pocket PCs of the future (like today's BlackBerries and iPhones, only better) will have plenty of memory for the times when yours fails, like when you need a phone number or you're standing in the middle of the supermarket and can't remember why.

But look at how technology is marketed and sold—you'll never see anybody over thirty in an ad or behind the counter of a store. And the product itself is unfriendly to older users, from the miniature keyboards to the type design on websites to the frequency with which printer and computer on-off switches are located in the back. Maybe some of high tech's appeal is lost when it's easy enough for your grandmother to use. But a couple decades down the road, when *we're* the grandmothers, there's going to be hell to pay.

ELEVEN

Kids

With gender revolt (or reconfiguration, at the very least) having changed so much about our lives, and men and women off boldly shopping new terrain, the effect on children today is quite simple: Kids go everywhere.

Where did they ever go? To school, of course, which left their mothers free to perform the myriad tasks of the domestic superintendent, high among them the acquisition of food, groceries, clothing and other supplies and services as needed. Dad bought booze, tires, cigars, lawnmowers, groceries (maybe once or twice a year) and Mom's birthday gift. Banking was done by either mother or father, depending on the household's particular division of labor. Only major purchases required the presence of the entire family, but how often did anyone get a car or a couch? Not so often that the children who came along for the ride required very much in the way of accommodation.

Today, both parents are almost certainly working at jobs, which means buying that cannot be done over lunch hours must take place during times the family might happily spend together. Shopping then becomes an acceptable leisure outing—less pleasurable, perhaps, than a week at Disney World, but not entirely without potential for fun, as we'll see. Also, divorce is common enough that the single parent (either one) in the company of the brood is a common sight in movie theaters, restaurants and stores. On any given Saturday afternoon, is there a Cold Stone Creamery or game arcade in America that goes unvisited by divorced dads with their weekend-custody kids? Kids go everywhere because we take them, but once there, they alter the shopping landscape in both obvious and subtle ways.

The older we get, the more we recognize that the ownership of any product, no matter what it is, isn't transformative. That dress, that lipstick, that iPod nano is not going to change you or anyone's opinion of you. The aging consumer is also better at ignoring pop-up ads online and TiVo-ing their favorite programs so they don't have to watch five annoying commercials in a row. Thus, the twenty-first-century marketer is focused on kids and teens. It's no surprise to note that the average four-year-old American child can identify more than one hundred brands.

There is also the fact that our children consume even more mass media than we adults do, much of it vying to sell them things. The marketplace wants kids, needs kids, and kids are flattered by the invitation and happy to oblige. They idolize licensed TV characters the way their junior forebears once were taught to worship patron saints, and they manage to suss out the connection between brand name and status at a very early age. It's just one more example of how capitalism brings about democratization—you no longer need to stay clear of the global marketplace just because you're three and a half feet tall, have no income to speak of, and are not permitted to cross the street without Mom. You're an economic force, now and in the future, and that's what counts.

All this, like every major upheaval, is both boon and burden. In practical terms, it means three things:

1. That if a store is somehow unwelcoming to children, parent shoppers will get the message and stay away. I can't tell you how many stores that depend on female customers fail to ensure that all aisles and paths between racks and fixtures are wide enough for a baby stroller to pass.

If they're not, at least half of all women in their twenties and thirties will be shut out at least some of the time. (A great many men shoppers will be, too.) We did a job for a department store and determined, using a tape measure, that the baby and children's clothing section was more crowded with racks and fixtures than any other part of the store. As a result, it was the most difficult part of the store to navigate if you were pushing a stroller; it was also the least-visited section of the store, which was no coincidence. Every year, Hallmark spends a small fortune on TV commercials for the Christmas ornament sections of its stores. In one prototype store we studied, the fixture sat on a narrow aisle. Every time a shopper with a stroller ventured there, the section was totally blocked off. As a result, our research showed, only 10 percent of the store's shoppers ever saw the ornaments. By store design and fixturing alone you determine whether you will be kid-friendly or kid-avoidant: Automatic doors, wide aisles and no steps make it easy on parents pushing prams or dragging (or chasing) toddlers.

2. That children can be counted on to be enthusiastic consumers (or co-consumers) as long as their needs have been considered. In other words, if you want to sell something to kids, you've got to put it where they can see it and reach it. That goes for obvious items, like bubble bath in an Arthur-shaped container, but also for things like dog treats, as I explained in an earlier chapter, since children (along with old people) are the main market for liver-flavored cookies. Conversely, if you don't childproof the store the way you would your home, you'll be in for many unhappy surprises.

3. That if the parent's sustained close attention is required (by, say, a car salesman or a bank loan officer), then someone must first find a way to divert the attention of a restless, bored child.

The first time I paid practical attention to the effect of children on the "adult" world was not in any retail emporium but in a temple of culture, the Rodin Museum in Philadelphia. I was wandering among the great one's larger-than-life bronzes, lost in aesthetic reverie, when I heard a young voice exclaim, "Look, Mom—a bottom!" I turned to see an angelic tyke gripping with both little hands the buttocks of Balzac.

I then gazed around the room and noticed that there were touch marks on all the statues, roughly at the height where this adorable child had grabbed poor old Honoré. Clearly, this little fellow was not the only touch-oriented art connoisseur in America.

That moment illustrated several truths about children. First, they are exuberant participants in the world of objects. If it is within their reach and it offers even the slightest inducement, they will touch it. A child's creative impulse is expressed in his or her search for the essential toy-ness in everything, from the most mundane objects to the loftiest. An ironing board? That's a toy. Balzac's butt cheeks? They're a toy, too. I realized that if you want children to touch something, you must only put it low enough, and they will find it. In fact, objects placed below a certain point will be touched by children *only.*

Supermarkets have been at the forefront of exploiting the hands-on shopping style of children. We have countless videotape moments showing kids in grocery stores begging, coaxing, whining, imploring Mom or Dad to choose some item (and when that fails, simply grabbing it and tossing it into the cart). If it's within their reach, they will touch it, and if they touch it, there's at least a chance that Mom or Dad will relent and buy it, Dad especially. Even this must be done with care, though— we once studied a market that had placed products with kid appeal on the bottom shelf, not realizing that for children riding in shopping carts, the shelf just below the middle one is ideal.

Supermarkets have gotten so good at appealing to children that parents are in semirevolt. In response to complaints about the candy and gum racks by the cashiers, some markets have begun to offer candy-free checkouts. (Now the confectioners are complaining.) We found an alarming trend in a study a few years back: a growing number of parents who assiduously steer clear of the cookie and cracker aisle in order to spare themselves the predictable youthful hue and cry. To counter that maneuver, our cookie manufacturer client began securing strategic adjacencies—with appropriate aisle partners (cookies on one side of the aisle and baby food on the other, for example) to guarantee that one way or another, families will have to confront chocolate chips.

In the '80s, General Mills devised a new product for callow palates: a microwave popcorn that came in different colors. They advertised the stuff heavily on kiddie TV, but then—in a classic example of the merchandising hand not knowing what the marketing hand was doing—failed to make sure it was being displayed within reach of its intended consumers. In fact, assuming that parents would do the buying, the firm's typical supermarket planogram had positioned it on the high side, and this, we felt sure, was to blame for the product's disappointing sales. We still show clients the video of a boy of six or so making repeated flying leaps at the shelf where the popcorn was kept, trying to knock one to the floor so he could show it to Mom. He finally got it down, but his mother refused to allow it in the cart. Dejectedly, he put it back on the shelf—not where it had been, but down at *his* eye level. And sure enough, the next kid who came by saw it, grabbed it and tossed it into Dad's cart, where it remained. A classic moment in the wisdom of watching the shopper.

It would be almost impossible for families to shop together if not for the advent of kid-friendly dining, and McDonald's, more than anyone, has prospered from this—the restaurants are part convenience, part bribery for the little citizens if only they'll behave through a morning at the mall. McDonald's realized early on that if it could appeal to children—through its menu but also with the toys and licensed character cups and playlands—it would get the parents as well. It's no coincidence that America's dominant fast food is also the favorite among kids. But even McDonald's doesn't get everything right. One glaring omission: The counters are all too high for children to use. A seven- or eight-year-old is certainly capable of going alone from table to counter to order more fries or another soda. But the design of the restaurants forbids it. Even the menu boards are so high that only an adult can comfortably see them. There should be kid-level menus that employ large photos of the food and as few words as possible.

I have my own personal kids-in-a-restaurant story. As I mentioned earlier, for a time I was one of the owners of a downtown New York bar and restaurant known as the Ear Inn. When we first bought the business, the bar was patronized mostly by aging printers and longshoremen—a rough-and-tumble blue-collar crowd. As the new owners, we were interested in reaching out to the homesteaders, artists and young families who were slowly moving into our industrial neighborhood, located only a block and a half from the Hudson River. We also needed to raise the prices, and to do that we had to—gently, unassumingly—change the makeup of the Ear's customer base. Our solution? We put paper and crayons on every table and at happy hour we invited our preferred patrons to set their kids loose inside the bar so that Mom could cook dinner in peace at home while Dad nursed a beer and kept watch. Thus, beginning at about five in the afternoon until after eight, the Ear Inn had a huge posse of toddlers and small kids underfoot. Happy hour became all about being happy, and not about scarfing down as many whiskey sours as you could. The longshoremen and printers disappeared. These weren't people you wanted to annoy, but they were scared off or turned off or both.

What we could never have foreseen was how the presence of children protected us in other ways. Almost every other new bar owner reported having trouble with the local mob: protection money, payoffs for garbage, staged fights, bookies camped out in their telephone booths jotting down bets. The Ear somehow steered clear of all these issues. Most mysterious.

In the ensuing years I got to know some of the neighborhood wiseguys. Two guys from that era of my life are now doing hard time in prison. Others I still see on the street and am always glad to run into. Even now I joke that if I ever needed someone whacked, I'd know where to go. One night about ten years ago I was walking down the street when I ran into, well, let's call him Tony. We retired to a local bar for a few drinks and a lot of talk about the old days. I asked why we got left alone.

"Paco, it was the friggin' kids. Three times someone was supposed to have a little talk wit you guys, but we walk in and you got old ladies and kids in the bar; we could do nothing. *Nothing.*"

Amazing what paper and a whole bunch of crayons can do for you.

• • •

No, you're not dreaming: There are more kids in bookstores today than ever before. Once, the children's books section consisted of a few shelves stuck way in back, behind the dictionaries. Today it may be the best-looking, most inviting part of the store.

Here's how smart booksellers stock the shelves: They place the books featuring characters from popular TV shows down low, so the little ones can grab Bratz, SpongeBob or Fairly OddParents unimpeded by Mom or Dad, who possibly take a dim view of hypercommercialized critters. Children's classics—*Grimm's Fairy Tales, The Little Prince* or anything that seems old and wordy—are displayed high, at eye level for adults, since that's who'll be choosing those worthies. In the middle go the books and characters whose appeal spans generations—Babar, for example, or *Curious George,* or Dr. Seuss. (DVD planograms should work the same way bookstores' do: the venerables that parents might choose—*Old Yeller* or *The Wizard of Oz*—displayed high, and contemporary favorites like *High School Musical* or *Hannah Montana* down where children can grab them and commence their noisy yet still somehow charming pleas.)

We always advise our bookstore clients to group sections by gender, acknowledging the tendency of men to cluster in sports, business, do-it-yourself and computers while women troll psychology, self-help, health, food, diet, home and garden. Place the children's books within sight of those women's sections, we counsel—and use low shelving for the kids, so that mothers can browse their books and look over from time to time to keep an eye on the children.

At the Barnes & Noble superstore near my office, there's a kiddie section with lots of miniature seating, which is good, but it ignores the fact that most children are accustomed to being read to while sitting in a parental lap. I'm always tempted to grab one or two of the large armchairs from elsewhere in the store and drag them into the kiddie section.

The publishers of children's books do a fairly lame job of making their product appealing for its main audience—adults. If you're buying books for your own child, whose tastes and reading level you know well, you probably don't require much direction. But what about all

those grandparents and aunts and uncles and friends of the family who
wish to buy books for the kiddies? They need some clear indication on
the books (and maybe on the bookshelves and other displays) about
for whom each book is intended—which grade (or age) reading level,
mainly. But few children's books or book displays carry this important
information. This is a classic example of a product's designers and marketers having no idea sometimes what shoppers require. You'll see potential buyers standing in the stores reading, as though they'll find a clue
there, and then, fatally uncertain about their choice, they put it back and
decide to get Junior something else instead. It may also be important to
find a way to let shoppers know about the focus of a particular book—
whether it's meant to teach relationship building or imaginative play—
as a way to signal a book's appropriateness as a gift.

Here's another way publishers fail shoppers at gift time: Kids' books
tend to be relatively inexpensive, meaning that if you're buying, you
may buy more than one. But even in the successful children's series,
such as Goosebumps or Lemony Snicket, you'll find few boxed sets, despite the fact that collections of four or five books would make a perfect
present.

Though technically adults are the ones who select and buy toys, the
kids are the real decision-makers. Even if Junior is still preverbal, you'll
see his parents take a toy from the shelf, consider it, and then dangle it
in the little one's face to get the opinion that counts. If he bites, they'll
buy—it's why most toy packaging now allows you to push the buttons
or pull the string without opening the box.

The principle, then, is simple: If adults are highly tactile shoppers,
kids are uninhibitedly so. As Balzac's buns discovered, kids will touch
anything. You've just got to watch them in action and then plan ac-
cordingly. But there are at least two troublesome aspects there, both of
which require common sense on the part of the retailer.

First, you've got to realize that the degree to which you are successful at getting children to see and touch and pick up and then desire items
is also the degree to which you will frustrate and annoy their parents—
the ones who brought the children in the first place. Like those adults
who avoid the cookie aisle or the checkout piled with candy and gum

and toys inspired by the latest Nickelodeon hit, for instance. Shopping is much more difficult when you're chasing after a child who believes he or she is the one doing the shopping. After a time, the experience of a store with too much kid appeal becomes one the adult wishes only to avoid. There's a balance there, one worth striking.

Second, if you're going to merchandise your store for kids, you've got to protect them from it as well. In other words, baby-proof it the way you do your home—wander it with your eyes trained on the area from the floor to about three feet off it, seeing exactly what kind of mischief can be created by an energetic four-year-old. The obvious dangers like electrical outlets and sharp-edged shelves should be easy enough to spot and address. But you've also got to make sure that heavy items can't be too easily yanked or toppled. We spent a day at a Burger King that controlled the line at the counter with a "hard maze"—a waist-high running ledge that doubled as a planter. In eight hours we counted a total of fifty-two boys and girls who climbed, clambered over, walked or jungle-gymed on that hazard, and I have no doubt that some kids have taken nasty spills there.

In one of my first assignments, before the popularity of cell phones, I studied three AT&T phone stores in different parts of the country. All were attractively designed. All had the same number of employees to handle roughly the same number of customers. One store, though, had a much lower shopper interception rate—the percentage of potential customers who were spoken to by a salesperson—and a much lower average time spent with customers. What made that store so different when all of the other numbers were the same? It took us a while to figure out that our underperforming store was the only one to employ a "waterfall" display system—a row of pedestals of descending height on which the equipment was shown. We watched various videotaped angles of the sales floor, and after a while a pattern emerged: In the underperforming store, staffers were constantly having to run to the rescue of phones and fax machines that were within easy reach of children in the store with their folks. The salespeople would be involved in a conversation with a shopper but with one eye always out to see what the little darlings were about to grab from that waterfall display. It wasn't just for the sake of neatness, either; the store only had one or two of each model in stock, so, for instance, if an expensive fax machine fell off its pedestal and broke, there were no replacements to sell. The poor clerks spent more time rescuing expensive telecommunications equipment than talking to shoppers. It was smart to place phones within reach of curious shoppers, but not so smart to put them within striking distance of children.

I sat one afternoon with a highly regarded designer of interactive video fixtures as he unveiled his latest prototype, a video game station to go in the play area of a fast-food restaurant. The first two kids sat in the contraption and played it without incident. The third boy took off his shoes, leaned far back in the seat and worked the touch-screen with his toes. The next child took the hard plastic toy that came with his lunch and began pounding the video screen with it.

"My God," the designer gasped, "look what he's doing!"

"He's interacting," I reminded him. Wasn't that the point here? The fundamental lesson? Any technology that's located on the floor of a store, and that's accessible to kids, has to be built to combat standards—as if it were headed to Kabul or Baghdad.

You don't have to be a Wiggle to keep kids relatively entertained. But especially in businesses where customers have to remain in one spot and pay attention, providing child diversion is a must.

That thought will seem painfully obvious to any parent. So it's amazing how few businesspeople make any allowance for it. I recently watched a two-year-old run wild while her mother tried to shop in an establishment that really should be aware of the presence of children in the lives of its customers: a maternity clothing store. Diverting a child can mean simply setting up a TV and some Disney videos in a little alcove, as is done in French hypermarkets. (I'm always amazed to see that of all places, video stores frequently fail to run kiddie programming on at least one monitor, leaving parents free to browse a few minutes longer.) Placing some plastic toys in a five-foot-square area where Mom and Dad can glance from time to time can suffice in a small store. Ikea is famous for its kiddie pen, the avalanche of colorful plastic balls having become a friendly icon. No surprise that a Swedish chain would be at the forefront here; Europeans—in particular, Scandinavians—are less paranoid about the safety of their children and will leave them in the custody of store personnel while they shop. A few years ago there was a ruckus in New York when a young Danish woman parked her sleeping baby in a stroller just outside a restaurant's window, then went inside (to a window table) to enjoy lunch. Police were called, child welfare workers descended and the woman very nearly had a custody battle on her hands.

For whatever reason, American parents *are* paranoid where their kids are concerned. Here, Ikea has had to institute a rigorous ID check for adults trying to retrieve their children from the play area. Many parents simply refuse to leave their children in play areas that can't be seen from the rest of the store at all times. A few years ago Blockbuster built a clever little drive-in theater for kids, complete with big-screen videos and tiny cars where the tykes could sit and watch. Unfortunately, it was positioned in a corner just inside the exit, giving most parents the willies. We don't really have much experience with public day care here. So it's no surprise that children end up traipsing through our stores and banks and other retail businesses.

We did a study for Wells Fargo a few years ago showing that 15 percent of all those entering its branches are under seven years old.

"What's your most effective selling tool?" I asked a loan officer there. She reached into her desk drawer and pulled out a lollipop. She said it could usually be counted on to buy her two minutes of uninterrupted face time with a parent, all she needed. The bank also offers a coloring book starring a puppy who lives in a Wells Fargo branch. That and a handful of crayons can add up to a brand-new home equity loan, no question. In New York, Citibank produces an activity book for children. In both cases, the banks are buying quiet today and—given how we like to fetishize our happy childhood experiences—loyal customers of tomorrow.

There are just a few principles of designing a good area (as opposed to a holding pen) for children. The sight lines must allow parents to see their children at any time, so it must be in an open area, unshielded by walls or obstacles. It must be safe. It must be large enough. And ideally, it would allow children of different ages to be segregated. Otherwise, the older kids will always dominate, making it an unhappy experience for the small ones who get in their way.

Car dealers tend to do a lousy job of diverting children, which is disappointing, when you think about it, because kids are already disposed to liking cars—toy ones, at least. A lot could be done, but the car business is far behind most. As a result, shopping for a car is more difficult for families than it needs to be. If no car dealer addresses this, then all are safe. But the minute Ford or Chrysler starts acknowledging the reality of kids in dealerships, the rest will be forced to respond. In Japan, Nissan is divided into Blue and Red dealerships, each selling different lines of cars. But both feature beautiful toy car displays in the front of the store that showcase the models and colors the dealership sells. Since a lot of the dealerships are small and don't have the sprawling parking lots we find in the U.S., the toy cars serve as an easy way for people to preshop. I tried to get Nissan to stock enough toys so that dealers could hand them out like lollipops. It's good, cheap, instantaneous advertising, and in the twenty-first century, even a six-year-old has a voice in the family automobile purchase.

Another place where children must be amused is in the pharmacy waiting area. There, among sickly adults waiting for prescriptions to be filled, the charm of youthful exuberance wears thin. Many of those children are likely to be ill themselves, which doesn't do much for their dispositions. Drugstores can easily stock toys or coloring books and crayons near the waiting area, creating an efficient adjacency. That's another great way of amusing children—give them something to shop while their parents do the same thing just a few feet away. Especially given how many parents resort to bribery as a way to quiet their progeny, this could be a smart strategy all around. Since women still do most of the shopping, it makes sense to place products for children near sections being shopped by their mothers. Is this child exploitation, or is it doing a mother a favor? Maybe it can be both.

• • •

A few years ago I read a news report about a convenience store that was having problems with teenagers loitering in the parking lot at night. Hiring a security guard to stand out there and scowl was an expensive solution. So here's what the store did: It began piping the smooth, suave sounds of Mantovani through the loudspeakers. No more loiterers.

Teenagers are still young enough to be total suckers for image, for all the blandishments of advertising, identity marketing, media messages, trends and labels. They still believe in a brand name's power to confer status, cool, charisma, knowledge. They construct their identities by the shopping choices they make—they're a lot like adults were back in the '50s, before we all became so wise in the ways of image hucksters. Kids also have fewer media choices than adults, so messages come through to them in concentrated form. They love to scour the world for icons or any other clues that something—some product, some store—is intended for them. They'll flee easy-listening music as if it were anthrax, while we can tolerate just about anything.

Which should make them fairly easy marks in the marketplace. But they have some built-in limitations, too. During a study of how jeans are sold, we noticed an odd pattern to adolescent shopping: Teenagers in groups spent a relatively long time in the jeans section (three minutes, fifty-two seconds) compared to teens with parents (two minutes, thirty-two seconds). And teens in groups examined one third more product. But the percentage of teenagers with parents who bought jeans was nearly double the number of teens in groups who bought, 25 percent to 13 percent. Then we realized: They come with their friends to browse—to preshop, as it were. Having made their choices and gained the approval of a jury of their peers, they return with Mom or Dad— the wallet bearer—and make quick work of the transaction, wishing not to risk the humiliation of being seen in public buying clothes with their ancient caretakers.

Does this not suggest that commerce in general and banking in particular can do a better job of serving young shoppers? How about inaugurating direct deposit of allowance, accessible by ATM/debit cards? Does any retailer still offer layaway, and should it become common again, but aimed at young shoppers? We've done some research for Crédit Agricole, the French financial institution, which is building branches for customers in their late teens and early twenties—the Gen Y bank. It won't look like a bank or sound like one; the design, graphics, operating hours, staffing, music and so on will all reflect its Gen Y target. It'll hold on-site seminars on how to rent a first apartment, how to finance a motorcycle etc.

That's a wise approach—remember, it's only one branch among many—for it acknowledges the fact that a product or service meant for youthful shoppers thereby declares itself off-limits to the rest of us. Clarion, the Proctor & Gamble cosmetic brand, no longer exists, but it was for a while a heavily promoted cosmetics brand. It was an early user of interactive computer fixtures—women would type in some information about their coloring and skin type, and the computer would tell them which Clarion products to buy. For some reason, though, the fixtures gradually migrated downward to low shelves, positioned perfectly for adolescent girls. They returned the favor by making avid use of the computers. Once adult women saw this, naturally, they assumed that Clarion was meant for beginners and steered clear. Thus was Clarion's reputation sealed, and before long it was withdrawn from the market.

IV

See Me, Feel Me,
Touch Me, Buy Me:
The Dynamics of Shopping

So far we've seen all that must be done simply to make retail environments user-friendly at the basic levels. The demands of anatomy must be obeyed just for shopping to be possible. The behavioral differences due to gender and age must be accommodated, or else stores, restaurants and banks will be best suited to a generic—sexless, ageless—human being who does not exist. Once all that is seen to, of course, things get really interesting. This third aspect of the science of shopping is where we find all the give and take, the back and forth—the romance, if you will. Retailing, for all we know about it, remains a mystery. Why does someone who walks into a store thinking Hewlett-Packard walk out lugging a Canon? (Or vice versa?) What induces someone who decides to kill a few minutes in a boutique to walk out $1,000 lighter but feeling infinitely more fashionable—more beautiful—than ever before? Yes, the simple answer is that he found something he wanted, but there's no easy explanation for how *that* happened. Good stores perform a kind of retailing judo—they use the shopper's own momentum, his or her own inclinations and desires, to get him or her to do something perhaps totally unplanned. In the end, it's not enough that goods be within reach of the shopper; he or she must want to reach them. And having reached them, he or she must then wish to own them, or all this effort goes for naught. Amid so much science, we discover in the end it's love that makes the world of retailing go round. What do shoppers love? A few important things, we've learned, such as:

TOUCH. We live in a tactile-deprived society, and shopping is one of our few chances to freely experience the material world firsthand. Almost all unplanned buying is a result of touching, hearing, smelling or tasting something on the premises of a store—which is why merchandising is more powerful than marketing, and why the Internet, catalogs and home shopping on TV will prosper and complement, but never seriously challenge, real live stores.

MIRRORS. Stand and watch what happens at any reflective surface: We preen like chimps, men and women alike. Self-interest is a basic part of our species. From shopping to cosmetic surgery, we care about how we look. As we've said, mirrors slow shoppers in their tracks, a very good thing for whatever merchandise happens to be in the vicinity. But even around wearable items such as clothing, jewelry and cosmetics, where mirrors are crucial sales tools, stores fail to provide enough of them.

DISCOVERY. There's little more satisfying than walking into a store, picking up the (metaphorical) scent of something we've been hunting for and then tracking it to its lair. Too much signage and point-of-purchase display takes all the adventure out of a shopping trip; stores shouldn't be willfully confusing or obscure, but they should seduce shoppers through the aisles with suggestions and hints of what's to come. The aroma of warm bread can be enough to lead supermarket shoppers to the bakery aisle; a big, beautiful photograph of a James Bondian stud in a creamy dinner jacket carries more levels of information than the clearest FORMALWEAR sign can ever convey.

TALKING. Stores that attract lots of couples, friends or groups of shoppers usually do very well. If you can create an atmosphere that fosters discussion of an outfit, say, or a particular cell phone, the merchandise begins to sell itself.

RECOGNITION. In that old TV show *Cheers,* the theme song went, "you want to go where everybody knows your name." This is a battlefield where the small, locally owned store can still best the national chains, and smart stores make the most of this advantage. Given a choice, people will shop where they feel wanted, and they'll even pay a little more for the privilege. Even the smallest stores can build customer loyalty just by keeping track of what people buy and giving price breaks when appropriate. Our studies show that *any* contact initiated by a store employee—and I mean even a hello—increases the likelihood that a shopper will buy something. If the salesperson suggests a few things or offers information, the chances rise even higher. Of course, shoppers don't love pushy salespeople, so there's a line here.

BARGAINS. This seems obvious, but it goes beyond simply cutting prices. At Victoria's Secret, for example, underwear is frequently piled on a table and marked five pairs for $20, which sounds like a much better deal than the $5 a pair normally charged. At even the poshest stores, the clearance racks get shopped avidly. Still, while shoppers expect a certain amount of elbow-to-elbow crowding around the discount table, they won't bite if the physical discomfort becomes too noticeable. They'll extricate a blouse from a jammed sale rack, for example, but if there's no room to back up and examine it as closely as the full-price merchandise, they won't buy.

On the other hand, shoppers tend to hate:

TOO MANY MIRRORS. A store shouldn't feel like a funhouse. At a certain point, all that glass becomes disorienting.

LINES. Not only do they hate to wait, they also hate to feel negative emotions while they do it—like frustration at watching inefficiency, or anxiety wondering if they're in the fastest line, or boredom because there's nothing for them to read, watch or shop while they wait. The memory of a good shopping trip can be wiped out by a bad experience in the checkout line.

ASKING DUMB QUESTIONS. New products especially should be out where shoppers can examine them, not behind glass. And there should be enough signs, brochures, instructional videos, newspaper articles, talking displays and whatever else is necessary for browsers to bring themselves up to speed before they ask a question. When stores work at making new or complicated products accessible, sales always increase.

DIPPING. Or bending, either, especially when their hands are full. If it's a challenge to reach down and pick up merchandise, shoppers will pass, figuring that another store will make the acquisition easier.

GOODS OUT OF STOCK. Self-explanatory.

OBSCURE PRICE TAGS. Ditto.

INTIMIDATING SERVICE. Also rude service, slow service, uninformed service, unintelligent service, distracted service, languid service, lazy service, surly service. Probably the single best word of mouth for a store is this: "They're so nice down at that shop!" When service is lousy, shoppers will find another store; bad service undoes good merchandise, prices and location almost every time. Regardless of how practical an activity shopping seems to be, feelings always come first, and good is always better than bad.

In the chapters that follow, we'll discuss what is probably the most powerful inducement to shopping—the opportunity to touch, try, taste, smell and otherwise explore the world of desirable objects, and how the artful juxtaposition of those objects can sometimes make all the difference in the world. We'll see how not just the merchandise but the displays, too, determine what gets noticed or ignored. We'll talk about how retailers can manipulate even our perception of time in order to control the shopping experience. We'll also take a look at what might seem to be the antithesis of sensual shopping—the future world of retailing via the Internet.

TWELVE

The Sensual Shopper

This might seem like an odd question coming from anyone at any time but especially coming here and now, in an inquiry such as the one we're conducting. But I need to ask it anyway: What *is* shopping?

I don't mean what is buying. I don't mean what is entering a public place where goods are kept until they can be exchanged for money. I definitely do not mean what is retailing, or what is commerce, or what is trade.

I mean: What is shopping? Who does it, and how? How does one go about this shopping activity?

For the purposes of this discussion, let's stipulate that shopping is more than the simple, dutiful acquisition of whatever is absolutely necessary to one's life. It's more than what we call the "grab and go"— you need cornflakes, you go to the cornflakes, you grab the cornflakes, you pay for the cornflakes, and *haveaniceday*. The kind of activity I mean involves a human being experiencing that portion of the world that has been deemed for sale, using her senses—sight, touch, smell, taste, hearing—and then choosing this or rejecting that (or choosing or rejecting it all, I suppose) on the basis of . . . something. It's the sensory aspect of that decision-making process that's most intriguing, because how else do we experience anything? But it's especially crucial in this context because virtually all unplanned purchases—and many planned ones, too—come as a result of the shopper seeing, touching, smelling or tasting something that promises pleasure, if not total fulfillment.

I want to repeat this, because I think it's key: We buy things today more than ever based on trial and touch.

Now, why might somebody wish to touch something before buying it? There are plenty of very practical reasons, the most obvious being that if a product's tactile qualities are what's most important, we must know how it will feel. For instance, we like to touch towels before we buy them—in a study we did, towels were touched on average by six different shoppers before they were actually purchased. (Which is why you really ought to wash them before you use them.) Bed linens—how sheets feel is pretty much the whole ball game. And clothing—we need to pet, stroke and fondle sweaters and shirts especially, but most apparel falls into this category. I think men's underwear makers are missing an opportunity by sealing the goods inside plastic bags. No women's underwear is sold that way, for good reason—women want to test anything that will go against their skin. Men would, too, if someone only gave them the chance.

There are also nontextile products that come into contact with our bodies and are therefore touch-worthy—lotions and moisturizers, lipstick, makeup, deodorant and powder, just to pick a few things from the health and beauty aisles. You need to touch something if it will be held or carried or wielded in some way. A hammer, for instance—you've got to heft it before you know it's right for you. Same goes for a handbag, briefcase or suitcase. An umbrella. A knife, a spatula, tongs. Anything you're going to carry around all day, like a wallet. Looking gives you a pretty good idea of how it's going to feel, but nothing takes the place of your own hand.

What don't you need to touch? Lightbulbs—*nobody* touches lightbulbs. But even they cry out to be experienced. You can buy them in a box in the supermarket or hanging from a rack in a hardware store.

Or you can go to a big home center and see those lightbulbs in action, glowing cozily inside lampshades. Which method sells more bulbs, do you think, or more expensive bulbs?

The rule of thumb in these matters is usually that shoppers want to spend time investigating and considering those products in which they have a high level of "involvement," meaning products that offer possibilities or invite comparison. In the supermarket, for instance, you might want to try a new brand of ketchup or cheese, or a pricey variety of apple or peach, before you buy. Salsa makers, for some reason, always seem to be conducting taste tests of new variations. Nobody needs to taste-test Budweiser, but if you're going to buy that expensive new lambic ale or that Armenian beer, you'll want to try a little first. How about sugar? Waste of time—sugar's sugar. Ditto vegetable oil, although people taste olive oil as though it's vintage wine. Twenty-year-old balsamic vinegar is always going to be a specialty item, but if stores let you try a little you might spring for it. Milk? As long as it's cold and the expiration date hasn't come and gone, you're convinced.

Close to 90 percent of all new grocery products fail, but it isn't because people didn't like them—it's because people never tried them. In my opinion, a new product introduction that doesn't include a well-funded, fully supported (with marketing) effort to give shoppers samples is not a serious attempt. Cigarettes may be bad, but until the 1990s the tobacco companies had a great method for getting samples out there: pretty boys and girls standing on street corners handing out freebies. Even nonsmokers took them, not wanting to reject such pleasant entreaties. Maybe we need to retrain those kids to hand out stuff on the supermarket floor.

Of course, a combined marketing-sampling effort still must properly decide on its target audience. In the earliest days of microwave popcorn, we were hired by General Mills to help expand the market for its product. "Who buys it now?" we asked. "Sixty-four percent of our purchasers are females," they replied. That was partly because back then men had yet to discover the ease of microwave cuisine, and partly because most of the marketing effort—the TV commercials and print ads—were directed at women and placed in women's programming and media.

"Whom do you want to reach with the sampling campaign?" we asked. "Well, women, of course," they replied. Which was the wrong answer—they had already reached a substantial female market. And when you think about microwave popcorn, you realize that it's perfect for men. It's the easiest thing in the world to make, it's a salty snack food and men are suggestible, impulsive shoppers who can be convinced to try almost anything. The product was being sold in six-packs for around $4. To gear it toward men, we advised, required less of a commitment— sell a two-pack for a buck and advertise it during hockey games.

Once you get beyond food, the involvement level drops. I'm convinced there's room in the marketplace for high-end toilet paper. People would spend more but only if it were possible to show them the difference on the floor of the supermarket, and there's the rub. Makers of brand-name plastic food wrap, aluminum foil and trash bags experience a great deal of frustration over this issue. Most shoppers will buy whatever's cheapest, and it's almost impossible to convince them that there's any point to buying a better (and more costly) trash bag. Why spend more when only your trash will know the difference?

Supermarkets are wisely becoming more sensual than ever. Most good ones now feature on-premises bakeries, which fill the air with warm, homey scents. You may be in the vitamin section when that aroma hits you, and before you know it you've followed the olfactory trail right up to the counter. Suddenly you're thinking, "I need bread"—but even more importantly, a good smell gets your saliva glands working, which translates into more sales. Stores have taken a tip from Starbucks and begun brewing and selling by the cup the expensive coffee beans they sell loose, another way of putting a product's sensory assets to work.

Scent is the new frontier of marketing. Martin Lindstrom, a prominent author and consultant, helps companies brand smells. In his book *BRAND sense,* he describes the special places fragrances hold in our memories, whether it's Play-Doh, Johnson's baby shampoo or a whiff of pure vanilla. Just as a baby animal recognizes the odor of its mother, we humans bond intimately with smells, too.

In April of 2007, I visited a new prototype store in Halifax, Canada, run by the Nova Scotia Liquor Commission. The store was divided by what they considered to be age preferences, and each section had its signature scent, piped in through air vents. There was a sweetly fruity, fragrant section for thirty-and-under imbibers filled with Pucker-shot concoctions, tequilas and flavored vodkas; another section of whiskeys for the mature palate (the piped-in aroma was smoky-dark and more sophisticated) and then extensive wine collections designed for the specific age groups of the customers, with different fragrances depending on the product and vintage. Just as our eyes age, so do our smell and taste buds. I loved the ad I saw once on a New York City bus shelter promoting a well-known Scotch whisky. The ad read, "You thought girls were yucky once, too." It's no accident that kids like sweets and sweet smells, and that the older we get the more we enjoy savory and bitter tastes.

In the new Best Buy consumer electronics store that opened just off Columbus Circle in the fall of 2007, the appliance section smelled of freshly ironed linen; these days, the dispersion of scent is done via machines. But when is enough enough? Will we start smelling eau de steak or essence of bacon-on-the-griddle in the frozen meat section of our supermarket? I'd like that. More meat would certainly be sold, but smells would also add something else to the overall shopping experience. It would become a sensualist's journey, not just another trip to the supermarket. Problem is, one person's perfume is another person's stink. I have an Italian friend who loathes the smell of oranges to the point where she's banned oranges in her office. The smell of roasting meat may get a lot of us salivating, but to many vegetarians it's nauseating.

In England, some infant apparel stores now pipe in baby powder through the air ducts, to put shoppers in mind of the sweet-sour smell of newborns, which is perhaps the most powerfully evocative scent of all. When we suggested to American baby powder makers that they add smell to their packaging, they recoiled, fearful that store managers would banish any product that threatened to contaminate the supermarket's sterile, odorless confines. And it's true that with the exception of the produce aisles, supermarkets here have no tradition of feeding our desire for sensory stimulation, for scent or taste or touch or even sight. They're still stuck in the early '60s, the time of frozen food, canned food, processed food, powdered food, packaged food and the germless ideal of blinding white cleanliness. I wish one would install a big open kitchen, like something you'd see on a TV cooking show, where the store chef can whip up snacks and pass them (and their recipes) out to shoppers. How about if the manager announced over the loudspeaker, "Attention all shoppers! For the next fifteen minutes, in the frozen foods section . . . free passion-fruit sorbet for everyone!" How about a DJ and a dance floor in produce, a puppet show in the cereal aisle, a jazz trio or the high school glee club at the checkout? It's possible to bring a little more life to a store that is the epitome of shopping puritanism.

Touch and trial are more important today than ever to the world of shopping because of changes in how stores function. Once upon a time, store owners and salespeople were our guides to the merchandise they sold. They were knowledgeable enough, and there were enough of them, to act as the shopper's intermediary to the world of things. We could take a clerk's word for something because he or she had been right so many times before. That was, not coincidentally, back in the day of grand wooden cabinets with glass fronts behind which goods were displayed, the heyday of the hardware store and the haberdasher and the general store, when space was clearly divided between shoppers and staff.

Today, the "open sell" school of display puts most everything out there where we can touch or smell or try it, unmediated by sales clerks. In 1960, 35 percent of the average Sears store was given over to storage. Now it's less than 15 percent. Today it's almost pointless to ask a clerk if an item you want is in the back room. Chances are, there *is* no back room. Everything is either on the shelves or in the little storage cupboards below. It's a brilliant innovation—what good is anything when it's in storage? You can't buy it unless you can find a clerk, and what do you do when there are too few clerks, or too few knowledgeable ones, or too few clerks who are actively trying to help you buy anything? It makes perfect sense to just put it all out there as invitingly and enticingly and conveniently as possible, and then let the shoppers and their good senses discover the stuff on their own.

Another reason touch and trial have become so important is the waning power of product brand name. When consumers believed in the companies behind the big brands, that belief went a long way toward selling things. No longer. This is an extreme example, but revealing: In a study we did for a national brand of skin and hair products, we found that of all ethnic groups, Asian-American shoppers were most aggressive about opening the packaging and touching the lotions, soaps and shampoos. In fact, 23 percent of those shoppers tore into the boxes or opened the bottles to test the viscosity and scent of the products. Clearly, this was due to the fact that the brand, despite having spent many millions on ads and media, still had not gained instant recognition and loyalty among an important and growing ethnic segment.

For that matter, we are all post-Nader shoppers—we'll believe it when we see/smell/touch/hear/taste/try it. Depending on what we're buying and what it costs, there's a healthy skeptic (or is it a nagging doubt?) in our heads that must be put to rest before we can buy at ease. We need to feel a certain level of confidence in a product and its value, which comes only from hard evidence, not from TV commercials or word of mouth. It's shocking how little stores seem to understand something so simple. We've done lots of research in computer retailing, and we've come upon this over and over: big sections of printers on display, but only some of them actually plugged in and working and stocked with paper, despite the fact that most printers make it easy to run tests.

And it's not just for big-ticket items like cars, stereo speakers or designer suits that we need to build our confidence. We performed a study of a newsstand design meant to accommodate a refrigerated soft drink case. One plan hid the cooler discreetly under a counter, then allowed for a display of empty cans to show customers what was available. A very unconvincing scheme, we soon learned—people don't believe the sodas are cold unless they can see the frost on them. The need for proof here (as elsewhere) seems almost instinctual. Once the cases were placed where customers could see inside them, lots of very cold sodas were sold. Convenience stores excel at this—they taught supermarkets that shoppers prefer to buy their soda or beer cold, even if they're not planning to down it on the spot. Warm beer just *feels* unnatural.

A great deal of our firsthand (ha!) experience of the world comes to us via shopping. Where do we go with the specific intention of closely examining objects? To museums, of course, but don't try touching anything that's not in the gift shop—a retail environment. Stores alone abound with chances for tactile and sensory exploration. Even if we didn't need to buy things, we'd need to get out and touch and taste them once in a while.

The purest example of human shopping I know of can be seen by watching a child go through life touching absolutely *everything*. You're watching that child shop for information, for understanding, for knowledge, for experience, for sensation. Especially for sensation, otherwise why would he have to touch or smell or taste or hear anything twice? Keep looking—watch a dog. Watch a bird. Watch a bug. You might say that ant is searching for food. I say he is shopping.

If you still don't believe all this, go to the home of a product fairly unconcerned with matters of smell, touch or any other sensual experience—a bookstore. There you'll be treated to the sight of shoppers stroking, rubbing, hefting and otherwise experiencing the physical nature of a product where no physical attribute (aside maybe from typeface size) has anything to do with enjoyment. Still, helplessly, we touch. We are beasts like any other, and despite all our powers of imagination and conceptualization and intellectualization and cerebration and visualization, we physical creatures experience the world only via our five senses (and maybe, if you're so inclined, our sixth sense—the übersense, the metasense, the sense that senses that which cannot be sensed). The world and everything in it reaches out to us and stimulates us through our senses, and we react. So fundamental is our ability to sense and our need to do so that even when we come upon something we can't know via our senses, we speak of it as though we can.

Do you see what I mean? Does this sound right? Do you feel that I'm making sense? Or does my reasoning stink?

Here's a final reason touch is so important. When does a shopper actually possess something? Technically, of course, it happens at the instant that the item is exchanged for money—at the register. But the register is the least pleasing part of the store; nobody is savoring the joy of possession at that moment. In fact, all that is experienced is loss (of money) and pain (of waiting in line, of waiting for credit card approval, of waiting for the clerk to get the thing into the bag so you can leave). So where does possession take place? Clearly, it's an emotional and spiritual moment, not a technical one. Possession begins when the shopper's senses begin to latch on to the object. It begins in the eyes and then in the touch. Once the thing is in your hand, or on your back, or in your mouth, you can be said to have begun the process of taking it. Paying for it is a mere technicality, and so the sooner a thing is placed in the shopper's hand, the easier it is made for the shopper to try it or sip it or drive it around the block, the more easily it will change ownership, from the seller to the buyer.

That's shopping.

So, then, the principle seems simple enough: Shoppers want to experience merchandise before buying it. Therefore, the main function of a store is to foster shopper-merchandise contact. Stores should be begging shoppers to touch or try things, though frequently they make it as difficult as possible instead. I don't care if we're talking about computer keyboards, shower massagers or a new flavor of Jell-O. If a product does something, it should do it in the store. If it has a taste, shoppers should be able to taste it. If it has a smell, shoppers should be able to smell it. In fact, even if its smell has nothing to do with its purpose, we should be permitted to smell it, for there are times when a product's primary use has absolutely nothing to do with how it will be experienced.

For instance: What do air conditioners promise to do?

Make rooms cool. How do we know if they can keep that promise? Oh, ask your friends, or read *Consumer Reports,* or rely on the sales-clerk's opinion. You can't tell by looking, or even by turning it on in the air-conditioned store. So, in the absence of hard evidence, you buy the brand you always bought, or the brand that's on sale. But there's another issue here: How does that air conditioner sound? Precisely because cool air *is* cool air does this matter. In the final analysis, sound is one of the few things that distinguish one air conditioner from another. The unit is going to be humming (or clattering) away in your house for a number of years, after all. In a typical summer, I'll bet I have three or four conversations about air conditioner decibel levels. That's what actual human beings care about when it comes to air conditioners, but you'd never know it when you're shopping for one. The manufacturers and retailers are missing an opportunity here: Maybe if the salesperson were encouraged to flip a few switches to show you how they sound—this one like a prop airplane, that one like a busted blender, this other, more expensive one like a very small kitten purring in its sleep—you'd have some new basis for choosing one over another.

The same holds true, to some extent, for all major appliances—refrigerators and dishwashers and vacuum cleaners and washers and dryers—and even some minor ones, like coffee grinders, food processors and can openers. We can stare at the box and see at a glance if it's the thing we want. We can read the spec sheet to know more or less what it will do. But then we can at least *hear* it in action.

Here's another way that stores miss the point about how we wish to experience products. Judging by how bed linens are packaged, you'd think the most important issue is something called "thread count." What is thread count? Damned if most people know, but it is posted on nearly every sheet and pillowcase package you see. Bed connoisseurs know thread count. Normal human beings, however, judge a sheet by this measure: How does it feel? The problem is that most sheets are sold in plastic bags, which allow you to look but not touch. So you tear open the bag with your nail and furtively rub the fabric. Now if you decide to buy, you'll choose another package, because who wants one that's been damaged (even if *you* did the damaging)? And either way, you still don't know how that sheet will feel, due to what is known as the "sizing." What exactly is sizing? Again, damned if anybody knows, but you have to wash it out of new sheets or they'll be stiff and scratchy. So why, then, are shoppers made to touch sheets at their absolute worst? There's a huge bed and bath emporium near my office where display sheets have all been laundered once to pillowy perfection, then hung from hooks so shoppers can know what the linens will feel like once you get them home. Which is all that anybody cares about.

Perhaps the most obvious arena for touch and trial is in clothing.

Today, it's a rare clothes store where shoppers can't touch and fondle and stroke all the goods, whether it's $3 sweat socks or $1,500 designer suits. You still can't go into the Museum of Modern Art and rub a Picasso, but you can walk over to the Calvin Klein or Armani store on Madison Avenue and have your way with masterpieces of ready-to-wear apparel. For the most part, the men and women who design clothing stores do everything possible to allow us to touch all that's for sale. But then, when it's time to design the dressing rooms, they show how completely they misunderstand what happens inside that store.

Where do they go wrong? They think of dressing rooms as bathrooms without the plumbing. They see them as booths where shoppers can strip, don the garment in question, emerge for a quick, dutiful glance into a mirror and then switch clothes again. They design dressing rooms with all the romance and glamour of changing stalls at public pools. It's the most misguided aspect of store architecture and design, a trade that at its best isn't terribly responsive to retailers or shoppers. They skimp on dressing rooms, I believe, because they don't want to "waste" space by making these rooms too large. They don't want to blow too much of the budget on rooms that will never be photographed by the fancier design magazines.

In fact, the dressing room may be more important than the floor of the store. It's a truism that improving the quality of dressing rooms increases sales. It never fails. A dressing room isn't just a convenience—it's a selling tool, like a display or a window or advertising. It sells more effectively than all of those combined, if it's properly used. I am an incurable dressing room visitor—I'll make a special trip into a store's dressing room if I'm anywhere in the vicinity. If the coast is clear, I'll even ask if I can look in on women's dressing rooms. The truth is that I could write an entire book about dressing rooms—there's that much to say. Here's a formula we've recognized after studying a great many clothing stores: Not only does shopper conversion rate increase by half when there is staff-initiated contact, it jumps by 100 percent when there is staff-initiated contact *and* use of the dressing room. In other words, a shopper who talks to a salesperson and tries something on is twice as likely to buy as a shopper who does neither.

Still, we did a study for a major national apparel chain, one that has been extremely successful, where the dressing rooms were just dismal. Stark, cheesy little cubicles, a long corridor of them, with a single, badly illuminated mirror down at the end of the row. In the store we measured, customers who bought spent between one quarter and one third of their total shopping time inside the dressing rooms. In other words, they were captives in a very small space with nothing on their minds but the desire to buy something that will make them beautiful. In any other business, such a time would be avariciously thought of as "the close"— the critical moment when the buyer is vulnerable and ready to take the plunge. In a car dealership, which is itself no great shakes at the art of retailing, there are rooms set aside just to orchestrate this critical juncture. Here, however, there was absolutely no effort to make the rooms even minimally pleasant, or to make the area conducive to seeing the clothes in their best possible light. Neither was anyone viewing this as the moment for bringing all the charm and service of the sales force to bear on the situation. I mean simple things, too, like the clerk escorting the customer to the dressing room, then going out to find a few belts that might go nicely with the trousers, or a shirt, or a vest, knowing that many times the right accessory sells the garment. When the customer is in the dressing room, he or she is in a total buying mode. But instead of taking advantage of that, most stores squander it.

In fact, I visited the couture floor of a major department store in New York and saw what may have been the most horrible dressing rooms I've ever seen. Dirty, shabby, worn rugs. Harsh, unflattering lighting. The same wall hooks and seats you'd find in a low-rent discounter. Mirrors that distort the viewer's body, and not for the better. When I pointed this out a saleslady sardonically asked, "Doesn't *every* woman want bigger hips?" The furnishings there should be what you'd want in your dream boudoir. The lighting should make everybody look like a million bucks. In fact, the illumination should have several settings, so you could see what a color or fabric would look like in daylight, or under fluorescent lighting, or by candlelight. The mirrors should be large, plentiful and first-rate—they should be like the frame for a flattering portrait, not just a slab of glass hung by clips on a Sheetrock wall. If there's space for a little anteroom outside the dressing rooms, so much the better. A shopper and his or her companion can really look the goods over out there. A shopper could actually see what it feels like to sit down wearing the garment, an important issue if it's to be worn at a special dinner, for instance. And there should be fresh flowers. Fresh flowers say that someone has paid attention to the room today, not yesterday, and that's the proper message.

Even outside the dressing rooms, apparel stores often mishandle something as simple as mirrors. Most commonly, there are too few of them, or they're placed badly. There should be a mirror anywhere there's merchandise that can be tried on or even just held up for inspection. If you pick up an item and can see in an instant how it looks on you, you might buy it. If you've got to search for a mirror, at least some of the time you'll decide it's not worth the trouble. If the hats are here, the hat mirror should be here, too—not five feet away. And I've seen more than one self-serve shoe department with no mirrors down at floor level. I've seen self-serve shoe sections with no chairs! This all seems so simple. Why is it ever wrong?

You need enough dressing rooms, and they must be clearly marked so they're easy to find, even from a distance. The farther the dressing rooms are from the clothes, the fewer shoppers will bother to make the trip. A truly determined shopper will always find the dressing room, but no store can survive only on the stouthearted. We've seen stores where you have to cross the entire selling floor and then go up or down a few steps to try something on. That's fatal. We did a study for a department store where our video cameras caught shoppers wandering uncertainly, garments in hand, searching (and searching) for the dressing rooms. There were enough of them, but they were hidden in corners, bare little doorways marked by inconspicuous signs. Finding a dressing room shouldn't be a challenge.

Okay, what have we here? A guy in an office supply store, one of the big chains. Looking for a pencil sharpener. Amazing that they still even exist—turntables are extinct but pencils and pencil sharpeners live on, thanks to the popularity of Sudoku. Anyway, the sharpeners are all together on a shelf, a few manual ones, some battery powered and some big plug-in jobs. He turns the handles on the manual ones to get their feel. Then he lifts a battery model and pries open the compartment to find . . . nothing. The thing won't turn on! He moves on to the plug-in models and lifts them, too, then looks around to see if there's an outlet. Nothing. Even if he had found a battery or an outlet, there's the small matter of pencils, none of which are anywhere in sight. He grabs a sharpener, then wheels away, out of the aisle, in search of an electrical outlet, I presume, and maybe a pencil, too.

Does this seem like a serious effort to sell pencil sharpeners? Clearly, there must be a difference in sharpeners, or else why would there be so many choices? But how can this poor guy choose one over another—or any one at all—without a test grind? It seems like the simplest matter in the world to anticipate what shoppers will want to do and where they'll want to do it: In the absence of a pencil-sharpener clerk, please allow me to figure it out myself. But bad stores get it wrong all the time, even large, sophisticated, profitable national chains of bad stores. In that same store, there is a ten-foot-high wall rack of paper sold in reams, which are encased in paper wrappers. Some of the paper is cheap, some of it more expensive—but there is not a single chance to actually see or touch the paper being sold. As a result, every fifth or sixth package has been torn open for some frustrated shopper's furtive inspection. This is a classic example of how a decision to be cheap (not allowing shoppers to touch even one sheet of paper) ends up costing money (lots of packages are torn and unsalable).

Making goods inaccessible hurts in other ways, too. We studied a jewelry store whose owner had recently scored a coup by hiring a designer well known for creating museum exhibitions to design some jewelry display cases. The result was beautiful but distancing—the guy was accustomed to making displays that allowed the public to see but kept them at arm's length, exactly what you don't want in a store where people are encouraged to take the goods home. The displays performed poorly compared to less exalted fixtures.

Here's how good stores do it. We were performing a study for

RadioShack just when the chain had decided to try to become America's favorite phone store. We watched countless shoppers approach the wall of telephones on display, look them all over, check out the prices, and then, almost without exception, pick up a phone and hold it up to an ear. What were they hoping for? Nothing, probably—it's just a reflex action, I think. What else do you *do* with a phone? On what other basis do you compare phones but by how they feel in your hand and against your ear? Well, we reasoned, if the first principle of trial is to make it as lifelike as possible, you can complete the experience by putting a voice in that phone. We advised RadioShack to connect the phones to a recorded message that would be activated when the receiver was lifted. Once that happened, the stores were alive with shoppers picking up display phones, listening a moment, and then holding the receivers out for their companions to hear—which was a bonus, because that would provide some basis for discussing the purchase, which greatly increases the chance that something will be bought. (People in stores love to talk about whatever it is they're shopping for.) This was also a good way for RadioShack to sneak in a commercial message. In another study, Sprint's cell phone stores used a counter display so you could see and heft the various models, but each phone was also activated, which is the only way to do it—customers picked up the phones and dialed a spouse or friend to discuss the very gadget they were considering. The phones sold themselves, which is the whole point.

Other stores, like Brookstone or the French beauty retailer Sephora, all understand the value of putting merchandise out there for shoppers to experience, damage be damned. If Brookstone displays a vibrating chair and after a few months it's shabby from shopper use, that's OK— they've no doubt sold more than enough chairs to cover the loss.

Store displays can be remade to allow shoppers to touch and try the merchandise. But if product packaging doesn't change as well, a great many opportunities will continue to be lost. In the health and beauty aisles, for instance, smell and touch are vitally important. What is skin lotion's first responsibility if not to feel good when applied to skin? Why does anyone buy deodorant except for its scent? And while shampoo's main job is to clean hair—something you can't really test in a store—it also must leave that hair smelling like the rain forest on a good day, and that's something you *can* investigate in the aisle, if only the manufacturer will permit it. Unfortunately, today's tamper-proof packaging thwarts every respectful attempt to experience the product.

Gillette made quite a splash with its clear gel deodorants for men—they come in a variety of scents, each with an evocative (yet manly) name. Somebody at Gillette was thinking correctly when they decided to give men more of a choice than Right Guard menthol or regular. But then the boys in packaging got their mitts on the idea. In the store you are faced with several varieties of deodorant, differing only in scent, and so naturally you wish to learn how they smell. You remove the lid from one and are confronted by a formidable strip of heavy-duty foil tape sealing the applicator. (Why? Can terrorists kill people through their armpits?) Now, if no one's watching, you might peel that tape back some and give it a sniff. But that would be wrong. So what's a shopper to do? If he's not terribly motivated, he'll put it back and walk away. If he is persistent, he'll glance up and down the aisle and, if the coast is clear, rip back that tape and take a whiff. Of course, if he then decides against buying the Alpine Morning underarm experience—maybe he feels like more of an Arizona Twilight kind of guy—how will the next shopper who comes along feel when he discovers that the tamper-proof strip has been tampered with? A lot of perfectly good deodorant is going to be ruined that way, by package designers who refuse to acknowledge how human beings shop.

One solution for this and all the rest would be for drugstores to create a sampling bar, a counter where new items can be freely auditioned. The tactile issues of body products are so important that resolving them would surely result in increased sales.

The biggest struggle in this area has to do with how cosmetics are sold. Manufacturers and retailers want to sell the products in as clean and orderly a way as possible. Women don't object to that, but understandably, they want to try before they buy, which is not always a clean and orderly impulse.

In days of old, most cosmetics were sold by the same kindly druggist who doled out prescriptions and fountain sodas. You'd ask for foundation, say, and he'd go behind the counter, open a drawer and begin pulling out boxes until he found your brand. It was kind of arm's-length, and no one would stand for that today, but it was efficient and neat. The world of cosmetics was liberated in large part by the Cover Girl brand, which was the first one to make wide use of the peg wall, allowing shoppers to touch makeup without an intermediary getting in the way. This was what moved cosmetics toward its future as a self-serve category. That also put a serious crimp in the prospects of another cosmetics tradition, the department store bazaar. There, even to this day, shoppers perch on stools at counters while Kabuki-faced representatives of makeup purveyors paint and daub them into perfection, the result of which is a small but costly shopping bag of makeup on the departing shopper's arm.

But even that method of selling cosmetics is passing from the scene—women are getting fed up, I think—and is being replaced by the open-sell layout. And so you have each manufacturer trying a different system that allows shoppers to look at cosmetics, and even, under controlled conditions, to try them. But not too much. And you have women who wish to undo those controls so they can test products as they please. The interests of seller and buyer shouldn't be at odds, but they often are. Designers of cosmetics fixtures are sometimes culprits, too—they build displays without considering that shoppers need simple amenities like tissues, for instance, which would actually improve the overall neatness of cosmetics sections. Or they don't put in enough mirrors, so women have to scramble around the store as they try out makeup. The designers of these sections never visit them at five P.M. on a Saturday afternoon, I can assure you, because if they did they'd design them differently, with more accommodation for the women who use them. Shopper-unfriendly packaging intended to prevent cosmetics trial is almost always a bad idea—bad because it discourages buying and because it encourages women to damage merchandise. In any product category, the best way to limit package destruction is to offer shoppers a way to try things without doing any damage.

The advent of shrink-wrap has made it difficult to experience a great many products firsthand. In fact, many products seem to be overly packaged, which is a pain if you're a hands-on shopper. We've come a long way from the simple listening booths once found in record stores. Today in the very troubled world of music, there are several rather complex electronic systems that try to make samples of recordings available to shoppers. Typically, these involve listening stations—headphones plugged into a board, and then a menu of CDs that can be dialed up. One problem is that you may be unfamiliar with these gizmos, and so you push the button for the disc you want, but then . . . nothing. In fact, there's a wait while the song cues up, but no indicator on the machine tells you so. You give it a moment and either shrug and give up, or you assume you've chosen a nonworking channel and push another button, and then more buttons, ultimately sending the machine into meltdown.

The best system is always the simplest and most direct one. There, a shopper just selects any CD from any rack and brings it to a listening bar, where a clerk opens the package and plays the disc. That's it—no gizmos, no buttons, no menus, no waiting. Instead of spending money on complicated, unreliable song-sample-playing machines, the store buys one shrink-wrapping device to repackage whatever's not purchased, and that's that. And such a system must allow shoppers to listen to music as human nature intended—meaning, nobody listens to music standing still and staring at the floor. In a store we researched in Alabama, listening station headphones were equipped with twenty-foot-long cords, so music fans could move around and even shop nearby racks. With that, the stores go from being places to buy records to places where one can listen to them, find out what's out there, what's new, who's playing what. It turns the store into an interactive radio station and makes shopping there a fun experience. Best of all, from the store's point of view, it lessens the retailer's dependence on the labels to market their merchandise properly. When a store allows access to merchandise, it is in essence doing its own marketing—one-on-one, to an interested consumer who is in a position to act on his or her desires on the spot.

Packaging often suffers when the shopper's desire for information is thwarted. We see this with electronics—the shopper for headphones, for instance, finds a stack of them, boxed, in a store. There's no display model in sight. If the box were properly designed—with a large, clear photo of the phones and all the features and specifications listed in read-able type—maybe seeing the headphones would be less crucial. But when the packaging forces shoppers to guess, it becomes easier to just rip the damn box open, pull out the headphones and see for yourself. No one's going to buy anything being sold in a shredded box.

Packaging need not always be such an impermeable barrier to touch, however. Toy manufacturers realized that adults wanted to try toys before they bought them. Maybe this was because so much toy advertising is deceptive, giving gullible kiddies the impression that this cheap plastic airplane is actually capable of zooming around the kitchen like a miniature bomber on an air strike. At any rate, the trend is now to design packaging so it allows toys to be tried without having to molest the box or the plastic wrap. You can push the button or pull the string and Cookie Monster sings from inside his cardboard prison. This suddenly made it a lot easier to know what you were buying in the toy store, and this was one of those instances where shopper con-fidence led to increased sales. I recently saw maybe the smartest toy packaging yet—a kiddie plastic tricycle that was boxed in a way that left exposed the seat, pedals, handlebars and wheels, thereby allowing a child to test-drive it without disturbing the box. If that principle were applied to all product packaging, shopping would be a lot more fun than it is now.

Security considerations are behind some reasons for placing mer-chandise off-limits. MP3 players are one such product. I guess any pricey item with lots of appeal for teenagers is heisted frequently. But the deci-sion to sell these behind a locked counter should be enough; instead, they're also packaged inside bulky, clear plastic "clamshell" containers, which makes it impossible to hear the player before buying it. I'm sure that shoppers would trade up to more expensive models if only they could comparison-shop a few brands—just witness the success of the Apple Stores, which invite you to play iPods and fiddle around with iPhones and other cool gear.

Costume jewelry is another category that's often guilty of this sin. You've got items that cost maybe $20 or $30 padlocked behind glass and steel, depriving shoppers of the chance to see how the chains and pendants would look and feel on a neck or a wrist. In the same store you'll see plenty of other merchandise of equal or greater value on open display. It's reflexive but makes no business sense. We see the same thinking about one of the hottest items to grow out of the computerization of America—ink-jet printer cartridges. Until very recently, in almost every major U.S. office product superstore (like Staples, OfficeMax, Office Depot and so on) they were displayed inside locked cabinets, owing to their small size and high price. But when you've seen as many frustrated shoppers prowling store aisles searching vainly for a clerk with a key as we have, you wonder if there isn't something self-defeating about all that security. Printer ink cartridges drive a huge percentage of office product store profits, and in the past ten years, most of the major chains have redesigned their stores around the ink-jet cartridge section.

Clothing retailers have learned a trick or two about placing goods on display without allowing them to be abused in the process. Let's go back to that beautiful Armani store on Madison Avenue, for instance. You've got shoppers whose hands have been who knows where, and they're groping costly Italian adornments like they already own them. Would you feel at ease knowing how many fingers have already had their way with your suit sleeve? Here's one strategy: If a suit comes in several colors, the store will place the dark shades down where they can be reached easily and display the beiges and pale grays and off-whites up high, where they can be seen but not touched. If a sweater displayed on a table comes in several shades, you'll always find the lighter ones on the bottom and the dark on top, where they'll be rubbed and grubbed, but who will know?

Selling is the main reason for making merchandise as available as possible to shoppers. But it's not the only one—there's also selling up. If you have no real basis for comparing one product to another, the normal instinct is to buy what's cheaper. But if a store sets itself up to educate shoppers, even just a little, a certain number of them will spend more than what is absolutely necessary. If given a choice of three brands, or three models, and given the chance to pit one against the others, the shopper will at least have a sensible reason for choosing the better item.

This is an issue for just about every product we've mentioned so far—men's underwear and coffee and stereo headphones and sweaters and skin cream etc. In mattress stores, too. There, typically, you find a whole field of undressed beds awaiting inspection. Some are cheaper than others, but it's just as expensive to stock and maintain the $1,500 mattress as it is the $4,000 one. So if you can get just one customer in five to start out trying the cheap number and work up to a better one, you're doing pretty well.

And how, aside from trial, can that be made to happen? Clearly, no other way. And the beds are all out there, ready for you to recline, isn't that right? Well, kind of. You really need to feel comfortable to try out a mattress. It's a vulnerable position to take in such a public space, in front of strangers. You may even wish you didn't have to lie down while the salesman stands there, looming over you. (He, of course, is afraid that if he backs off five feet and stops sending you telepathic "Buy this mattress now!" messages, you won't purchase anything.) And you're on a mattress that has been helpfully positioned in the front of the store, where your supine form can be seen easily through the front window, and where, if you are a woman in a dress or skirt, your modesty will be severely tested. How much worse can this experience be made? How about no sheets on the bed, so you never even see how it will feel if and when you get it home, and no pillow either, so you get no idea of the comfort this baby will (or will not) provide?

It seems that if the better mattresses were positioned away from public view, maybe even partly partitioned, to give the experience a little of the feel of a dressing room, maybe shoppers would be encouraged to upgrade their bedding desires. More thought is given to the trial experience when you're buying a pair of $40 jeans than when you're buying a $4,000 mattress. We did a study of mattress retailing, during which we asked a manager whether pillows of various thicknesses and firmness could be provided, along with freshly laundered pillowcases, for mattress try-outs.

"But we don't *sell* pillows," was his flat rejection of the idea. Never mind that pillows have a much higher margin than mattresses even, or that selling pillows was a way of adding on accessories to a product that had few opportunities for such novelties.

Similarly, at AT&T phone stores, the focus was on selling the main product; almost as an afterthought, they sold a dopey little item called the SoftTalk phone holder. It was a soft plastic cradle designed to make it more comfortable to keep your phone jammed between your neck and shoulder. The thing didn't look like much of anything, but once you tried it you learned that it was ingenious and truly effective. Without trying it, however, it looked pointless, and because none were on display there was no easy way to actually try it, and thanks to the sales staff's lack of effort nobody ever did. Sure, it was only a $5 or so item, but the margin on it, as with most accessories, was obscenely high—the most profitable thing in the joint. We computed that if every third customer bought one, the profit would cover a store's monthly rent.

Another glaring example is wireless services, where customers can compare the costs of handsets and services online. It is a very competitive market where margins are small and where the money is made by selling accessories, from ringtones to carrying cases. Best Buy, for example, has struck a deal with Liz Claiborne to develop slick cell phone and laptop cases. At one recent store opening, they staged a fashion show exhibiting carrying cases for phones, computers and digital cameras. None of them were cheap. Great idea. I just wish they'd been smart enough to realize that if you want to sell high-priced laptop bags, you also need mirrors. In Japan you can "tattoo" your phone or iPod—you pick out the skin and for about $40, someone carefully applies the decal to cover your phone. Add to that spare batteries, a charger for your car and a hands-free device, and the transaction is that much more profitable.

There's one final issue regarding the sensory and tactile nature of shopping. Oddly, it involves letting shoppers know that it's *all right* for them to touch. At Hallmark stores we studied, some front-end Christmas ornament displays were so artfully designed and painstakingly constructed that shoppers didn't know if they were supposed to take or just gaze adoringly. Bookstores, too, sometimes run into the same problem when tabletop displays show a little too much effort. People know how hard it is to get anything looking nice, so they can be reluctant to undo somebody's hard work. We ran into this while helping Einstein Bros. Bagels test-drive a prototype restaurant in Utah, of all places. A brilliantly anomalous decision, by the way, inventing a new way to sell bagels in a place where there is no bagel culture to speak of—if you can get it working there, it'll work anywhere. At this store, a wall rack holding bags of variously flavored bagel chips was positioned so that customers standing in line to pay would be able to reach out and grab something on impulse. The problem was that the bags were stocked so neatly, and with such an orderly eye, that customers were never quite sure if they were meant to touch the thing. The solution was to have an employee come out every so often and mess the shelves up, pull a few bags out so there would be obvious gaps. *Then* the customers touched. (People are awfully polite in Utah, aren't they?) Actually, the clerks would create a total sensory experience by grabbing a bag, ripping it open and proffering it to those waiting in line, as a way to introduce the locals to the wonders of jalapeno-cheddar whole wheat bagel chips. Which may sound like a joke, but don't laugh until you've tried them.

THIRTEEN

The Big Three

I've got a brilliant idea: Let's save money! We're in charge of merchandising and display for a chain of stores here, so let's make an executive decision to replace our expensive old wooden shelving with a cheaper new wire grid system. The difference in cost goes directly to the bottom line. There. Done. Next?

What? Oh. Well, look at that. Yikes. Who knew? The wire shelving seemed perfectly beautiful and functional—until actual product was placed on it. At that point (or minutes after, I should say) the main drawback to the wire grid became clear: Every time a customer touches something, it tilts. Sometimes, to be honest, nobody touches a thing and it tilts. I think the damn boxes may be tilting each other. And you look down the long expanse of wire grids and every fourth or fifth thing has tipped, and it looks like hell, I'll be the first to agree, so somebody needs to go straighten it. The boys over in Operations are screaming like wet chimps: We're now paying people $8.00 an hour to straighten boxes. On a busy Saturday night, as the lines grow long, we're talking an hour or more per store of wasted labor. How many stores? How many hours? How much did we save? Uh-oh.

And that's not a hypothetical scenario, either—it's verbatim from the Envirosell playbook. It illustrates one of the most important principles of shopping. Retailing 101 starts with the notion that a store has three distinct aspects: design (meaning the premises), merchandising (whatever you put in them) and operations (whatever employees do). These Big Three, while seemingly separate, are in fact completely and totally intertwined, interrelated and interdependent, meaning that when somebody makes a decision regarding one, a decision has been made about the other two as well. In this particular instance, the mistake was one that's made all the time: Display designers never go into stores to see their creations in action, so they don't have a firm grip on what happens in the real world. The larger lesson here is that if one of the Big Three is strengthened, it takes some of the pressure off the others. If one is weakened, it shifts a greater burden onto the remaining two. This is not a good thing or a bad thing—it just is. It's the geometry that rules the shopping universe.

Here's an example. The Gap's trademark is that you can easily touch, stroke, unfold and otherwise examine at close range everything on the selling floor. A lot of sweaters and shirts are sold thanks to the decision to foster intimate contact between shopper and goods. Obviously, that merchandising policy dictates the display scheme (wide, flat tabletops, which are easier to shop than racks or shelves). But it also determines how and where employees will spend their time. All that touching means that sweaters and shirts constantly need to be refolded and straightened and neatened. That translates into the need for lots of clerks roaming the floor rather than standing behind the counter ringing up sales. Which is a big expense, but for the Gap, it's a sound investment—the cost of doing business. The main thing here is that it was a conscious decision.

Sometimes it's not a decision so much as a response to a fact of life. Revlon's merchandising must work in a variety of settings—mass merchandisers, cosmetics specialty stores and drugstores. In the latter, typically, the aisles are narrow and jammed with stuff. Because of that design reality, the dreaded butt-brush factor—the fact that women don't like to be bumped from behind while shopping—comes into play. Revlon's drugstore merchandising must be clear, bold and direct, so that women can spot the brand name, find what they're looking for and be on their way as quickly as possible. If the signage and displays were more subtle or oblique, those women would have been butt-brushed out of the aisle before they chose a single thing. This issue comes up all the time because the people who design packaging and merchandising materials don't spend enough time in stores, visiting their creations where they live. For instance: We all know that college-educated shoppers tend to read everything that's printed on a package. That's how they prefer to info-load before deciding whether to buy. So a company selling herbal remedies should instruct its package designers to incorporate a fair amount of text on those bottles. The designer follows orders. But small type is hard to read for older shoppers, who are a prime market for vitamins and herbal supplements. And these products tend to sell well in drugstores, where aisles typically are narrow, which discourages shoppers from reading any package for very long. That's how a good decision (adding more information to a package) results in a not so good effect (no one can read it). In Chapter 17, I'll explain a potential solution to the small-type issue.

The point here is that whenever a decision is made, it should be examined closely for all its farthest-reaching implications. In real life, however, it doesn't often happen that way. It doesn't happen in small firms, where a few people are run ragged making all the decisions. And it especially doesn't happen in big firms. Frequently, we'll go into some company's conference room to deliver our findings, and chiefs of Store Design, Merchandising and Operations will be present. Sometimes, it's clear that they barely know each other. They may even be based in different cities. The suspicion, hostility and turf-warring can actually seem palpable. The executives either don't know what the others are doing or don't care to know. As a result, a lot of shortsighted decisions get made.

Here's a good example. In a big, famous department store, the boss of ladies' shoes decided that he needed more display space and that he'd get it by shrinking the register area. As a result, the clerks who once used the counter for bagging had to start placing the bags on the floor and lowering the shoes in. This added several steps to the process and made ringing up sales more arduous for the clerks, who usually wore pretty fancy shoes themselves. By the end of a day these women were hurting and dragging—and a little bitter, understandably. As part of our research we trained video cameras on the register and then, back at the office, we timed transactions with a stopwatch; at 4:30 P.M., it took almost twice as long to ring up a sale as it did at 11:00 A.M. Shrinking the counter space also added to the general clutter, making transactions less crisp. The overall result was that a mild improvement in merchandising required a change in design, which hurt operations quite a bit. In order to show off a few more shoes (like maybe a dozen pairs), transaction time grew longer, customer patience grew thin and employee energy and morale grew short. Considering that employees sell shoes better than any display, this was a very bad decision—all because someone who should have known better forgot that when you change one thing, everything changes.

Another client, a video chain, made some interesting decisions about how its stores would look. The dominant color would be a deep burgundy. And the lighting motif would be rows of lightbulbs, such as movie marquees once employed. It all looked good on the drawing board, maybe, but then real life happened. The burgundy kept getting scuffed and dented and chipped, meaning the store got dingy-looking fast, meaning the painters were spending an awful lot of time on the premises doing touch-ups. That's usually the fate of any surface painted a rich, dark shade—every scuff shows. Also, the dark walls and display racks required quite a bit more illumination than off-white would have needed. Which was expensive just for the electricity, nevermind the fact that all those lightbulbs had the habit of burning out, which meant they had to be replaced at once or risk looking like something from Times Square—the old Times Square. In the end, bad design decisions added quite a bit to the chain's overhead and maintenance, which came right out of the bottom line.

Relations between the three aspects of retail are under a fair amount
of stress today for one main reason: Most North American businesses
are constantly looking to save money on labor. From the businessperson's point of view, this falls under the heading of operations. From the
shopper's perspective, it means service. Retailers try to maintain service
while cutting labor, which is usually impossible to do. Back when stores
were properly staffed and employees were encouraged to stay in their
jobs and learn their business, the demands on design and merchandising
were few and simple. A store could even be cluttered and disorganized,
because there was always a clerk available to help, and he or she always
knew where everything was kept.

Today, when many retailers underpay and undervalue their sales
staff, the opposite is true. The burden falls on design and merchandising, which are sometimes up to the job, but not always. For example,
retailers try to make up for staff cuts by using interactive computerized
fixtures to answer shoppers' questions. The only problem is that the fixtures are frequently badly designed—they're confusing, or don't answer
questions fully, or are so slow that you'd think they stopped working. So
what do shoppers do? We've seen lots of them give up and walk away
grumbling. Some just grab a salesclerk and drag him or her over to figure out how to use the thing. That's some labor-saving device.

At a department store we studied, the beleaguered staff saved time
by overstocking the fixtures—jamming more clothes onto the racks
than they could comfortably handle. Some shoppers didn't even bother
trying to extricate garments, it was such a struggle. Customers who
did wrestle a hanger out invariably pulled other garments along with it,
dragging them to the floor. And whose job was it to pick them up, dust
them off and rehang them? The time saved by overstocking was wasted
in maintenance. Even worse, while the clothes lay on the floor no shopper would touch them. You should have seen the lingerie section—
would anyone buy underwear off the floor?

But it is possible to use design and merchandising to save operations
some work. One example comes from the United States Postal Service.
A few years ago we tested prototypes for their new post offices. In one

of the "stores," the self-serve section—you buy stamps and envelopes from machines, weigh your own packages and apply your own postage—was positioned beyond the traditional counters staffed by postal workers. In another configuration, the self-serve was right inside the entrance, beyond which were the counters. The first store had a fairly low rate of self-serve; people who were used to dealing with clerks just got in line and never saw the machines in back. The second prototype had a much higher self-serve use—customers would enter fully intending to stand in the teller lines, then see people quickly taking care of things on their own. Banks find the same pattern—if ATMs and automatic deposit machines are in view of the teller lines, full-service customers "migrate" over to the automated side.

The second example comes from a giant drugstore chain. Pharmacies have changed a lot in the past two decades, but one thing remains constant: the large burden on staff to stock all those little bottles, jars and boxes in perfectly straight rows in aisle after aisle of shelving. Every time a customer picks something up to read the label, you're guaranteed that the thing needs to be straightened or turned so it faces front. It's a lot of work. Not long ago, Wal-Mart tried an experiment: It began replacing traditional shelves with a system of bins. Instead of a shelf facing of six little aspirin bottles, say, the shopper would see a blow-up of the aspirin label. Under that blowup was the bin, into which the aspirin bottles had been dumped.

This made an enormous difference. First, it solved the problem of stocking—a clerk could just roll a trolley of merchandise to the aisle, open the bin, dump in the goods and move on. No more straight lines. The shoppers liked it better, too—instead of facing a row of bottles with tiny print, they saw a large, easy-to-read version of the label. It was much easier on the eyes, especially for older shoppers, who carry a lot of weight in drugstores, as you can imagine. Wal-Mart's main concern in making the change was whether shoppers would perceive the bins as being somehow cheaper and lower in quality than the shelves. In fact, just the opposite was true—shoppers interviewed said they thought the bins were an upgraded display system. A very elegant solution. The next problem was who would pay for the new system—the store chain or the vendors whose product was being sold? A big fight ensued and the system wasn't implemented. Two years after we did the study I saw the identical system used with great success in Auchan, the French hypermarket chain.

FOURTEEN

Time

In stores, as in life, there are good times and there are bad times. Good times—meaning any time a customer is shopping—you want to stretch. Bad times you want to bend.

Bad times are whenever the customer is made to wait. Understandably, they don't like it, but as reasonable beings, they'll do it—up to a point. Beyond that, though, comes trouble. In study after study, we've seen that the single most important factor in determining a shopper's opinion of the service he or she receives is waiting time. If they think the wait wasn't too bad, they feel as though they were treated capably and well. If the wait went on too long, they feel as though the service was poor and inept. Quite simply, a short wait enhances the entire shopping experience and a long one poisons it.

But it's possible to "bend" waiting time—to alter how shoppers perceive it. You can even turn bad times into good times.

First, a word about the whole issue of time and perception. There's the watch on your wrist, which is probably a highly accurate instrument, but there's an even more important clock inside your head. That mental timepiece is highly susceptible to outside influences, and yet it counts more than any Rolex. We've interviewed lots of shoppers on the subject and have found this interesting result: When people wait up to about a minute and a half, their sense of how much time has elapsed is fairly accurate. Anything over ninety or so seconds, however, and their sense of time distorts—if you ask how long they've been waiting, their honest answer will usually be a very exaggerated one. If they've waited two minutes, they'll say it's been three or four. In the shopper's mind, the waiting period goes from being a transitional pause in a larger process (purchasing goods, say) to being a full-fledged activity of its own. That's when time becomes very bad. Time is a cruel master in the world of shopping. Taking care of a customer in two minutes is a success; taking care of a customer in three minutes is a failure.

The obvious appeal of drive-thru shopping (or banking, or dining) is in its convenience and efficiency—you save yourself the trouble of finding a parking spot, then parking, then getting out of your car and going inside and then having to do it all over again in reverse. (One of our favorite pieces of videotape shows a bank drive-thru in Whittier, California, where the cars in line were joined by one time-stressed man on foot.) But even if going to the drive-thru didn't move things faster, the comfort of waiting in your own car, sitting in a comfortable seat with the CD player and heater or air conditioner on, would without question make it *feel* faster.

Most of this matter of time centers on the cashier area, when shoppers are standing in line to pay, or to see a teller, or to order a meal. And it's there that measures can be taken to bend waiting time. Such as:

Interaction, human or otherwise: The time a shopper spends waiting after an employee has initiated contact actually goes faster than time spent waiting before that interaction takes place, our studies have shown. Having an employee simply acknowledge that the shopper is waiting—and maybe offer some plausible explanation—automatically relieves time anxiety, especially when it comes early in the wait. I once visited a big chain drugstore where the manager clearly loved customer contact. When the checkout lines got a little too long he'd leave his office and work the front of the store like some combination expediter–standup comic. His presence seemed to make the cashiers move a little faster, and he was entertaining, too. If, during busy times, I had a choice between deploying three cashiers or two cashiers and a line manager, I'd go with the latter. The line manager can serve as a kind of precashier—he or she can gently suggest to shoppers that they have their orders ready or can offer to answer any questions the customers may have, thereby shortening both the perceived and the actual wait. This can be a great way to train even your customers to be more efficient.

Another related way to bend time is to tell shoppers their wait will be finite and controlled rather than open-ended and subject to the vagaries of fate and chance. Some banks do this by posting an electronic sign that announces how many minutes the wait for a teller should last. These signs are never accurate, but that's OK—just being told that your patience must last for only two minutes makes the four minutes you actually wait go faster. I recently called a computer manufacturer's telephone technical help hotline. A recorded voice informed me that my wait for a human being would last "an estimated one to five minutes." Which is a hell of a long span, when you think about it, but they were placating my time anxiety while playing it safe, a smart move.

Orderliness: European shoppers don't seem to mind queuing up in a great, heaving mass of humanity, but Americans like their lines single-file, crisp and fair. Making people guess about where to stand frustrates them. Allowing chaos to reign causes anxiety. If customers see that they're being helped in the exact order they arrived, they relax, and the time spent waiting seems shorter. This is the secret to bending time: get rid of the uncertainty and you cut the perceived wait.

The organization of cashier lines is still one of the great ongoing quandaries in the world of shopping. Without question, the fastest, most equitable system places customers in a single checkout line. This way guarantees that shoppers are taken in the order they arrive, and there's no angst about whether they've chosen the swiftest line. There's just one problem: You will sometimes have one *very* long line—a worrisome sight for a shopper in a hurry. Somehow, three lines of five customers each promise less of an ordeal than a single line of fifteen people. It's irrational but true, and such is the difference between perception and reality.

Just as important is the fact that when the cashier is positioned near the front door, a single long line drives incoming customers away. A common sight in our work is the shopper who enters a store (or merely peers in through a window), sees a long line at the checkout, takes that as a sign that the entire place is mobbed, turns on a dime and exits. In fact, the store may be empty past that checkout line, but who can tell? (And this, as we say elsewhere in these pages, is a good argument for not positioning cashiers within sight of the outside world.)

Two major American merchants changed their line system in the hope of making it more efficient and less daunting: Best Buy, the consumer electronics chain, and Whole Foods, the grocery store chain. Best Buy runs you through a maze where the walls are high enough so you have no idea as you enter how many people may be waiting in front of you, and those walls are merchandised with batteries, cheap video games and office and computer supplies. It works remarkably well. Whole Foods has been rolling out their new queuing system, a series of minilines with flat-screen televisions above them indicating which numbered cash/wrap the first person in each line should go to. What's good about this system is you're breaking up a big, snaky, short-tempered line. And it's clear that a technological system is overseeing the whole thing. With the knowledge that someone is minding the store, and maybe even paying attention, customers' anxiety levels drop off. Is it a terrific system? No, but it's a system, and an obvious improvement over the old chaos.

Companionship: The wait seems shorter if you've got someone to talk to, no surprise. A store can't do much about that, except to recognize that the lone waiters are the ones who need employee contact most.

Diversion: Almost anything will suffice. One bank we studied used a TV tuned to soap operas to entertain the line—a bad idea, we thought, because to enjoy a soap you need to see the entire half hour. A much better solution was used by another bank, in California, where a big-screen TV played old Keystone Kops shorts during the afternoon, when most customers were retirees. Everybody's considering video systems these days, but some low-tech entertainments work just as well. Many food stores serve free samples, a good time-killer that promotes new products. Positioning racks of impulse items so they can be shopped from the cashier line is smart merchandising, but it's also good time-bending. Also keep in mind that the first person in line doesn't require much diversion—he or she is in the on-deck circle, just waiting for the sign that they're up. Merchandising materials, signage, shoppable racks and anything else should be positioned for the second person in line and back.

The racks of sleazy tabloids at the supermarket checkout are a great use of diverting merchandise, allowing you to absorb all the trashy news you need without having to watch Jerry Springer. Another popular form of shopper diversion is, believe it or not, signage. Customers perceive waiting time as shorter if there are signs to read, our research shows. In fact, smart retailers view waiting time as a kind of intangible asset—it's one of the few opportunities when you have your customers standing in one spot, facing in one direction, with nothing much else to do. This is when bad times can be turned into good times: Waiting may be a necessary evil, but you can use it to communicate some message and, at the same time, shorten how shoppers perceive it.

Even away from the cashiers, waiting time is a problem in stores today. Retailers typically cut costs by cutting back on labor, which means that shoppers now spend more time than ever searching for a clerk who can answer a question. This is a particularly deadly form of waiting time; we've watched countless shoppers dart back and forth in stores looking for help or directions. After they've wandered in vain for a minute or so, you can see the steam coming out of their ears. Male shoppers are particularly vulnerable to this—if they can't get an answer fast, they give up and go home (or to another store). We studied a department store that had just made a change in staffing policy: Instead of keeping cashiers stationed throughout the place, in the various departments, the registers were consolidated in front. (*Fewer* registers, naturally.) As a result, waiting time in line instantly became quite a bit longer. Plus, it suddenly was very hard to find an employee on the sales floor. *Plus,* the mob of impatient-looking shoppers lined up to pay just inside the front door gave entering customers the impression that the store was packed. In all, saving on a few salaries created a lot of expensive new disadvantages to overcome.

This equation pops up all the time in retailing today: At what point does saving money on labor end up costing money in shopper frustration? Banks in particular are vulnerable. They tend to hire part-timers for minimum wage, meaning they're not getting workers with seasoned math or people skills. As a result, wait time increases. At some point, customer dread will take its toll. We studied two businesses—a bank and an electronics store—that, mainly for security reasons, used a single cash drawer. At the bank, tellers had to run back and forth from their windows to the drawer for even the simplest transactions. At the store, shoppers beheld the spectacle of salesclerks jostling each other out of the way to get at the register. Neither setup did much for consumer confidence, and the effect on waiting time was just what you'd expect.

We've studied quite a few stores where time-consuming antishoplifting policies ended up costing sales, we felt sure. In each example, the merchandise was small in size but not inexpensive: prestige perfumes in one case; computer printer ink cartridges in another; video game players in a third. All three stores decided to display the items in locked glass cases, meaning that shoppers had to make their selection without being able to touch their choice or see it up close. That alone guarantees that purchasers are being discouraged. Shoppers then had to track down an employee, praying they had found one who was permitted to carry the magic key in question. In all those instances, we watched customers search in vain for help, then give up on the purchase altogether. Did fewer thefts make up for the loss in sales? Probably not.

There's no question that shrinkage issues (meaning products that can't be accounted for) are serious. But they tend to be focused in select stores, rather than in all stores. If you're a chain like Staples you'll have a few with huge shrinkage problems, others with minor and many with none. Shrinkage comes in three forms: It can be a product that walks out the back door (employee theft); a product that's stolen by pros whose intent when they woke up that day was to rip you off; and theft by amateurs, who are writing their own discount programs. Wal-Mart claims a less than 1 percent shrink rate. But that can add up to a lot of money where a chain that enormous is concerned.

So the stores instituted security everywhere. On one hand, you have the little old lady perched at the entrance, cheerily greeting customers, on the assumption that you're less likely to swipe a sweater or a pair of barbells if someone has acknowledged your existence. Another deterrent some stores use is to blare over the store loudspeakers something like "Security to aisle six!" even though the store probably doesn't have a manned security system in place. The stores with the biggest ongoing shrinkage problems need to bring in professionals.

We once worked for a drugstore chain in South Carolina with a corporate return policy that was the very definition of generosity: They would refund the price of any return, no questions asked. While I was there, the manager took me to a section of the store that sold hair products and equipment for women. "This is the most expensive hair dryer I sell," he told me, pointing to a swanky multivolt model. "I've taken four of them back as returns in the past month." He paused dramatically. "Problem is, in the past month, I haven't sold a single one."

Obviously, some devious souls had been stealing the same hair dryer over and over again, then returning it for cash. Unfortunately, the manager was handcuffed by the company fiat: "We accept all returns—no questions asked."

Which blows.

Back to time. Restrained by corporate decree, the poor manager has to write up the return, refund money he shouldn't be refunding, vet the item for damage and restock it. Part of what is painful is that the time expended here is so clearly bogus. The return policy costs valuable minutes at the register, and rather than creating goodwill, it's actually poisonous to the staff. One instance where taking the time just isn't worth it.

FIFTEEN

Cash/Wrap Blues

The cruel reality is that most shopping leads to paying.

It's a necessary evil. Maybe someday it won't even exist. Stores will all offer self-service options, as gas stations and toll booths and banks now do. Shoppers will feed their purchases into a computerized gizmo where a scanner will read the product code, total up the damage, add on the taxes, then swallow a credit or debit card, get the approval and emit a receipt, a bag of the appropriate size and a tinny "Thank-you-for-shopping-at-Paco's-*beep*-please-accept-this-coupon-for-ten-percent-off-your-next-purchase-of-men's-accessories-*beep*-have-a-life-affirming-day-*beep*-Thank-you-for . . ."

Part of the technology is already in use—like the portable scanners used by FedEx and UPS drivers. Many supermarkets already depend on shoppers to perform the ritual debit card swipe. In Europe, some restaurants present the diner with a portable scanner instead of a check, so the credit card transaction can be done right there at the table. Here's another rare example of innovation: ICA, a Swedish supermarket chain, has portable scanners you pick up at the door along with your shopping trolley. You scan your olive oil and your ice cream as you load them into your trolley or inside your shopping bags; swipe your credit card at the store exit, where an employee weighs your trolley to make sure the price and the weight of what you scanned match up; then you take off into the night. A pretty cool system, especially when you compare it to most other self-scan checkout systems.

And let's face it, for all the glamorization and glorification of the twenty-first-century shopping experience, for all the art and science that have been brought to bear by geniuses of commerce, nobody has found a way to make the cash/wrap lovable. Retailers try to exploit it by stocking high-profit, high-impulse merchandise there. They create distractions to take shoppers' minds off the fact that they're waiting in line for the privilege of handing over money. That's ultimately what's so frustrating about the cash/wrap: In theory, since it's where the shopper is being separated from his or her dough, it should be where all the dazzle goes. Instead, it's the dreariest part of the process. It's also the source of most shopper anxiety. "Where do I stand? How long will this take?" The rest of the shop seems so well designed and user-friendly. Here, the illusions fall away and the true function of a store is revealed—it is a machine where goods are exchanged for money. If the machine is badly designed, or poorly built, or misunderstood by its operator, here is where it shows.

As we've noted, the biggest single quandary in cash/wrap is where to put it. Up front, near the door, is the logical choice. You enter the store, make your way around, choose a few things, then return to the front, pay and leave. From the staffing perspective this also makes the most sense. A small store can be run during off-peak times with one employee if the register is near the door. If it's not, then you need two employees, or a clerk and a guard at the very least. We once studied a shoe store where the misguided architect had placed the cash/wrap in the rear and the register itself facing the back wall. This guaranteed that during every transaction there was a moment when the clerk's back was to the entire store and all the shoppers in it—a setup that practically guarantees theft.

But it's a mistake to position the cash/wrap so that it's the first thing an incoming shopper sees. It's like entering a restaurant through the kitchen. It just doesn't do much to stoke your anticipation of the store. And if things are a little slow there, and shoppers are stacked up, it's the kiss of death for incoming customers. Countless times we've watched shoppers peer into a store, see a line at the registers and just walk away. A cash/wrap is just the promise of misery—it says that even if you do find something you want, you'll have to undergo a little bit of torture to get it.

When pondering its location, you must also consider the effect of cash/wrap on the rest of the store. You'll look at the blueprint for a new store, or the artist's rendering or the architect's model, and you'll see a beautifully ordered, serene space. That's how designers prefer to imagine their creations—devoid of human clutter. This is how every magazine devoted to architecture depicts stores: empty. But then the store opens, customers actually show up and suddenly you see that the lines at the register cut the space in two. The shoppers waiting to pay snake around in a direction the designer in his aerie never anticipated (his wife does all the shopping). And there you have it—a wall of shoppers that makes half the store difficult to see and inconvenient to reach. If those shoppers in line are pushing carts, you've really got an obstacle. Most incoming customers can't even see over the line, meaning that if what they want is back there, they may never even know it. We measure shopper movement patterns in several ways, among them by department density. Every hour on the hour, we tour the entire floor and count how many shoppers are in each area. During busy times in stores where the cash/wrap has been badly positioned, the number of shoppers to be found in the rear of a store is low. The line of people waiting to pay acts like a human barricade.

Ironically, crowding at the cash/wrap is often no indicator of the state of the rest of the store. In other words, a few time-consuming transactions can give the false impression that the store is crowded. So you've got a mob up front, behind which is total shopper paradise, if only someone were there to enjoy it.

What causes problems at the cash/wrap? Mainly the fact that retailers fail to recognize how an efficient cashier system affects the overall shopping experience. That is a dangerous way for businesspeople to think, as you know if you've ever done a slow burn and vowed never to return to a store because the cash/wrap was so badly bungled. Retailers and the architects they hire stop trying to please shoppers when they design the cash/wrap area. They don't give it enough space, they cut corners whenever possible, and too few employees are stationed there most of the time. I can think of two instances where management tried too much piggybacking at the register, to the ultimate misfortune of the store.

One was at Hallmark, which does quite a bit of business at Christmas, you may be surprised to know. A large part of that business is in fancy, high-priced tree and other ornaments. Many of these are given as presents—so many that the stores end up gift-wrapping quite a few. The wrapping is done at the cash/wrap by the same clerks who ring up sales. Have you ever been in a card shop around the holidays? Can you imagine what happens when a clerk must stop ringing transactions for the two minutes required to wrap a box and tie a ribbon? It's worse than the airspace over O'Hare on the night before Thanksgiving. Meltdown. Gift-wrapping should be done from its own site, but every year fewer stores do it that logical, old-fashioned way. Instead they try to save on a clerk's wage and create gridlock at the register. One truly efficient way to handle gift-wrapping is to set up a do-it-yourself station, complete with paper and ribbons and tissue and scissors and tape but no employees at all.

The second instance was at RadioShack. There, the cash/wrap shared a counter with repairs and returns. This meant, of course, that there would be lots of extraneous traffic slowing down shoppers who wanted only to buy something and be on their way. But it also meant that happy shoppers who were about to acquire a camera, say, or a computer monitor had to stand elbow to elbow with unhappy shoppers who had some complaint about cameras and computer monitors—the very same cameras and monitors, sometimes. This setup did not do wonders for consumer confidence. Put repairs and returns somewhere else, we counseled—somewhere in back, away from the main flow of shoppers.

I have a personal stake in at least one little corner of the world of cash/wrap—hotel check-in and checkout counters. Like lots of people these days, I spend roughly half my life on the road. The hospitality industry is booming as a result of the peripatetic nature of modern business. Yet the most problematic part of the hotel experience has remained more or less unchanged. The scenario is always the same: you arrive late, tired, jet-lagged and looking forward to the shortest possible transition from the road to your room, where you can begin e-mailing or reading or writing or phoning or just ordering room service and a movie. Instead, you spend eternity standing in a line when all you really need is your key, the rest of the transaction having been managed in advance over the phone or the Internet or through a travel agent.

One hotel I visited had progressed to using small circular check-in islands in the lobby, where guest and clerk can sit side by side at the computer terminal. That's a start, but some hotel is going to score huge points with business travelers by taking it further. Then there will be a check-in section of the lobby consisting of some comfortable easy chairs. When a clerk sees you sit there, she or he will come over with a portable, palm-sized computer, a credit card reader, a room key and your choice of beverage, and the paperwork will be handled in that civilized way.

SIXTEEN

Magic Acts

In the science of shopping, to the extent to which there is magic, to the degree to which there are tricks, it's mostly all in what we call merchandising. The rest of this book concerns itself with sensible subjects such as ergonomics, anatomy, kinetics and demographics. This chapter is all about getting products to jump up and hit shoppers in the eye.

The world of merchandising breaks down into two distinct aspects. One is the effort to get products off the shelves, where they are forced to compete on equal footing with their competitors. Who wants to settle for that? So a great deal of effort and money is expended on finding ways of getting products out on their own. Shelves are fine for libraries, everyone agrees, but elsewhere they are to be avoided if at all possible. And in fact, in a bold move in the late 1970s, the Baltimore library system tried displaying some books face-out, and borrowing increased dramatically. This is now standard practice for many bookstores and libraries. There's a lesson in there for bookstores, which do a fairly uninspired job in the display department, at least for the majority of titles. The downside would be a big decrease in the number of books available, which would no doubt raise a cry from woebegone authors and publishers.

The other aspect of merchandising is the subtler art and science of adjacencies—how placing one item next to another creates some spark and sells more of one or even both. Part of what adjacencies attempt to deliver is add-on sales. Sometimes this is just the typical cash register impulse buy, like the box of tangerine Altoids or pack of batteries tossed into a shopping basket at the last second. But add-ons can happen anywhere in a store. Retailers pay too little attention to this, in my opinion, and their businesses suffer as a result. Because add-ons typically have a high profit margin, they can make the difference between a store that just gets by and one that prospers. They can make a failing store into a success. At the New York bar I used to co-own, the proceeds from the jukebox, cigarette machine and coin-operated video games covered the rent. Retailers must accept the fact that there are no new customers—the population isn't booming, and we already have more stores than we need. The usual figure is that 80 percent of a store's sales will come from 20 percent of its clientele. So if stores are to grow, it will be by figuring out how to get more out of existing customers—more visits, more time in the store, more and bigger purchases.

It isn't just a clothing issue either: New computer mouse? Try this mouse pad. New car? Try this stylin' floor mat. The Gap now sells fragrances and candles. Victoria's Secret sells cosmetics, reasoning (wisely) that women will shop for makeup wherever they are, especially if they're already in a store designed to enhance their comeliness. The U.S. Post Office branch in the Mall of America sells USPS-branded toy mail trucks, leather jackets, teddy bears in mailman uniforms and other related items, and while they don't make money delivering mail, the retail items carry a healthy markup. Someday that's what will keep the whole system afloat.

Another good example of this is in my favorite bookstore, Book-People, in Austin, Texas, which sits across the street from the flagship Whole Foods. BookPeople is a happy store filled with lots of personality, and it delivers the unexpected, starting with good, cheap visual effects. An old stove anchors the cookbook section. The seating, scattered throughout the store, reflects what's being sold; the sports and technology sections have old barber chairs, and aging Barcaloungers are used judiciously. Around the store, the owners have added merchandise categories themed to each particular section—puppet hats and masks in children's books; relevant clothing, jewelry and candles in the spirituality section—and even the stairs are lined with wrapping paper and gag gifts. The checkout area has "Keep Austin Weird" T-shirts, unusual confections and BookPeople-branded chocolate bars. This store isn't just selling books—it's selling to people who *like* books. At heart it's still a serious place that, among the tchotchkes and kitschy humor, has reinvented categories and subsections. For example, the Insurrection and Conspiracy section sits next to the Journalism shelf, and there's a pair of stuffed roosters flanking Homesteading & Farming—a nice touch.

Yet another admirable example is the Apple Store, which lays out impulse products at their cash/wrap that cost upward of a hundred dollars: a cool game, a designer backup hard drive, a great-looking USB hub. Placed in various locations, these good-looking inessentials fly off the shelves. It's like selling you accessories for your new car. The company figures that if you're spending thousands of dollars, what's another couple of hundred when you already have your wallet open?

Let's say we have a clothing store where the typical sale is a $30 shirt. If you can convince that typical customer to also buy a $6 pair of socks, you've just increased sales by 20 percent. Not too shabby! If she takes a $20 belt, sales just rose by 66 percent. You're a genius! Now you just have to figure out how to make it happen. One good way is to gently suggest to the shopper that she is not buying enough for her purposes, and doesn't she need a mousepad to go with that mouse? Another good way is just to place the mousepad next to the mouse so that the juxtaposition does the talking for you. A lot of this is as simple as can be. Where do belts go? Near trousers. How about socks? Near shoes. (But where do shoes go? On your feet.) Tomato sauce? Near the pasta. Department stores do well selling neckties on the ground floor, mainly to female shoppers. But ties also have to be near suits and sport jackets, and surprisingly, they often are not. That's a big mistake, because sometimes you need to actually see and touch that amazing Technicolor tie to imagine yourself in that somber gray suit. And anyway, nobody wears just a suit—you need the shirt, tie, socks, shoes, cuff links and belt before you can leave the house. So why sell the most expensive part of the package in such unnatural isolation? Computer stores make an even bigger botch of this. Typically, they'll display the computers themselves in one section, the printers elsewhere, the furniture in a different spot and then the accessories, from cables to wrist rests, in yet other places. Could anyone devise a less sensible, less inviting display system? That organizing scheme is right for the warehouse, not the selling floor. It all needs to be shown as people use it—computer, monitor, printer and accessories, all hooked up, plugged in, turned on, and placed on furniture so that a shopper can sit down and give it a test-drive.

There's a similar issue back in the supermarket, starting with this urgent question: Where do we put the taco shells? With the rest of the Mexican food? That's how it's usually done. Not near the ground beef? It might require the combination of tacos and meat to trigger "fiesta" in the mind of a shopper wondering what to make for dinner tonight. How about stocking taco shells in both places? And while we're at it, how about just over the meat counter also being a good place for bread crumbs, steak sauce, tenderizer, peppercorns, sea salt and fresh herbs? In Italy we tested an urban supermarket that was organized by meal groups. Breakfast ingredients here, lunch stuff there, dinner makings over there. A concept made possible by two innovations—the energy efficiency of small refrigerated units and a redesigned store that put electrical power everywhere you looked. In many cities across the world, both the rich and the poor shop one meal at a time.

What about something truly tricky—say, packaged cake by the slice? You could decide to stock it in the cake section, but why would anyone looking for a whole cake buy just one piece, and vice versa, for that matter? It could go with other refrigerated desserts, such as pudding, in the cooler. But how about if a slice of cake could be found by the salad bar, as a reward for choosing an otherwise virtuous meal? Such placement alone would identify the cake as something other than the stuff for callow kiddie palates over in the cooler. In chapter 12, I discussed how name-brand aluminum foil makers have a tough time convincing shoppers to spend the extra money on better quality. One way to get around this is by merchandising it better—in summer, for instance, supermarkets could sell charcoal, barbecue sauce, funny aprons and aluminum foil all from the same fixture, somewhere near the meat counter. Men especially would be likely to grab the whole kit at once rather than have to assemble it aisle by aisle. And in this context, the superior strength of the name-brand foil might seem relevant.

In a drugstore, where do the books about vitamins and dietary supplements go, with books or with vitamins? It's easy to say both, but at some point your store is going to run out of room. And all those multiple placements are pointless if they don't increase sales. Also in the drugstore, and on the subject of multiple placements, where do you stock the sample sizes of shampoo, conditioner and so on? Typically they get their own display case, but they really should be sold from the same shelves as the full-size products. That may be all it takes to get you to try a new product, something you wouldn't attempt if you had to buy the big bottle just to see if you like it. Common sense says that if I hit the shampoo shelf first and buy my usual brand, I'm less likely to pick up something new when I arrive at the sample shelf.

Adjacencies are also about order—coming up with a sensible sequence of things. We once were hired to study how potato chips are sold in employee cafeterias. In one, the rack of chips and pretzels was positioned at the head of the line, right where you picked up your tray. In another, the chips were down at the end of the line, just before the cashier. Did it make much of a difference? When the chips were near the end, sales were dramatically higher than at the head. How can you decide what kind of chips you want before you've chosen your sandwich? What goes with pimento loaf and Swiss on white, corn chips or barbecue-style potato chips? Similarly, one December we studied a department store where a Christmas wrapping paper fixture was positioned just inside the entrance, and it wasn't selling much because nobody buys the paper before they buy the gifts. It was moved so that it was one of the last things shoppers came upon, and sales went up. Supermarket planograms are designed to make the most of adjacencies, the thinking being that if a popular item like Corn Flakes is positioned correctly, at the bull's-eye, it will help sales of other Kellogg's products arranged around it. Because most shoppers are right-handed, the best spot should be just to the right of the bull's-eye, to make it as easy as possible for the quick grab.

Sometimes, though, it's the irrationality of combinations that provides their power to grab our attention. Consider how expensive chests are sold in a furniture store as opposed to how they're sold in a newfangled home and hardware store. In the former there were dozens of chests neatly lined up, nothing but chests, one after the other, chest chest chest, with all the charm of a warehouse sale. In a Restoration Hardware store, the chests were treated like furniture, placed next to a chair, or in a corner, with a lace doily or a picture frame or a mirror on top. Sitting on one chest was a big old-fashioned glass jar containing chrome-plated ball-peen hammers, of all things. So maybe the jar or the shiny hammers caught your eye, and you picked one up, and suddenly you noticed the chest, really noticed it, and you realized it wasn't just there to hold the hammer jar but it was actual merchandise, with a discreet price tag hanging from a drawer pull. You didn't feel overwhelmed by forty similar pieces of furniture to study. You could actually see how the furniture would look in a home as opposed to a showroom. And the fact that you could start out looking at hammers and end up considering furniture satisfied your love of discovery—it kept you on your toes. Anybody can sell furniture to people looking for furniture; it takes a little ingenuity to sell it to people who aren't. I'd wager that more than one doily shopper has gone home with a new maple dresser.

You can figure out intelligent adjacencies just by standing near one thing and asking yourself, what else is on my mind here? In the paint section, there should be some cross-selling of power tools, even if it's only a poster or some literature or a chain saw just lying on a table—who could resist picking it up? As I discussed earlier, in the bookstore we advise clients to group sections by the gender of their likeliest readers, meaning that computers, sports and business books should flow from one to the other, as should self-help, diet and nutrition and health and home. We were consulting on how to sell computer printers and advised the retailer that maybe they should be grouped by manufacturer—Hewlett-

Packard here, Epson there. Then we saw that shoppers don't buy that way; they're more interested in comparing all $300 printers than seeing what one manufacturer is offering, so we quickly changed our recommendation. Golden Books, the children's book publisher, was organizing its sections by price point until we saw that with such inexpensive goods, price doesn't matter to anyone, and that the books should be grouped by character—little ponies here, teddy bears there.

How's this for a bright merchandising idea: We'll take pantyhose and sell them in plastic eggs! Pretty weird, I agree, except that this signature package turned L'eggs into the country's number-one brand in its category. Famously, blind tests were run in which women preferred the No Nonsense brand, which is usually sold right next to L'eggs. Still, L'eggs rules, which makes it a true merchandising victory, since, in theory, any fool should be able to sell the superior brand.

If you're not involved in retailing, you might not be aware of the size and scope of the industry that provides all the in-store merchandising materials—signs and display cases and impulse goods fixtures and all the rest. From supermarkets and drugstores to home centers and auto showrooms, what became known as the point-of-purchase business— PoP for short—has come a long way in a short time. PoP materials have existed since forever, of course, going back to the first cigar-store Indian or red-and-white-striped barbershop pole. But since the early '80s, PoP has really become a player, and it now commands a seat at the selling table right next to marketing's.

Until then, though, merchandising was the stepchild of the marketing trade. The marketing geniuses called all the shots for how a product would be presented to the world, and the boys in merchandising were left to work out the petty details of how it would work at the retail level—the in-store signage and displays. Then the two sides began to change places. Suddenly, retailing realized that to a growing extent, shoppers were making their buying decisions on the floor of the store. As was noted elsewhere, surveys showed that more than half of all supermarket purchases were unplanned. And this all happened as

marketing's influence was coming down from its peak—the monolithic
TV networks gave way to many viewing options, and consumer devo-
tion to brand name yielded to a more skeptical, independent-minded
shopper. That all added up to more of a dependence on merchandising,
which led the industry to grow from a $5-billion-a-year pushcart to a
$35-billion-a-year roller coaster almost overnight. Traditionally, it's been
a business of smallish (and now some not-so-small) family-owned firms,
meaning it's been short on sophistication and long on guts, verve and
energy. It's a cowboy business, and I mean that in the best way. Owing
to its youth, there are still lots of lessons its practitioners are learning,
and they have to learn as they go. In fact, a great deal of our work in the
past two decades has been just in testing and measuring the effects of
in-store signage, fixturing and display systems, trying to figure out what
works and why.

Here's a good example of the terrible magic that smart merchandising can perform. I once heard a talk given by the vice president
of merchandising from a national chain of young women's clothing
stores in which she deconstructed a particular display of T-shirts. "We
buy them in Sri Lanka for three dollars each," she began. "Then we
bring them over here and sew in washing instructions in French and
English—French on the front, English on the back. Notice we don't say
the shirts are made in France. But you can infer that if you like. Then we
merchandise the hell out of them—we fold them just right on a taste-
ful tabletop display, and on the wall behind it we hang a huge, gorgeous
photograph of a beautiful woman in an exotic locale wearing the shirt.
We shoot it so it looks like a million bucks. Then we call it an Expedi-
tion T-shirt, and we sell it for thirty-seven dollars. And we sell a lot of
them, too." It was the most depressing valuable lesson I've ever had.

Car dealerships aren't anyone's idea of how merchandising is supposed to work, which makes them good lessons in what not to do. We
studied a foreign car dealership that was practically a college course in
itself. The salespeople would load shoppers down with literature but fail
to give them folders, so you ended up walking around that showroom,
arms burdened with pieces of paper. There were plenty of brochure
racks but no brochures, which is a problem, not because shoppers love

pamphlets so much, but because empty literature racks give shoppers the (correct) impression that the details don't get taken care of in this place of business. One-sided posters were taped to exterior and interior windows, meaning that shoppers frequently found themselves staring at blank white rectangles. In one dealership, as I mentioned earlier, we saw a sign heralding the new cars—the previous year's new cars. The signs that did receive prominent placement were "awards" to the dealership from the car manufacturer—just the kind of thing to leave shoppers yawning. The display that showed buyers available colors was a real mess—the spiral-bound portfolio was held together by duct tape. And instead of being able to see a picture of the car in each color, shoppers were given a tiny swatch book more appropriate for choosing drapes. Signs meant to hang over cars were placed on tables instead. Some favorable auto reviews were clipped from newspapers, but they were simply taped to walls rather than displayed properly. Some of the articles had begun to yellow and curl up. And all this to support merchandise costing $20,000 and up!

Retailers aren't alone in screwing up the design and deployment of merchandising materials. Many times the firms that design and make them (and sell them to hapless retailers) screw them up before they get to the floor of the store—simple things, too, like using displays made from uncoated cardboard. We saw one such fixture, for sun products, arrive in a big drugstore on a Friday night. It hit the floor immediately and sold well. Then the cleaning crew came in and, as cleaning crews will do, mopped the floor without moving all the fixtures and displays to one side. The base of the suntan lotion display got a little wet. By Saturday afternoon it was listing. After the floor was mopped that night, it had begun to tilt seriously. By Sunday night it was in the trash.

Often nobody has devoted any thought to the question of what a display will look like when half the merchandise is gone. Will what remains look like a hot item, or will it look unattended and forlorn? Some of this has to do with what shoppers see after a ketchup bottle or whatever has been removed—will brown kraft paper be visible, or will there be some kind of message or a photo of the bottle? It makes a difference.

And other questions: Can you read it from twenty feet away? If it only works when you're on top of it, it seems to be doing only half a job. Is the back of it blank? The sides, too? Because the designer of that display has no idea how it will be positioned in a store and so can't really be certain which surface shoppers will see first (if any).

Endcaps and freestanding displays are staples of American retailing. Some of them succeed and some fail, depending on how they work once they are placed in the store. As with signs, you can't say which are good and which are not until you see them in action. The latest trend in displays is the so-called activated fixture—one that uses movement, especially moving lights, to get the attention of shoppers. Our testing of types of fixtures has yielded some impressive results: In soft drink coolers, the activated version was noticed by 48 percent of shoppers, compared to 6 percent for the nonactivated one. An activated endcap got 37 percent notice, compared to 16 percent for the old-fashioned version. But at a certain point the displays begin to cancel each other out. There are so many fixtures screaming for the shoppers' attention that they become the visual equivalent of a dull roar, with nothing discernible amid the clutter. Merchant prince John Wanamaker once famously said (and I paraphrase) that half his advertising was waste—but he couldn't figure out which half. Same goes today for merchandising materials and strategies.

We were hired to study a terrific idea for solving all confusion regarding over-the-counter cures for indigestion, heartburn, nausea, gas and other even more wretchedly human gastrointestinal maladies. The shameful nature of these conditions is what engenders such woeful ignorance of how to treat them, the medicine company's research showed: Shoppers were a little reluctant to approach the cashier or even the pharmacist with problems such as these. (Personally, it was an extremely illuminating job, since I, too, was never quite sure which product was for which form of gastrointestinal distress, and I had no great desire to ask. Perhaps, like you, I was taking cures for burps when I had farts and confusing the relief for the runs with that for the pukes.) The cure for this was a signage system, a horizontal cylinder with a dial on one end: You'd dial up your symptom—say, heartburn—and in the little window the name of the drug that cures it would appear. Can't miss, we all thought. Then a few prototypes were installed and we studied how shoppers interacted with them.

Well, actually, how they *didn't* interact, for the fixture went all but unused. Maybe shoppers were less confused than the research showed. The fixtures were perhaps a little too tastefully rendered, so the gray tubes didn't stand out on the shelves as much as they might have. It was even a little unclear that the dial on the side was meant to be turned—a big red arrow would have helped a lot. In any event, gastric uncertainty is going to be with us awhile longer, for the idea was a bust.

Here's another example. The question wasn't whether one of America's leading marketers of spices was going to get a fancy, expensive new system of supermarket fixtures to display its wares. That part had already been decided, to the tune of more than a million dollars' worth of displays as proposed by a major PoP firm. The prototype was a beauty—it organized the company's products by whether they were spices, extracts, essences or flavorings, something that hadn't ever been successfully done before. Everything's a battleground in supermarkets and spices were becoming a two-horse race; this was surely looking like a way for one company to distinguish itself where it counts, on the floor of the store.

The fixture's prototype was brought into the firm's headquarters for all to see, and there, in the flesh (as it were), it got raves from all concerned. And so into the stores it went, where it had, in essence, no positive effect on sales.

It had no negative effect either, which was a good thing, but for all that it cost, it did no better than the old displays it was meant to replace. What had gone wrong? Well, for one thing, the distinctions the display made—spice, extract, essence, flavoring—were more or less meaningless to the shopper. Who cares which it is? What it does to food, how it tastes and smells, are all that count. What exactly do I do with turmeric? Where does the rosemary go in a chicken? There was a lot you could tell people about spices, and some of that might actually encourage them to buy more. What does saffron smell like? A fixture that could manage to answer that question would be a genuine advance, but this display was not that. And although the displays were a feast for the eyes when seen in the monochromatic gray (or was it beige?) headquarters of the firm, the swirling, heaving, dizzying visual cacophony of a supermarket was something else again. It is tough to get noticed in an environment in which even Cap'n Crunch himself must shout to be heard.

So say good-bye to those nice new fixtures. Maybe some new display system for spices was warranted. But the process that yielded this one was flawed from the start. The major decisions about how a company's goods will be presented on the floor of a store are made by the firm itself and then by three outside entities—the ad agency, the package designer and then the PoP agency, which usually has no input into what the first two decree. Those three all have their own agendas and their own priorities, none of which have any meaningful contact with what happens to displays once they reach the selling floor. Until the many agendas are settled into one sensible, practical-minded one, resolved, there will be plenty of flawed display systems.

Here's a final tale. A big-name soft drink maker had just spent a lot of money on new supermarket displays and hired us to test the prototype. When I arrived at a supermarket with the client, we looked in through a window and saw a giant pile of soda cases just sitting on the floor—a huge, bright, monochromatic mountain of pop.

"I wonder why they left it there like that," she said. "It sure looks like a mess."

Before she could arrange to have the sodas stocked properly, I asked if we could just videotape it as it was for a day. By our measure, 60 percent of the people who passed that mountain noticed it, a higher rate than much of the firm's in-store merchandising materials ever scored. Clearly, that big mass of color was all that was required to stop shoppers in their tracks. There's a lesson in there somewhere.

V

Screen Savers, Jet Lag
and Whirling Dervishes:
The Culture of Shopping

SEVENTEEN

The Internet

Back in 1997, when I wrote a chapter for this book that didn't exactly trumpet e-commerce, and by extension the Internet, as the greatest invention since cheese and crackers, a lot of people reacted as though I'd just insulted a newborn who'd already been crowned a combination of Mozart, Einstein, Newton, Tolstoy, Galileo and Jackie O. Basically, I said that e-commerce would never replace bricks-and-mortar stores, that it wasn't the final word on anything, that it was clumsy and annoying and—I almost forgot—that it was designed by a bunch of Silicon Valley geeks for a bunch of fellow Silicon Valley geeks.

Boy, did the hate mail ever start coming in—you can read some of it in the previous edition of this book's early reviews on Amazon. A lot of it accused me of not being able to accept the Brave New Digital World, and I just didn't get it, and my head was in the sand, stuff like that. I even got booed off the stage at Internet conferences. No one in the crowd of techies and software designers and true believers wanted to hear about the downsides and limitations of this kick-ass new revolution. They just wanted me to echo the party line—that the

Internet and e-commerce were the most remarkable discoveries since, well, *ever*. They would allow us to conduct business, trade stocks, buy all this cool gear, meet our soul mates and sit around in chat rooms swapping opinions about antique furniture, medieval Christianity or Duane Allman's slide guitar technique—all within the context of a united global community.

That the Internet and particularly e-commerce might not be the Wizard of Oz but instead some befuddled guy crouched behind a curtain, or that it was a work in progress, that it was, in fact, human and young and imperfect—well, no one was terribly eager to hear that message.

So when the dot-com bubble blew up in early 2001, I wasn't happy, but to be honest I did feel a little bit vindicated. At the same time, I wasn't surprised when the phoenix that is the World Wide Web 2.0 rose up out of its cinders. But there's a seminal issue that hasn't changed since the web came along in the early '90s: Internet shopping has grown in places not because it's all that good, but because the things it's replacing or trying to improve upon have gotten that much lousier, clunkier, more expensive and/or inefficient. The online world can chalk up whatever success it has today mostly to the failure of offline avenues and mediums and processes and delivery systems. In 2008, a decade after I wrote that first Internet chapter, I still think the Internet and the world of shopping online has miles to go.

If we look back at the web when it was first starting out, we can't help but be reminded of its big-bang origins. Essentially it was, and still is, an enormous data dump—a place where you and I can sift through massive amounts of unfiltered information, goods and people, to which nowadays we have unprecedented access. Want to hunt down the ISBN number of a crime thriller a buddy recommended? Need directions from your house to the racetrack in Pasadena? What about the Amtrak train schedule for this Thursday afternoon? Want to take a virtual tour of Berkeley College, find out who won the 1976 Super Bowl or the 1981 Tony Award for Best Musical, or figure out Best Buy's Sunday hours of operation? By giving consumers entrée to basic, useful information (as opposed to, say, knowledge) about products, places, schedules and people to a degree that we've never had before, the Internet has democratized information. Better yet, we can track down whatever information we need from our kitchen tables, from a suburban campus or, increasingly, from our BlackBerries and iPhones.

The infinite glory of all this indiscriminate exposure—e.g., the absence of any filters, other than the finger-wagging kind that prevents school-aged kids from stumbling onto sites parents would rather they not visit—is, as it happens, also one of the World Wide Web's biggest disadvantages. The uncensored nature of the web has created a world where anyone can cheerfully disseminate the Protocols of Zion or share detailed instructions about how to build a homemade bomb without a grown-up stepping in and saying, "Hey there, wait a minute . . ." Type in, for example, "Eric Clapton," and a second later, a gleaming, pulsating, almost madcap oil spill of Claptonia—roughly seventeen and a half million websites—will stun your senses. If you have roughly forty-eight hours to kill, you'll be able to scan everything from the guitarist's official website to fans' tribute pages to every interview Eric has ever given, to guitar tabs, chords, bass tablatures and lyrics, to YouTube videos, to ticket-vendor sites selling ducats to this summer's Clapton tour, to chronological listings of Eric's side work, to Eric's Cream years, to Eric's John Mayall years, to Eric's Yardbird years, to Eric's Derek and the Dominos years, to Eric's love life, to Eric's drug use, to Eric's sobriety, to Eric's astrological chart, to the pros and cons of Eric's recently published memoir, to autographed Eric memorabilia for sale on eBay, and honestly? You've barely scratched the surface of this guitar behemoth. It's truly astounding how much pure *data* Eric Clapton has generated since he picked up his first ax at age thirteen (and I know he was thirteen because I read it a few times on one of the seventeen and a half million websites).

The problem begins when you're trying to figure out a) what exactly are you after here? and b) what's true and what's not? The Internet, after all, is a repository for rumors, half-rumors, quarter-rumors, errors, speculations, hypotheses and racy untruths. These coexist along with, well, *facts* (things that derive from what at least appear to be valid sources). How do you tell the two apart, especially when they occasionally share space on the same website? Take Wikipedia, the collaborative, ongoing encyclopedia. Students using the site as a resource for their term papers are never sure from one hour to the next whether the entry they're reading won't have entire chunks removed, altered, updated, reattributed or even eliminated during tomorrow morning's upload.

So the lack of any filtering is both an embarrassment of riches and sometimes just an embarrassment. It's given consumers access to spectacular amounts of data (and *stuff*) but no reliable way to discern what's worthwhile and what's not, what's trustworthy and what's louche.

Within this smorgasbord of information and data, many consumers have come to believe that if they can't find something on the Internet, it doesn't exist. They're usually surprised to learn that if a website tells them there are no rooms available at their favorite hotel, no airline flights leaving this afternoon for Singapore, or no alternate routes to Yankee Stadium other than the one MapQuest proposes, that a simple phone call to the hotel, the airline or AAA will often prove the Internet wrong. Ninety-five percent of the time, absolutely, chances are you'll find what you're after online. The other 5 percent of the time, though, a hotel advertised online as sold out often does have a spare room, and there *is* a flight that leaves when and where you want it to leave from that's simply not listed on Travelocity.

The lack of any filtering process on the Internet, as well as its margin for error, suggests the need for some kind of expertise—someone to winnow down the possibilities into a good dozen or so. Part of the problem these days, as most consumers are aware, is that there's too much choice in the world. Too much product. Too many different kinds of ink cartridges. Too many shaving razors. Way too much *stuff.* Where does one even begin? Often consumers are looking for the most rudimentary guidance—someone who will come forward if only to decrease the range of available inventory. The Oprah Winfreys and Martha Stewarts of the world have intuited this and have posited themselves, among their other roles, as agents or doorkeepers. Like the third ghost in *A Christmas Carol*, the one who could see into the future and prevent Scrooge from making goofs, they point to a particular book or musical recording or comfy mattress or long-burning candle or flat-screen TV that in their opinion has all the right moves. Addled, overwhelmed consumers respond.

Matter of fact, many are outright relieved to let go of the burden of decision-making—which in my mind contributes to the popularity of online best-of lists, whether it's the Amazon books bestseller list or the category-specific start pages that show up onscreen when you pay a visit to the Apple iTunes Store. From decades of work, especially with music stores and bookstores, we know that among the most popular and effective merchandising tools are lists—*Billboard* magazine lists, *New York Times* bestseller lists, The VH1 top 10 hotties list.

1. It's
2. A
3. Fact:
4. People (and particularly Americans)
5. *Love*
6. Lists.

They love lists even though the list in question may not be one that a team of in-house experts has thoughtfully assembled, but rather a rundown of the most popular items other consumers bought. "Most popular," as any artist or consumer will tell you, doesn't often match up with "the best." But many consumers are perfectly content to eat what everybody else is eating, just as they have no qualms about naming their babies Emily and Jacob, this year's most popular girl-baby and boy-baby names. Among the top-purchased items on the iTunes most popular classical music downloads list you'll always find five or six titles displayed right there on the iTunes Classical start page, including recordings by several shapely young violinists and comely pianists. Again, consumers love the idea that a bunch of other consumers have pre-vetted what they're about to buy. Regardless, it moves product.

Far more valuable, as I see it, are those lists put together by entrepreneurial Amazon readers. Ranging from extremely quirky to dead-on, these lists seem sincerely meant to help out first-time or overwhelmed book buyers interested in an author or a subject or a specific genre. I also get a kick out of the public-forum aspect of Amazon, where readers can engage in a genuine dialogue about the merits of Eckhart Tolle's new book or the latest Janet Evanovich. Some five-star reader recommendations are no doubt phony and posted by friends and close relations of the author, but they can't all be, can they?

Still, Amazon has its definite downsides. For one thing, try contacting them if you have a problem with your order (entire websites are devoted to this common quandary). If you have a problem, it's hard to ignore the little voice in your head telling you that Amazon's powers-that-be haven't the slightest interest in hearing from you. Try to contact them via e-mail, and you'll get back a terse yet genial automated response. You can spend days fruitlessly trying to track down a customer service number. The price we pay for convenience, one-click shopping and a ritualized retail experience is that no one recognizably human sits at the other end of our Amazon transactions—just a seamlessly calibrated database of e-mails that roll toward our in-boxes.

This issue got a little personal when Envirosell started working for Microsoft, a company that has become one of our largest and most enthusiastic clients. For them, we deconstruct the software and video game sections of stores across the world (as someone who can't get past the first series of screens in Halo—a classic Xbox game—I know more about how Xbox 360 is shopped globally than anyone really has a right to know). At one point early on in our Microsoft relationship, one of the company's executives called me in a panic. Was it true, as per Amazon, that I was the coauthor of a new manual on Unix/Linux, their rival operating system? Of course not, yet there I was on Amazon (for God's sake, how many Paco Underhills can there be in the world?). Our colleague was relieved but made it clear there had been a few waves in Redmond, home of Microsoft's corporate headquarters, about a vendor who might be a spy.

What to do? E-mails to Amazon led to more automated replies. Finally, exasperated, I managed to get hold of the company's general counsel, who told me there wasn't a whole lot he could do to resolve my problem, that the issue lay with one of their many distributors.

When I made it clear that they *had* to do something, that Amazon's mistake was jeopardizing my business, the most he could offer was that he would remove the offending coauthorship immediately; however, Amazon couldn't guarantee that as subsequent uploads came along, my name wouldn't reappear as the Unix/Linux manual's coauthor. To this day, I check the site pretty vigilantly.

As I alluded to earlier, today's tidal wave of websites, products, choices, stuff, information and outright misinformation is a dilemma that suggests the need for some future "Ask an Expert" service, someone who will condense two thousand websites into the dozen or so that are of vital assistance to you, the shopper. Certain websites such as Head Butler are on top of this already. Its proprietor simply handpicks stuff he likes, from Shure E3c Sound Isolating Earphones to the new Levon Helm album; writes a short, witty essay on why these things are so great; then directs interested consumers to Amazon. How terrific the future of the web would look if we could rent an expert to help us make our way around the net and by so doing, shrink it. Our colleagues at LivePerson.com have launched a new online service where aside from getting shopping advice, consumers can, say, rent a microbiologist or a distinguished software engineer and pay them by the minute to field their questions. As the literacy of the web's latest generation begins to develop, we may find that the monopoly on information that the Googles and Microsofts and Yahoos possess will break down into processes that are far more discriminating than what we have right now.

But I'm not crossing my fingers.

From my perch studying the buying habits of consumers both online and off, for a long time I've considered the web as analogous to water. It inches and flows and streams and pools into ditches and culverts and creeks and channels and puddles where someone has already done the surveying and architecting and ditch-digging. And the net, with a good sixth sense for this pre-dug inventory of opportunities, makes its way there intuitively. It fills up those holes. Now and then it even plugs them up pretty well. But it still hasn't resolved the same issue that's facing today's retailers, namely, what's global and what's local? Can a global process have any relevance to you as a local individual?

Me, I'll take the news my local radio station gives me any day, whether on-air or online, versus what Excite or Google or Yahoo delivers. Sure, I can custom-design a start page—sports, business, national and international news, a weather forecast and so forth—but except for me now knowing it's going to rain next Tuesday, customizable doesn't mean a whole lot here. It doesn't really touch me personally. I need to know about what's happening in my city and neighborhood, whether the Yankees pulled off a late-inning win last night and what's playing at the Angelika Film Center six blocks south. So what a lot of people, including myself, get frustrated by is the very same universal software solution that Internet types keep claiming is the medium's biggest strength. The germ of the idea is already here—but what if we could get to a point where we're developing processing engines that are eminently more local, i.e., locally targeted, than what we have right now?

I point the finger here at venture capitalists. Instead of putting their bucks into $10 million businesses, most of them are worshipping at the altar of a $100 million business, something that will grow ten thousand percent over the next three years. Everybody has set his or her sights on being the big bucks behind the next online behemoth. Which isn't to say those companies don't deserve their wild success or their billions. But the result's been that even with Facebook, the concept of a socially integrated network still hasn't been customized to the person, the place or the environment. After all, while the Internet may be in the public domain, Google, MSN, YouTube and the other huge internet players are all businesses answerable first and foremost to their shareholders.

My ideal local online process? One in which you could pick and choose your processing engine based on your own interests and beliefs, so it ends up far more responsive to you, the user. Periodically I'll pick up a copy of *The Villager*—one of my neighborhood rags—since their ads and listings have direct relevance to my actual lower-Manhattan existence. Fashion clothing emporiums on the web might consider doing the same. After all, New York City females dress differently from the way females dress in San Antonio, Texas, and the way females dress in Los Angeles. The "favorite" or "recommended" outfits on the Macy's and Eileen Fisher websites run the risk of looking great on a Texan matron but ludicrous on a forty-year-old Hollywood executive. These sites might consider doing what Netflix does, which is supply a list of the most popular titles within its subscribers' zip codes. Again, "most popular" rarely coincides with "the best," but such a system would come closer to wedding a local solution to a global process.

A website called DailyCandy, which is geared toward trendy twenty- and thirtysomething women, is another encouraging example. Subscribers can select among a dozen or so cities, ranging from San Francisco and Chicago to London. If you live in or near Miami, DailyCandy will not only tell you where the coolest place to buy lingerie in South Beach is, but also tells you what's going on culturally in the city over the weekend, what to do with the kids, as well as the latest, coolest places to eat. To me, that's at least a start.

Another issue I continue to have with the web: How is it supported? What are its basic economic underpinnings? Does advertising keep it going? Does the government? Do local institutions? The jury's still out. If it's advertising by companies, we can point to examples like Samsung, which devotes large chunks of its marketing budget to Internet ads on fly-fishing websites and other places where it seeks its demographic. Samsung has gotten terrific mileage out of this, too. But again, Samsung came to that decision the hard way—because the viewing public generally ignores, bypasses, gossips during or TiVos their way through traditional thirty-second TV spots. Plus, televised ads cost an arm and a leg to produce, and newspapers and magazines aren't much better, since they're no longer dominated by five or six periodicals that 60 percent of all Americans regularly glance at week after week.

The bottom line is that it's the failure of the traditional engines for selling and delivering products that's created the opportunity for the engine known as e-commerce to exist.

Which really isn't high praise when you think about it.

• • •

The question remains: Why has this second generation of the web succeeded better than the first go-round? As I've said, it isn't that the Internet has gotten any cooler, sleeker, faster, sexier, better or more efficient.
One big reason is because women have begun devoting serious—and I
mean *serious*—time to the Internet. E-commerce Generation II is doing
just fine.

The January 2008 Nielsen Global Online Survey reports that more
than 85 percent of the world's online population has used the Internet
to buy something—that's up 40 percent from 2006. The world's most
ardent Internet shoppers come from South Korea, where close to 100
percent of all Internet users have bought stuff online, followed by Germany, the United Kingdom and Japan. The U.S. lags in eighth place. The
most popular online purchases are books, followed by clothing and accessories; then shoes; then videos, DVDs and games; then airline tickets
and electronic equipment bringing up the rear. Online shoppers are a
loyal bunch, too. Sixty percent of them claim they buy products mostly
from the same sites.

Among the things females do online, aside from actually closing the
deal? I call it *sort of* shopping. Here's how it breaks down:

The Pre-Shop: The retail equivalent of a blind date. Nothing heavy
goes on here, just a lot of flirting and data gathering. As she surfs away,
your wife or girlfriend or sister or daughter can acquaint herself with a
dress from Target.com, new binders for school or the latest model of
fluffy moccasin from L.L.Bean. The phenomenon of the pre-shop is
particularly prevalent when women are in the market for automobiles,
to a far greater extent than men. Since Dante would have to invent a
tenth circle of hell to mirror most females' experiences inside car dealerships, women go online, figure out how much that new Prius or Sienna
or Civic costs, with or without automatic transmission, XM radio, a
satellite-linked navigation system, splash guards, moon roof and other
goodies, then walk into a dealership with confidence, armed with facts,
figures and prices.

Thus, almost incidentally, the web serves as a resource for actual
bricks-and-mortar stores. If consumers are feeling lazy, tired, time-
crunched or antisocial, they can look up the book, movie, TV or

preferred Cuisinart model beforehand, maybe scan a few consumer reviews, then make an unimpeded beeline for the thing when they reach the store, which saves them from having to do a half-hour walkabout or ask a clerk who may or may not know, or care much, about the difference between one model and the next. Alternately, if consumers don't feel like going to the bookstore or the local Blockbuster, they can save themselves a drive by using Amazon and Netflix and simply strolling to the mailbox at the end of their driveway.

Secondary Shopping Therapy: Just imagine it—no crowds. No malls. No snaking lines. No young moms blocking the aisles with their gray Bugaboo Cameleon strollers. It's the wireless equivalent of paging through *Vogue*—the ultimate fantasy maker and time killer. It gives women instant access to boutiques and high-end baubles they might not otherwise feel comfortable shopping for. In this case, there are no Hermès clerks giving them the once-over. No saleswomen with attitude. Online, they can stroll into Harry Winston, duck into Louis Vuitton and check out the Canyon Ranch in Tucson, the Ritz in Paris or the Mandarin Oriental in Singapore. It's like being invisible *and* having wings. They can even do it naked, exhausted, in need of a shower or while simultaneously watching a rerun of their favorite TV show.

The sense of today being the first time a lot of consumers have had access to goods without having to buy them mimics the sense that the first department stores gave their consumers in the 1850s. Among other things, the department store served as an impetus to middle-class upward mobility. Up until that point, it was assumed that if you walked into a store you were there to buy, or at least had the means to purchase. Thus many people were exposed to a life they'd never seen before, in many cases fueling their appetite to succeed. Then and now, the department store is a very democratic institution. It invites everyone in to take a look and/or gawk to his or her heart's content.

Time Savings: An excellent example: Christmas. Consumers can skim all the good stuff from the most wonderful time of the year while avoiding its horror-show aspects—crowds, jammed parking lots, frenzied parents elbowing one another aside for Wiis or Flip camcorders or whatever the gizmo du jour is. Online, they can point, click, add to cart, checkout and boom, a bonsai tree is on its way to a nephew, a red sweater to a niece, and two quarts of Legal Sea Foods' clam chowder overnighted to an uncle in Florida who misses nothing about living in New England other than the occasional local specialty.

Still, shopping on the web doesn't always fall into one of these categories. The net has had its notable success stories. How do you explain the popularity of merchants like Bluefly, which sells discounted designer fashion for men and women? It's like an even more animated version of the Home Shopping Network. Bluefly has overcome the human need to smell, touch, taste and feel that C3 cashmere sweater or that pair of Marc Jacobs pants, and based on great copy and nice pictures and an ever-changing exhibition of good-looking stuff, they're able to move product consistently through their portal. It's the ultimate in cyber-window-shopping, and the price is right.

The next thing you know, though, you're a woman who finds herself with forty-three designer handbags and no place to put them.

Which is where we get into one of the great pluses of the web—its ability to create secondary markets, a comfortable, reliable system for recycling possessions that would otherwise rot, mildew or rust in the garage or attic. Whether it's a previously owned Mercedes or a slightly scratched Les Paul tobacco-sunburst Gibson guitar that you place on eBay, the Internet has institutionalized a virtual flea market of sorts. I have a number of colleagues who supplement their incomes by specializing in certain categories of goods in a way that would have been unthinkable a decade ago. Old railroad books, estate wineglasses, Moroccan tiles, antique postcards, it doesn't matter—someone out there wants it. More power to them.

Even Amazon has gotten into the game, because often the profit margin on selling used products is higher than selling new. Amazon gives you the option of buying many books, new or used. For out-of-print volumes, Amazon connects to a network of used-book dealers who may make as much if not more money on the shipping and handling charges than they do on the sale of the book itself.

Outside of the virtual flea market environment, how do merchants get people to buy online? Well, there's the easy way, and it goes something like this: You are enamored of a certain brand of running shoes or cut of khaki pants, you've been wearing them for years, you know your size, and that's that. Checkout—and a replacement is zooming its way toward you.

Another way the Internet has worked well is in children's online communities, like Club Penguin, Webkinz or other sites where kids are entreated to buy, tend and shower their love on virtual pets. If you buy a penguin, well, hell, a penguin needs an igloo, right? He has to eat, too. Despite the tariff—five bucks here, five bucks there—these clubs help grow kids' computer and keyboarding skills (though they remain extremely sedentary experiences). Luca, the young son of Gustavo, who runs our data department, could turn on a computer, get online and make his way to his favorite game site by the time he was three years old.

What puzzles me, frankly, is how well visual artists have managed to sell paintings online, and sometimes for thousands of dollars, too. Up until now, artists could either sell their paintings at art fairs or street shows, or else exhibit at a solo or group show where the opening price starts at, say, $2,000. By going direct and virtual, artists have created a new category equivalent to a farmer's market, one that combines the street fair and the art world. The success of this model may be attributable to the desire on the part of artists to bypass the protocol of art galleries, and to customers' discomfort with the art world's snoot factor, or to consumers' sheer geographical distance from the hubs of the art world, but it also comes down to a kind of naïve trust. Still, I'll be damned if it doesn't work, as the idea of someone shopping for art online without actually seeing the thing in person leaves me a little incredulous. Nonetheless, I'm glad that a lot of artists have managed to pull this off.

If someone has a clear-cut sense of focus, it's not only possible to sell stuff online, but you can also do incredibly well.

A friend runs an online vehicle for a small boutique housewares store in New York. He sells more than half a million dollars a year online off a little laptop in a back office. He finds great-looking stuff in small quantities—books, toys, tabletop junk etcetera—and gets it featured in magazines. People fall in love with it and buy it. He'll sell until he runs out, then starts the process all over again. I love going onto his website,

because it's one of the best gifting solutions I know. Why does he succeed? In part it's because he's known in the magazine world, and the
magazine media design editors have come to admire his cherry-picking
ability, his revolving inventory, his good taste.

Had enough shopping? Let's go mingle.

Poke me. Write something on my wall. Glance at my friends list and
the roughly three hundred digital photos and home videos I've up-
loaded. Send me a virtual potted plant, a virtual cupcake. Find out my
relationship status and, if I'm not attached, what it is I'm looking for—
friendship or the real thing.

If you thought social networking was limited to cocktail parties and
private clubs and business seminars, have a look at Facebook, today's
virtual incarnation of the electronic tribe—one created by those two
visionary villains Frank Lloyd Wright and Henry Ford.

Yes, an architect and an equally well-known carmaker. The way I see
it, Facebook is a direct extension of the popularization of the suburb
and of the automobile. Both have created enormous physical distances
among people. As the world gets more and more de-urbanized and we
spread out across the country and the world, with a lot of us toiling
away in isolated corporate campuses, we still can't get away from our
basic human need to reach out and connect with other people (housing
is often key to understanding a lot of new phenomena, social networking sites included). Across that shadowy, gaping void of alienation and
risk and uncertainty comes Facebook, a virtual passport to intimacy. A
kind of intimacy, I should say.

Once again, the web has found itself identifying and fixing a hole
in our physical world. By doing its usual watery thing, it's allowed us
to meet and chat and feel as though we're a part of something bigger
than our high schools, college campuses, bedrooms and office cubicles.
Facebook is not only a social networking site, it's a voyeur's dream. It's
like reading a loose-leaf, picture-filled diary someone has left splayed
open on a couch. It's a way of seeing what your friends are doing, in real
time, even if you have no desire, reason or inclination to call, e-mail or

in some cases lay eyes on them ever again. It's a Google map of your entire social network. For some users, it provides an opportunity to show
off how many friends and connections and wall-postings they have, and
to cement their social status in public. For others, it's just plain convenient, like an illustrated address book that's constantly self-updating. It's
addictive.

Facebook has created an entirely self-contained miniuniverse in
which my sixteen-year-old nephew, say, can have an online conversation
with a girl who, under normal circumstances, he'd be too tongue-tied to
talk to face-to-face. The intimacy that's created by not having to look at
someone physically has its parallels in the retail environment, too—for
example, we've migrated from the nose-to-nose relationship of dealing
with a saleswoman at Bloomingdale's across a makeup counter to the
open sell at Sephora, where you and the person helping you are on the
same side of the counter and seemingly on the same team. Part of what
we're seeing is the early stages of a transformation in communication
and intimacy. From my cynical standpoint, Facebook users are triangu-
lating through the social network because they lack the courage, opportunity and geographical proximity to come face-to-face with an actual
living, breathing human being.

But how long will the Facebooks of the world last? Will Facebook
end up turning into a semipermanent virtual village? (The standard line
in social science buzz is that almost everybody lives in a "village" made
up of approximately two hundred people.) At what point does a Facebook user decide that since he or she hasn't spoken, e-mailed, texted or
called a friend in her network in three years, that person might as well
be given the boot? Does a user ever "graduate" from Facebook? Most
people I know who use it say they can't foresee a time, date, place or age
when they wouldn't be invested, somehow, in their Facebook accounts.
And as we come out of the suburbs and are faced with the mobility
in our culture, social networking—a means of finding some kind of
cyber-permanence within the context of our ongoing lives, as well as
a common identity—may always have its place. Lacking an anchor in a
transitory world, your life can disappear, *poof,* like that. The only question left, then, is do you give two hoots if it disappears?

Still, Facebook and other social networking sites are famously having trouble justifying the cost structures that keep them up and running,
namely, ads. Can we scribble virtual notes on our friends' walls and pay
attention to soda entreaties at the same time?

I get many invitations each year to join one online social networking
site or another. I never bite. Still, at age fiftysomething, I have boxfuls
of business cards I've been handed from across the world, so many that
if I laid them end to end, I could build a cardboard stairway to heaven.
Maybe that's my version of Facebook.

People's spread-out-ness works at the other extreme, too. There are
cultures in which economic prosperity may have provided gleaming
gadgets and connectivity, yet people are still living in small, crowded
spaces. Which is one reason why in a sense, the Japanese and Koreans
use technology to wall themselves off—to create a sense of virtual privacy. In a crowded Japanese home or apartment, the ability to vanish
inside the Internet or into your mobile phone is like ducking inside a
pup tent or adding on an extra wing.

Another thing the Internet has accomplished in Korea and Japan is to
conduct a nifty end-run around social restrictions and manners. In these
two countries, where it's impolite to actually look someone straight in
the eye, Facebook and instant messaging are ways of staring and not staring at the same time. Also, if you think about Japanese kids on a mobile
phone, they use a minimal amount of strokes to create a complex de-
clarative sentence. As they start typing a word phonetically, the character
pops up, making it infinitely speedier to communicate. Contrast this to
American teenagers, who've had to come up with their own homemade
abbreviations to cut down on the keystrokes—LOL—while their parents
continue madly thumbing away at their BlackBerries. All of which makes
communication in Asian countries faster, and is one reason why the role
of the net-enabled phone has found a natural home there.

Another difference in Japan, Korea and many emerging markets:
Public transportation isn't the exception, it's the norm. The average
citizen may spend two or more hours a day commuting. It's bad manners to talk on the phone as they ride the train or bus, but with a web-
enabled phone they can surf and text-message to their hearts' content.

It isn't just a time-saver, it's another cyber body-bubble. In Europe and America, we can drive and chat on our phones in the privacy of our cars, but we can't stare hypnotically into them or we'd topple over the guardrail. Why should we be surprised that cyber applications will have varying degrees of success based on the markets they serve?

I wonder what will happen now that our thumbs (rather than our forefingers) are doing all the work. Whoever designed our hands made them so that the thumb is the source of strength and the other fingers are in charge of the delicate stuff. What happens when arthritis sets in— are our IM days over?

Facebook isn't the only electronic tribe out there, and in theory, it's more about friendship and belonging and creating a giant alumni association than it is about actual meeting up and settling down. The Internet has become, in essence, a kind of modern-day Jewish matchmaker, creating sites such as Match.com, where a red-haired guy in Des Moines who stands five feet one inch tall can tell the world he's six feet four inches' worth of tawny, easygoing California beach boy. That is, until he meets up with an actual woman who just can't believe she fell for it again.

The problem with Match.com and with every other look-up-hook-up-and-settle-down site is that they're founded on mutual compatibility. Remember the questionnaire you were possibly given once about what sort of roommate you'd like to have your freshman year in college? Nonsmoker, vegetarian, likes Metallica etc. These same standards go hand in hand with online mating services. You play tennis? Me too. We're both not-very-serious Buddhists. We both love Italy and Monty Python and cats and . . . you get the picture. In the end, the whole thing becomes a potential orgy of self-love, a union of mirrors. When we fall in love, are we *really* looking for a person who's exactly like us? If I had to date myself I'm pretty sure I'd announce, "This isn't working," after about a day.

This is one of the chief limitations of the web. It thinks and perceives and processes data like a computer, because it *is* a computer. It lacks the capacity to be thoughtful or inventive or intuitive in an original way. Even Amazon.com is guilty of this. Its predictive mode is based on the premise that past behavior (you like John Grisham) defines future behavior (you'll keep on liking John Grisham). Now, this is very likely true for many readers, but at the same time, a lot of us are always on the lookout for novelty. Just because I love James Lee Burke novels doesn't mean I won't get a kick out of a new book on hang gliding in the Galapagos or a new bio of Sir Richard Burton (not the actor, but the wonderfully weird nineteenth-century explorer).

Come to think of it, some of the strongest unions I know are between two people who are completely unalike. There's this couple I know, Richard and Stacy. Richard is my market research mentor. He likes the New York Mets, basketball, a few beers and Chinese takeout, and he knows more about Finnish cinema than anyone I've ever met. Stacy, who's the love of his life, is an aficionado of five-star restaurants and gourmet vacations, and has never gotten off an airplane without knowing that a deluxe hotel and a megavolt hair-dryer were waiting for her at the other end. But Richard and Stacy adore each other. It's the second or third marriage for each of them, but this one's going the distance. And what keeps them together, in my opinion, is that every day they have to compromise and roll their eyes skyward at each other's foibles.

They would never have met if Match.com had set them up. Not even close.

There are lots of people out there who've carried off the whole *When Harry Met Sally* thing. They meet in college, break up, get together again, bust up a second time, then reunite—this time forever and ever. Those guys and dolls who were meant to be tootsified got married at twenty-seven, and that was it. I'm happy they knew what they wanted when they wanted it. For the rest of us who failed that standard practice, we're back on street level, back in the churning mill. We recognize with a touch of bittersweetness that if we haven't settled down by age thirty, there's probably a good reason why—that there might be something a tiny bit faulty with us. For all its imperfections, the net has at least been able to facilitate hooking up for the over-forty set.

The triumph of hope over experience—it's just a couple of clicks away.

• • •

Generally, so much of what we spend money on is so predictable that if we thought about it too much, we'd question whether or not we were conscious. For most of us over age forty, 80 percent of what's inside the fridge at home is routine purchases. Yes, we may change the cheese, vegetables and meat based on the season, but the basics remain the same. By now I know what I like: Tropicana orange juice with pulp. Skim Plus Parmalat milk. Low-fat plain Dannon yogurt. Cream cheese with scallions. French mustard. Malaysian chili sauce. A few beers. I've even settled on a label and vintage of white wine my significant other and I both enjoy drinking.

But is there any reason why we can't endow the web, or our kitchens, with the power to carry out our most routine shopping purchases? The Japanese are working on a refrigerator that allows you to scan the bar codes and radio frequency identification tags of items going in. The machine knows when they're missing or that the weight has declined. It then sends you a daily or weekly text message asking your permission to place an order with an online emporium. The same thing goes for the laundry room, where a web-empowered shelf or storage system keeps accurate track of your soap, bleach and fabric softener. Unfortunately, the lifespan of most appliances is ten years or more, while the typical software lifespan is less than two years. The problem is making the hardware and the software truly compatible.

The future of the Internet as I see it: *convergence.* It may sound a little sci-fi, but all I'm talking about is the linkup between the physical world and mobile technology and the web—an improved union between stores, the online world and the mobile phone. Recently I was struck by an interesting way to quantify any customer's potential value to a retailer. If I'm a store owner, and my customers only shop my products out on the floor, they're "worth" one unit. If they shop the store and also glance through my catalog, they're worth 1.5 units. If they shop, read the catalog and also visit the website, they're worth two units— meaning that my relationship to customers in terms of the amount of money they spend is in direct proportion to the number of ways they interact with me.

As an example of convergence, consumers could take their web-enabled mobile phone into their local drugstore and point it, say, at an over-the-counter drug. The shelf would then direct them to a website that tells them what the drug does and doesn't do, its dosage, its side effects etc., which they scan on their phones. Simple, right?

Convergence also advances a phenomenon that's already making inroads in online shopping: the Internet as a green tool. A friend of mine recently caved in and bought an iPhone. Instead of reading a fold-out instruction manual that told him how to use it, the box it arrived in directed him to an Apple website which screened an instructional video. Same thing happened when I bought my new, fancy-schmancy Casio watch from a Japanese department store. It came with a web address from which I could download the instructions onto my desktop. That way, I wasn't frustratedly parsing an instruction book in twenty-three languages from French to Serbo-Croatian.

So whether it's instruction booklets or boxes and bags, convergence is among other things a great way to eliminate excess clutter and paper and packaging, just as the web-connected refrigerator that I described earlier streamlines shopping trips and merchants' distribution processes. And somewhere out there, the world's landfills will be breathing a sigh of relief.

The second function within this system is its ability to replace our wallets and *become* a wallet (and a bank) at the same time. At the Do-CoMo store in Japan and in the Philippines, you can preload your mobile phone with cash or your mobile phone can accept wire transfers. Particularly in third-world countries like the Philippines, this provides an end-run around banking institutions, a valuable perk to say the least for people who don't have a bank account. Think of it as the currency of mobile phone minutes. At the same time, it also serves as a safety net for worried parents in a scary world. By loading money onto their kids' mobile phones, at the end of the month they can see how that money has been spent, whether it's on cheeseburgers and the movies—as the little ones claimed—or on a half-ounce of high-octane pot. Another bonus? Safety. Once you start putting cash into electronic form, crime plummets.

The third and final bonus of a web-enabled mobile is that it would also work as a form of personal ID. It would connect somehow to your physical self in a way that would allow the phone to work only when it was in your vicinity. Meaning if you drop the thing in a gutter by accident or someone steals it, the phone becomes for all intents and purposes useless.

What the web-enabled phone also does is create a network that bypasses the traditional media of both the web and of face-to-face communication. The elections in Spain in March of 2004 were influenced partly by all the instant messaging provoked by the deadly terrorist train bombings in Madrid that happened on the eve of the election. No one was debating political issues, but an online community was able to shore up its allegiances. So we now have the tools to disseminate information in a way that transcends phones, magazines and newspapers—and that connects us all locally.

To take convergence to a retail level, it could also mean that the bricks-and-mortar model, with its distribution systems and supply chain management, might be ripe for overhaul. The era of the big-box merchant, at least in the first world, has reached its apogee. Stores may be getting bigger, but that doesn't mean consumers plan on spending a correspondingly increased amount of time, or money, in them. Scaling down stores makes both economic and ecological sense. If we start ordering our staples online—and even if we only swing by and pick them up at the store—do we *really* need that laundry aisle?

Come to think of it, when we reach the point of convergence, the entire purpose of a physical existence may have to be dramatically reconsidered. The United States is investing huge sums of money in nation-building outside the country (think Iraq), but in the meantime our docks, ports and bridges are rotting, our passenger railroads are vanishing *and we've all but lost the capacity to think big or be bold*. We are backing into the future. At a time when we need to get beyond our addiction to fossil fuels and take better care of our planet, we are stuck. A hundred and fifty years ago it took vision to push our railroads across the country; a hundred years ago it took guts to conceive and build the Panama Canal. Today, America is a follower, not a leader—so convergence will happen somewhere else first.

Convergence will initially find its footing in someplace like Africa or India where someone doesn't own, or have access to, a landline. Part of what I find interesting about visiting India is that for reasons of space, density, primitive retail and an absence of things that Americans and Western Europeans take for granted, it's a country that's managing to leapfrog the traditional landline. Visiting Delhi recently, I was struck by the number of people whose mobile phones were always in their hands—far more so than in New York City. Mobile phones weren't just for calling; they served as their owners' pivotal identities. People's mobile phone numbers were at least as, or more, important as their names.

This makes sense when you contrast India's path with the evolution of technology followed by most Americans. First we had our landlines. Next we had our computers, followed by the Internet, followed by the first mobile phones. (Recall if you will that the first mobile phone stores didn't appear in the U.S. until the late '80s and early '90s, and were used mostly by business guys. I can remember once attending the opera with a friend who'd never used a mobile phone before. She glanced down at mine as if it were an exotic mango. When she called her daughter, the first excited words out of her mouth were, "Guess what—I'm calling you on a mobile phone!") After that, some of us graduated to PDAs, which ushered us into the first mobile Internet world. Oh, and incidentally, the next time I saw the woman from the opera, she was the proud possessor of both a mobile phone and a BlackBerry.

If you ask most people, they'll tell you that mobile phones have been around forever, rather than since the early 1990s.

Compare this technological journey to that of an emerging country, where someone is going to migrate from having nothing—no landline, no laptop—to suddenly, overnight, having the Internet at his or her fingertips. In Delhi, it was almost comical overhearing people calling each other on their mobiles. *Where are you? I'm going to be three minutes late.* Made me wonder how people got along before mobile phones appeared.

But that's why I'm positive convergence will take place first in an emerging country. At which point, someone in the U.S. will exclaim, "Hey, why the heck don't we have that here?"

One of the most remarkable things about the World Wide Web is that even its most grizzled veterans lack a clear-eyed understanding of how it works. Most of us have accepted it, embraced it and sworn at it, but it's in our homes and in our coffee shops and in the air, whether we use it for Hollywood gossip, stock trading, or simply as a combination electronic post office and gigantic animated *Encyclopaedia Britannica*.

So what would happen if there were a cyber war and the net collapsed? What if an organization or foreign nation decided that the best way to assault the United States would be to sabotage the web? If we think about terrorism and the fallout from 9/11, what happens when the terrorist moves beyond dreaming up simple stupid viruses and figures out some way to make the web disappear? What happens then?

Rather than sitting around figuring out what the next Facebook will be in this money-crazy culture, it's worth setting aside a little time to think about that.

But enough with worst-case scenarios involving nefarious plots. Let me leave you humming a few bars of music.

I have a professional friend, a guy I don't see as much of as I'd like, but someone I'm always happy to run into when I do. He has three interconnected vices—he runs marathons, smokes a half-pack of Marlboros a day and is a total music junkie. Every time we meet up at some conference or another, he'll pass me a fervent note that says, "Check out these guys," before listing off a few musicians he stubbornly believes no contemporary iPod owner should live without. The last band he recommended was called Balkan Beat Box—a fusion of Middle Eastern music tangled up with electronica, with a heavy bass beat behind it. Terrific dance music that sounds just as good when you're bopping down the street with headphones on.

So I went to the iTunes store, typed in "Balkan Beat Box" and up they came. Two albums' worth, some twenty-five songs in total followed by a ten-line description of what the music was about and a few customer reviews. That was it. Hardly enough to chew on—extremely frustrating. I ended up buying three or four songs at ninety-nine cents a pop, plus some songs from a couple of other bands my buddy told me about, and I put together a mix, which I've been enjoying, as it's pretty complex, wonderful stuff.

But if my friend hadn't brought the band to my attention, chances are high that Balkan Beat Box and I would've never found each other. Why? Because for all the talk about iTunes being this revolutionary new medium for sampling and downloading digital music, let's face it, it's a pretty limited site—and I'm a lifelong Apple fan.

Example: Why doesn't iTunes offer me any song samples longer than thirty seconds? Sometimes the vocals or the melody don't even begin to kick in by then. Why doesn't the site request more personal information, including where I live and what kinds of music I'm interested in, so it can tip me off to local concerts based on my preferences or on the music I've downloaded already? Why doesn't it permit me to buy, say, a three-play version of a song for twenty-five cents, so I can decide whether I want it in my permanent music library or not? iTunes also can't seem to figure out why a guy who buys Balkan Beat Box also gets a kick out of vintage Eartha Kitt. Plus, where are all the liner notes? I love reading liner notes. It turns out I can peruse them only if I buy the whole album for $9.99 or $11.99 or $18.99, or however much the site is charging me.

Where's the information explosion here?

There's another issue: I'm at a point in my life where I own four iPods, each with its own speaker system. I keep one such sound device in my living room, another apparatus in my kitchen, a third in my office and a fourth . . . well, it migrates. But why hasn't Apple recognized the revolution it's created and facilitated it? It should be selling me—all of us—much broader solutions than it does now, other than just simply being the latest, coolest new distribution system. Because the site is preoccupied with selling me songs for ninety-nine cents—as well as audiobooks, TV episodes, music videos and just-released DVDs—it isn't giving me the tools to manage my fleet of iPods. I want Apple not just to sell me content, but to expedite and simplify the role of its products in my life.

Recently I met up with a senior group of executives at Sony BMG, the global music conglomerate. As a lot of people know, CD sales are in a downward spiral, and in 2007 they declined again by some 30 percent. Strange fact: The only places where CDs are doing okay are in niche markets. For example, polka is holding its own. Same goes for Latin music. Little indie stores with focused and dedicated clientele are surviving. But the rest of the industry is suffering.

There's a lot wrong with this picture. Because today we find ourselves at a time in history where there's never been a more voracious appetite for music. A typical fifteen-year-old kid in 2008 has a working vocabulary of all different varieties of music. He or she knows something about trance, blues, rock, reggae, heavy metal, country, rockabilly, stoner music, the British Invasion, contemporary, hip-hop, world music, even the Christmas Peanuts soundtrack. Yet in spite of the knowledge and appetite out there, the Internet doesn't have the tools yet to indulge it wholeheartedly. It can't penetrate its outermost edges. It can't get us psyched about listening to good new stuff.

I know, I know, online music sales are booming, but the thing is they're not even close to matching the falling sales of CDs. Again, that's not because digital downloading is anything terrific, or the quality of the sound is all that excellent, or managing your MP3 sound files is any easier than juggling your ancient vinyl collection.

To blame file sharing or online piracy is a copout, too. In 1959, the typical American household had 1.7 sound reproduction devices—the parents had their stereo and maybe the kids had a portable record player upstairs. We placed the needle reverently on vinyl, cocked our ears and listened. We couldn't move (or dance), because the needle might skitter across the record. Today we do just about everything to music—cook, read, work out, make love. Music has become the soundtrack to our multitasking lives. Yes, I have four iPods of various styles and sizes, but in total, my house has twenty-three sound reproducing devices. I've bought one particular Doors album four times, on vinyl, cassette, CD and as MP3s. Yes, kids are trading music—for God's sake, why wouldn't they if for almost twenty years we made them buy pricey CDs rather than 45s that conformed to their budgets? Problem is, the music industry has historically been closer to the musicians than the consumers.

Music has flourished online because of the failure of the music industry to recognize that consumers don't want to buy the whole cake—we want to buy the stuff by the slice. We don't want to shell out $13.99 for *The Best of the Troggs* or $24.99 for *Arthur Rubenstein: Chopin Nocturnes*. Maybe we just wanted "Wild Thing" and Nocturne op. 15, no. 3 in G-Minor. Did the music industry intuit this about us? No—they're still putting out music the way they did back in the days of Chuck Berry, and now they're paying the price.

That said, if iTunes is the only music portal out there, I think we're all in trouble. If Sheryl, my significant other, who's a professional musician, is hunting down an obscure piece of chamber music, she isn't about to find it on iTunes. There was a time not so long ago when she could pay a visit to Tower Records near Lincoln Center, and some shy, knowledgeable clerk would know exactly what she was talking about, and the various versions, and why the 1962 studio version recorded in Vienna was superior to the one done live in 1978 at the Concertgebouw. But Tower is gone, Barnes & Noble is unlikely, Wal-Mart is out of the question and Sheryl is stuck.

One of the questions I put to the Sony executives was, can you figure out a way to put your catalog in a place where people can access it? It almost suggests the need for a company portal for their entire classical backlist. As I said, the appetite for music today is overwhelming—it's just a matter of helping consumers find it. If I want a classical compilation with a title like *Chill with Beethoven* or *The Most Relaxing Classical Album in the World,* I can download it off iTunes, no problem. But wouldn't many of us pay a premium for a Sony-led chat room, where, say, we could pick and choose from a complete catalog of music, and the host—some distinguished, goateed professor of music from Berkeley or Juilliard—would ask us what type of recording we wanted, if we preferred a live or studio recording, how old we are, what our ears are like and all that, before directing us to the perfect piece of music? Whether we walk away with something digital or a real CD—or even a bracelet with earphones attached to it—it's an opportunity that's just waiting for someone to invent the process. Techies?

A music store or bookstore of the future—couldn't it be similar? It might resemble the comic-book clubs they have in Japan, where you can go in, rent a chair and read all your favorites. You would pay a small admission fee. In return, someone whose taste you admire and appreciate would serve as the emcee. Your fellow members would be men and women who like and appreciate the same music you do. Maybe the club could serve drinks and feta-stuffed olives and a wheel of Epoisses cheese. The people who run the place would know what you like and even hand-sell you stuff, including vintage collectibles.

Imagine—you could cyber-experience a concert, anything from Balkan Beat Box to Maurizio Pollini. You could rent it, buy it, mix it or go to a club and actually attend a concert. An expert would guide you every step of the way. And your connection to the place would be fostered by an online community.

Now *that'd* be music to my ears.

EIGHTEEN

Come Fly with Me

Here's a boarding pass. Step on it—the gate's closing. Pop a Xanax, fasten your seat belt, extricate that blue blanket from its shrink-wrap.

Oh, and the aisle seat is mine, an anatomical necessity for a guy with long legs.

Time for a trip around the globe, from Italy to India, with a few stops in between. Business *and* a little pleasure.

In the late 1980s, Envirosell found itself at a fortuitous crossroads, in that whatever direction we chose to take was going to lead us *somewhere* new and promising. We could either plow time, energy and resources into expanding our business here at home, or we could train our binoculars on the great big world out there. A trade-off, absolutely, but for me the decision was easy: go global.

If we'd stayed put, we'd probably be a lot bigger in the U.S. than we are today. But from a strategic point of view, transforming Envirosell into a business that understood the needs of international retail and shopping was a huge plus in terms of what we could bring to the table in the U.S.

I'm also totally at home traveling—about as comfortable boarding an airplane and navigating the wild world as just about anyone I know. Having a fiercely independent live-in significant other and no kids freed me up to spend good chunks of time on the road, too. Once I've cleared customs, my adaptive skills are up to speed as well. I'm not talking about backpacking in the Himalayas or finding the best B&B in Chiang Mai. I'm talking about being able to competently go around the world in ten days, in and out of multiple time zones, and stay more or less sane, healthy and in a good frame of mind. Plus, it's a thrill to be able to fold up your American glasses and try on your new *gafas,* your *magane,* your *occhiali,* your *óculos.* You see everything in a new light. Such as, what are some of the things that make this store or mall here in Cape Town or Shanghai work that wouldn't go over in Colorado Springs or Austin, Texas? Or, why the heck hasn't an American retailer ever thought of this? Truly, under the best of circumstances, and even the worst, it can be a revelation.

My only wish? That I slept better on airplanes. Sleeping in public is hard, and I'm no good at it. My theory is that the people most at ease doing it grew up sharing a room with a kid sister or brother and got used to it. I slept alone back then.

Buckled in? Up we go. First, though, let's backtrack a little.

In the early '90s—remember, this was before e-mail—my fax machine whirred out a sheet of paper. The fax came from Alberto Pasquini, who was then the managing partner of Creativity Italia, a point-of-purchase agency. He'd read about Envirosell in one of the trade magazines and invited me to visit him in Milan. I was already sold on the idea of opening up a European office and was commuting back and forth across the pond, trying to scare up business. I happened to have a trip planned the following week and was able to get my airline ticket changed so that I could fly into Geneva and back home to the States from Milan. Ten days later, I took the train from Lausanne, Switzerland, to Milan to meet up with the guy who'd sent me the fax.

Alberto was born to have an exclamation mark at the end of his name—maybe half a dozen. Flamboyant, snowy-haired and in his late forties when I first met him fifteen years ago, he was a sort of

Mediterranean P. T. Barnum. On that first visit to Milan, Alberto took it upon himself to introduce me to a woman he knew by the name of Giusi Scandroglio, who ran a small market research company called QT. "Here," he said in his charming fractured English, "is your future partner." I can remember thinking, *What are you talking about here, Alberto?* But Giusi and I shook hands and made all the right small talk. And things went no further than that. Over the next year or two, I found reasons to go back to Italy. Each time I went, it dawned on me that Alberto had managed to choreograph my schedule so it involved—somehow—Giusi.

Italy as a concept is only one hundred and fifty years old. Then and now, the country is a collection of city-states, each one with its own distinctive character. Giusi is Genovese by birth and Milanese by choice. The Genovese historically wandered the Mediterranean mostly as merchants and occasionally as pirates—call it the light and the dark sides of the Genovese identity—whereas Milan is a city of industry, persistent, hardworking, focused, controlled. Almost everything of interest or significance in Milan happens behind a high wall or a closed door. It isn't so great a city to visit as a tourist—in twenty-four hours, you can see just about everything—but with a guide or mentor by your side, Milan can be a magical place.

Thanks to Alberto, meetings happened and before I knew it I needed an Italian office sooner rather than later, and who else to run it? Giusi Scandroglio. A woman who by taking the reins of Envirosell Milan has turned out to be exactly the person we needed, as well as purely Milanese in her values—focused, independent, knowledgeable, tireless and tenacious. Not an easy combo of attributes to come by, particularly for a female living and working in a male-dominated country like Italy.

Rule of thumb: With international expansion comes worry, tossing and turning at night and readjusting your vision to the local ways of doing things. In Italy, the payment system is enormously complicated. Every project you take on first has to be financed by a third party, typically a bank. That means that when someone signs a contract with you, it's more than likely you may not be paid for 180 days or so. I was willing to take a fall personally, but I didn't want Envirosell itself to be jeopardized. So I took an ownership position in our first overseas office. Like so many journeys, the scariest step is that first one.

Once we'd broken into the Italian market, one thing led to another. One of our first Italian clients was Levi's Italia, and while we already had the company as a client here in the U.S., Levi's Italia led us to the jean market all across Europe. Within a few years, we were looking at Levi's and Dockers sales in Amsterdam, Stockholm, Lisbon and elsewhere. Before long, thanks to an alliance Envirosell had formed with the John Ryan Company, a Minneapolis-based retail bank marketing agency, we were introduced to the world of Brazilian banking; our first effort came when we worked for a company known as Banco Itaú.

Itaú is a completely vertically integrated bank. They make the furniture that goes into the bank, they assemble their own ATMs and computers, they own the construction companies that build their branches and they operate the complexes that house their staff. It's a privately held company that throws off more than a billion dollars a year in profits. Though who really knows—it's nothing at all like Chase, Citi or Bank of America. But then, it *is* Brazil. The typical Itaú branch could have as many as a hundred tellers. The first branches we saw had towers in the middle of the floor with hard-eyed security guards equipped with machine guns keeping close watch on the floor.

In Banco Itaú, we were looking at in-store signage issues, points of service, the design of teller stations and so forth, but instead of doing it at a three-thousand-square-foot Citibank in midtown Manhattan, we were carrying out our research in a twenty-thousand-square-foot Brazilian bank. Also, in Brazil, people's concepts of wait time are different. As I said earlier in this book, in the U.S. our internal clocks begin to ding after about three minutes, signaling impatience, but Brazilians' internal clocks swell to about five minutes, since they're far more accustomed (or resigned) to waiting. Another thing that surprised me was the complete absence of privacy, or more likely the resigned indifference to the fact that your most intimate affairs will be made public. If you're applying for a loan or a mortgage in the U.S., typically you take a seat at a bank desk and some officious vice president will ask you what your annual salary is, what your monthly credit card payments are, whether you have any additional sources of income etc. In Brazil, you'll be asked these same questions, but the thing is there'll be half a dozen other customers awaiting their turns a foot away from you, and no one blinks an eye. It's not an ideal culture for someone who has a lot to hide.

In Brazil, like in many developing countries, much of the economy functions on cash. The employer might issue a check, but the check is then taken to the bank to be cashed. Many companies have a prescribed day and time when their employees descend en masse to get their checks cashed, and I can remember one afternoon when five hundred bus drivers turned up at our test branch. Also, in Brazil many people pay their bills, including rent, electricity and phone service, with cash at the bank. The branch is divided up according to different classes of trade. The lower-class cash-based customers, known as "Amigos," go to one part of the bank, while the middle-class "Star" customers make their way to another. It's a noisy, hectic and altogether difficult environment. We loved it, though, and it turned out that Itaú loved us back. Within a year John Ryan had moved on, but Envirosell was invited to stay. Soon we added Brahma, the huge Brazilian brewer, to our client mix and found ourselves shipping members of our New York staff down to São Paulo left and right.

Not much opportunity to come up for air in those days. But when we finally stood up and took a big collective gulp, we found that almost 20 percent of Envirosell's work was coming out of Brazil, accounting for nearly 30 percent of our total profits.

So what about opening up a Brazilian office? But this time, we all agreed, we'd do it as a licensee.

To set up a successful licensee in a foreign country, obviously you need to find a reliable partner. So we promptly began shopping around for the right person. Our search was narrowed down to women who'd had some experience owning and running a market-research business. What's with the reverse sexism? Quite simply, our experience in Milan had taught us a few things. Giusi had succeeded in a male-oriented culture, and we were eager to find her Brazilian equivalent—a woman who wasn't a stranger to facing those same odds and staring them into submission. Also, the product we were selling wasn't exactly your everyday commodity.

Into Envirosell's life strode Maria Cristina Mastopietro, though everyone called her Kita. Big brain, big heart, broad shoulders and a memorable laugh. She had a master's degree from Stanford University and matched our profile to a T; she was, and is to this day, exactly the person we were looking for and more. Her business partner is a young, smart industrial engineer named José Augusto Domingues. They're a great team.

I won't ever forget the day when Giusi and Kita met for the first time in our New York offices. They were wearing identical outfits. Their purses were the exact same style. They carried them the same way. They owned the same type of car—same color, too, I might add. The similarities extended to the way each woman described her husband. They might have been talking about the same guy, though luckily for all of us, they weren't. And they also got along like old friends.

Typically when we license a business abroad, we fly our overseas partners to New York, where they spend a month or so with us learning the ins and outs of our business. Then the process is flipped. We ship some of our people abroad to help our offshore licensees set up shop and get rolling with their first projects. We provide training and marketing systems and control their Internet presence, and in return, our off-shore partners agree to share a percentage of their revenues with us. We also have the right to review their performance. If things aren't going as well as we hoped, we take whatever steps we need to deal with what's not working and figure out how to fix it.

That's about the long and the short of it.

For a lot of our New York–based staff, working in Brazil was their first exposure to a developing country. Eye-opening, to say the least. Definitely an experience, particularly for some of our Midwestern-born employees who'd never left our shores before. Nothing bad ever happened, but there were a couple of incidents involving one of our blonde female employees being followed on the streets by wolf-whistling males.

Ten years or so after we set up our São Paulo office, Brazil is front and center in our category management work. "Cat-man," as we call it for short, examines how a category of goods is shopped at the point of sale. It could be baby products, canned soup or cell phones. Thus, rather than working for a retailer, we're throwing our energy behind a consumer goods manufacturer.

Cat-man work is booming in South America as companies like Johnson & Johnson, Unilever, Nokia and Motorola expand their offerings. Envirosell Brazil is now in charge of doing business in other South American countries, and we're currently in the process of changing them from a licensee into a joint venture. A tribute to all their spectacular work.

Unavoidably, though, our São Paulo office finds itself mixed up with currency, politics and soccer. It just can't be helped. There's no getting around that three-headed monster. Which means that if it's a crazy political year, or if the Brazilian currency, the real, takes a hit against the dollar or vice versa, well, fasten your seat belts, we may be in for a bumpy few months. Also, did I mention the World Cup? The entire country shuts down for three months. It tacks up the football equivalent of a GONE FISHIN' sign. Nothing anyone can do about it either, except wave the yellow, green and blue flag back and forth for the home team.

Our first bout of world-class publicity came to Envirosell thanks to a young science writer at *The New Yorker* magazine named Malcolm Gladwell (yes, the very same guy who went on to write the two mega-bestsellers *The Tipping Point* and *Blink*). His piece, entitled "The Science of Shopping," profiled what we do and went on to become one of the most reprinted pieces in *New Yorker* history. Moreover, it made this book possible.

After the Gladwell article appeared in the fall of 1996, the queries from potential licensees from all around the world multiplied. Every week a new call would come in from someone who wanted to partner up with us. It was very flattering stuff. One of the most wonderful things about our business life around that time was the number of clients who showed up on our doorstep ready to hire us. They were presold, first on the *New Yorker* piece, and second on this book. For a guy who'd once saved money on hotel rooms by napping in his car and washing up the next morning at the nearest gas station, after all those years of not knowing whether this business would fly or go crashing to the ground, it was gratifying beyond belief.

In the wake of the *New Yorker* article, one note that showed up in the mail grabbed my attention. The letter writer—I consider him now my white knight—was a Japan-based licensing agent named Kaz Toyota who represented a number of top-tier clients in the U.S. and was responsible for licensing their offices across Japan. He'd read the *New Yorker* article and found out more about our business online. And he not only offered to scout out for us the right Japanese licensee but volunteered his future daughter-in-law, Momo, as a guide.

During the first four years of my Japanese business life, Momo Toyota became my mentor for all the ins and outs of Japanese culture. She'd spent part of her childhood in the U.S. and Australia and understood the cultural gaps I was coming up against. We'd visit different shopping districts and go to malls and even a shrine or two. She'd answer every question I asked, no matter how dumb or personal it was, with a little giggle—followed by an honest, thorough, thoughtful answer. When Momo got married, I sent her and her new husband tickets to come visit me in New York. They took me up on the offer and stayed in my apartment. She has two children now, the oldest named Emma, and I keep up with her through her private-access website, Let's Go Emma.

If it was keys to the Japanese culture I was looking for, then Momo handed me a big, valuable set, and for that I'm forever grateful. She taught me everything from the Japanese family structure to the nation's preoccupation with keeping clean to the unspoken protocol of gift giving, and about the nuances of bowing, and knowing when to show your back to someone and when not to, how long and how low to the ground your bow should be when one person is leaving, when to turn and who turns first, when you can feel free to cut your bow short—in essence, how best to do honor to your hosts. I actually grew up in Asia. My father was a diplomat and my sport of choice through my teenage years was judo. I had a head start in Japanese culture compared to most foreigners, but Momo gave me an accelerated course in technique and finesse. Every day, I'd stow away more and more information, which no doubt made me come across as more of a sophisticate than I usually felt on the inside.

There was only one speed bump: my name.

When I went to Japan for the first time to work, it became clear that the Japanese faced an uphill climb with the word "Underhill." Something about it just wasn't easy for them to say. One day, I just came out with it: "Please—call me Paco-san."

Now, you have to understand that for the average Japanese businessman, this was a radical suggestion. For Americans, it would be like addressing your beloved grandmother with "Yo, Gloria." No one in Japan ever addresses anybody by his or her first name. But once we'd gotten over that little name hump, we could all relax.

Looking back, I'm sure a lot of my ease within the Japanese culture, and their ease with me, had to do with my being physically big and friendly, but also with the fact that I'd picked up a few cultural nuances thanks to Momo. Little things such as adding "chan" to a woman's name—an affectionate suffix that sets up a chummy but respectful relationship with a younger female. For a boy, the equivalent is "kun." With a few of my Japanese clients, I've said, "If you want to call me Paco-kun, it's okay with me." Usually they're shocked that I even know these terms, never mind that I just suggested they call me that. At the same time, I think they enjoy the novelty of it. I'm both being playful about their culture and revealing my genuine interest in Japan at the same time. This is a country where people are always amazed that someone not only speaks even a few words of their language but actually *processes* how the culture functions on a daily basis. Those little things count for a lot.

This new informality I have in Japan even includes my wardrobe. On my first few trips there, I wore a coat and tie everywhere I went, or a suit. Then one day it was very gently pointed out to me that I was Paco-san and could wear a bathing suit and a bunch of kiwifruit on my head for all anybody minded.

For comfort, I have to say that nothing beats a buttoned-up white shirt and a nice pair of khakis when you're strolling along the streets of Tokyo.

In a totally male-dominated society such as Japan, our managing director, Uchida-san, stands out like a lotus flower. Some people collect Beanie Babies, or Coke cans, or driftwood. But along with her ability to function on no more than two or three hours of sleep a night, Uchida-san has what must be one of the most elaborate frog collections in the world, and it even carries over to her person. I'm talking about frog earrings, frog pendants, froggy necklaces. Even at traditional company meetings, Uchida-san will arrange to have someone wearing a frog costume greet you at the door and usher you to your seat. Thank you, frog.

Tom Waits, the American rock and roller, has a song I can identify with. The chorus is "I'm big in Japan / I'm big in Japan." When this book first came out, it sold very well here in the States but especially well in Japan, Canada and the Netherlands. I chalk this up to the fact that these are all countries where manners matter a great deal. Which is one of the major concerns of this book—how to decipher manners and behavior.

One question we get asked all the time is what makes shopping different in other countries. My first response is to point out what's the same all over—which I like to think is the basic subject addressed by this book. Our eyes age the same way whether we live in Tokyo or Chicago or São Paulo. Our basic human measures fall under the same parameters: the length of our arms, how our hands work, the fact that almost all of us are right-handed. We love our children and like our spouses most of the time. We tend to move in similar groups made up of friends, couples and nuclear and extended families.

That said, there are some fundamental things that make shopping and the physical environments we live in different based on where in the world we live. The first is the relative density of the population. Tokyo, and to an even greater extent Mumbai, is a crowded place; Dallas and Los Angeles are extremely spread out. The sheer luxury of space alters the mix. After all, one of the key measures for the success of a store is sales per square foot. If I'm looking at a Japanese store in Ginza, the sales per square foot may be at least ten times as high as the same store located in a strip mall outside Chicago. The denser the physical environment, the less hard management has to work to get people inside a store. In Tokyo, some department stores are ten floors high, with one escalator after another. In the same city, you'll even find high-rise restaurant buildings, with a different restaurant on every floor. No one in the U.S. would even think to open up an Applebee's on the fourth floor of a high-rise.

The second factor is the level of economic prosperity where you live. North America and Western Europe have a very high standard of living, and while poor people live everywhere, you won't find the same level of poverty here in the West that you do in parts of Asia and Africa. The contrast between rich and poor often sets up security issues that have a profound effect on the physical environment. For example, a Brazilian shopping mall offers a degree of safety and security that the street can't.

A third factor is the weather. The difference between Dubai and Helsinki is that in one place you have to manage the heat, and in the other, the cold. And then, of course, we face issues of national culture and customs.

Place your tray table in its upright position—we're touching down in Bangalore, home to Envirosell India.

An intriguing place, India. A country that's currently on the roll of a lifetime. The sense of national pride and patriotism—the belief that now is their time—is pervasive. Nothing to argue about there. Just take a look at Mumbai's or Bangalore's state-of-the-art factories, plastics industries and petroleum processors. At the same time, the country's core infrastructure is coming apart at the seams, and India still has the most primitive retail of any country in the emerging world. From clothing to groceries to cars, the overwhelming majority of retail is still being sold in ma-and-pa stores. Thus you're subject to the vicissitudes, prices and variable standards of whoever's operating those stores (there's no quality control and, as of 2008, no big-box chains). The country is still under the hard-to-shake shadow of three hundred years of British colonialism and domination. In fact, one of the things I find utterly charming when

I'm over there is hearing the same expressions I remember from when I spent the fifth and sixth grades in the British Army School in Kuala Lumpur. Like "What a cheeky guy." It's as though all those 1950s locutions are locked in time.

India may be showcasing its new industrial stardom, but a measure of civic pride is still waiting to show its face. In most Indian cities, brownouts and blackouts are an everyday occurrence. Generators hum at all the major hotels, while the rest of the city flickers like an old unreliable lightbulb. Just as in Brazil, there's a high level of prosperity, but on the other hand, the images on the street can be a shock if you're not steeled against them—lepers; eunuchs; scrawny cows; ulcerous dogs; people wandering across the highway, barely noticing the oncoming traffic.

For all its problems—its lack of civic cleanliness, its obsession with status and caste and pecking order (have a look sometime at the amazingly detailed and snobbish personal ads in the local newspapers)—India is a fascinating place. Sometimes off-putting, but always fascinating. Even if we hadn't been approached by India's largest retail consulting firm to license a Bangalore office, which has serviced a mix of consumer product manufacturers and technology clients, I ask myself every so often, would I go back there?

Yes—in a heartbeat.

We've taken a U-turn, heading back home. But first a brief sojourn in Moscow. Snowy, sure, gray, sure—but as exciting a destination for retail as exists nowadays. Alexey Pryanishnikov heads our spanking-new Envirosell Moscow office. An avid diver and cyclist, Alexey also has one of the most complete commands of colloquial English I've ever heard—which he claims he's picked up from watching American movies. Our Russian partners are brand new, and as Alexey might say, I think this is the beginning of a beautiful friendship.

Next stop: smoggy, wonderful-as-all-get-out Mexico City. Seventy percent of all market research taking place in Mexico happens here—so if you want to open up an office in this country, you're in the right place. Needless to say, drink all the beer you want, but the water's off-limits except for snorkeling and coral gawking.

In 2002, Manolo Barberena, the well-connected, U.S.-educated son of the former governor of the state of Aguascalientes, approached us on behalf of Pearson, a Mexican full-service market research firm he'd founded. The firm's roots were in political polling, and Manolo also served on the boards of ESOMAR, the European market research trade association, and CASRO, its American counterpart. He had an impressive command of the research business, and among the things I liked best about him was his encyclopedic knowledge of rock 'n' roll. Pearson was already working with Johnson & Johnson and Procter & Gamble, and Envirosell rolled in seamlessly as part of the suite of services that Pearson offered its clients.

Today, our Mexico City branch is one of our most autonomous, classically focused market research offices. Like our colleagues in Brazil, they're extremely proud and extremely capable. One of the things we'd like to see more of in the future is a greater collaboration between our Brazilian and Mexican licensees. There's a language barrier there, both real and imaginary. Or it might just come down to getting two very able overseas heads—one an alpha male, one an alpha female—to work more closely side by side.

Bangalore. Toyko. São Paulo. Moscow. Milan. Mexico City. Despite the leg cramps and the stiff back and the rotten movie we had to endure about the teenage ice-skater, that wasn't so terrible, was it?

I think about it this way: Being able to stand up in front of a U.S. audience and talk about retail overseas is, I believe, one of the things that makes Envirosell distinctive. To be able to address a Midwestern mall owner and say "I was in the new Tokyo Midtown Shopping Mall two weeks ago, and this is what they did," or, "I've been to Dubai five times now, and they look at that problem this way." It's not to be confused with bragging, and I'm pretty sure it doesn't come across that way. It's just a fact of life for a road warrior who's always been fascinated by how the rest of the world ticks.

We've also made a concerted effort to hire employees who speak more than one language. Today in our New York offices, we have people who are fluent in Italian, French, German, Spanish, Japanese, Hindi and a bunch of Asian languages and dialects. I consider having a language skill a critical part of a career in business. If the only language you speak is English, you're frankly at a disadvantage.

I can't help but wish more people felt that way. It bothers me sometimes how downright *uninterested* so many Americans are in leaving our shores and expanding their foreign knowledge base. Or that so many people are scared to travel. Part of it has to do with the shaky times we're living in, but another part comes down to just plain lack of interest. A shame. Especially since one of the true highlights of my life is accompanying either a friend or an Envirosell colleague overseas for the first time. Watching someone I care about discover the third dimension gives me a true kick.

One guy in particular sticks out. His name is Tony Trout. Our destination was Paris, and we were working with the French bank Crédit du Nord. It took Tony about an hour and a half to realize, *Hey, this is fun!* We rode in from Charles de Gaulle airport on the train, switched over to the *métro,* bought our *carnets,* and on the first day of the job, Tony felt completely at ease ordering a coffee at the café next door.

When you arrive in a new place, fold up your old glasses and put on those *gafas, megane, occhiali* or *óculos,* I tell you—doors pop open. Windows appear out of nowhere. I've seen it happen again and again. Traveling someplace new improves your processing skills. It helps sharpen the old tacks. It reminds you that no matter who you are, you'll probably end up coping just fine.

Our next flight is leaving tomorrow afternoon at four—I'll be there waiting at the gate.

NINETEEN

Windows of the World

As I said before, if you're looking for the cutting edge of retail today, you've got to go to places where money is young.

Young as in just hatched, freshly minted, just plain . . . *young*.

In cities like Dublin, Moscow and São Paulo, among others, the retail world belongs to people under the age of forty who have just come into their money, and they're spending it on stuff left and right. By 2010, the vast majority of growth in the retail marketplace will take place in emerging markets, where well-trained merchants are serving emerging customers.

Dubai is a bright and shining example. Maybe you've seen those images of the city's mirage-like skyscrapers and sandy beaches. But did you know Dubai has also transformed itself into a twenty-first-century shopping crossroads? New shopping malls are sprouting up across Dubai like exotic mushrooms, and some are like nothing you've ever seen before. The new Mall of the Emirates has a ski slope, for heaven's sake. Ten bucks' admission gets you a parka and the chance to sip hot chocolate in what must be the world's largest deep-freezer. Seventy bucks rents you skis or a snowboard, a truly hallucinatory experience in midsummer, when the temperature outside hovers around 115 degrees. My favorite new Dubai mall is named after Ibn Battuta, the legendary Islamic traveler. Each section of the mall celebrates a different architecture of the fourteenth-century Islamic world, from the Silk Road to Andalusia. Truly breathtaking, with a history lesson very softly thrown in, too.

In the coastal town of Durban, South Africa, stands Gateway Mall, where among the other retail offerings is a surfing school with a wave machine, as well as a Tony Hawk skateboard park (after all, it is a beach town). So as you're eating your lunch, you get to watch people learn how to re-create *The Endless Summer* or do crazy-eight leaps and spins. My client Old Mutual, a life insurance company, is investing in commercial real estate across Africa and the Middle East. With a dynamic CEO, its young crew of architects, marketers and managers have millions of square feet of malls and town centers both under construction and on the drawing boards. One of its South African malls offers an innovation that's breathtaking in its simplicity: a stadium for high school sports adjacent to the food court. It's secure, it's protected, it's extremely well maintained. And in a sports-mad culture, does it ever drive traffic. It also makes the mall a cool destination for teenagers. For parents it's a winner, too; they can drop their kids off in a sheltered environment, do a little shopping, retrieve their spawn and drive home. Please add South Africa to your global retail tour, and plan on a little wine tasting, too.

After apartheid's cruelty, the new South Africa is an example of the curative properties of economic growth. While crime, corruption and AIDS are a part of any objective portrayal of twenty-first-century South Africa, no one can overlook the growing prosperity, either. I would wish that same prosperity on Kabul, Gaza, Darfur and Baghdad.

Grafton Street in Dublin is the epicenter of Ireland's red-hot retail industry. Thanks to the country's skyrocketing economy, sad old Danny Boy has given way to exultant, stomping Riverdance. Practically everyone you meet in Dublin seems flushed with success. For a long time Grafton Street's anchor has been the venerable department store Brown Thomas, mecca to dowagers and dukes, who make a seasonal pilgrimage there for shopping, lunch and a dose of fashion worldliness beyond the home-grown uniform of tweeds and brogans. And just as Dublin has become one of the hippest, most happening cities in Europe, Brown Thomas has gone through its own transformation. A few years ago, it moved across the street to a bigger, brighter, sleeker location, so today, it's an upmarket, cutting-edge, spanking-new department store, as opposed to, say, a thoughtfully renovated one. As a perfect emblem of Ireland's new prosperity, the new Brown Thomas all but hollers with taste, joy, opportunity and sheer fashionableness. They're selling to thirty-year-olds rather than forty-five-year-olds, and the younger demographic gives sections of the store a nightclub-like vibrancy you'd never find in Bloomingdale's. Do whatever you want to Saks—tear down walls, rejigger the lighting, pipe in Amy Winehouse—but the population base will remain stubbornly conservative. Whereas Brown Thomas is a truly *modern* department store.

But for a store that really takes my breath away—and as a globe-trotting retail wonk, that's never happened until now—I'll take Daslu, in São Paulo. While the owners are presently experiencing tax problems with the Brazilian government, Daslu for the past two decades has been the preeminent purveyor of luxury goods in the world. The new store is a mammoth one-hundred-fifty-thousand-square-foot colossus that functions like a series of artfully linked mansions. Stand back, Louis Vuitton. Too bad, Neiman's. Eat your heart out, Harvey Nicks. You ain't even playing in the same arena, much less the same game.

A Daslu membership card and a no-exceptions valet parking–only policy control access to the store. For cardholders, parking is free; for non-cardholders, parking is exorbitant. The average wait for your car is less than three minutes. Most shoppers are greeted by name, and a concierge positioned in the doorway calls their very own longtime personal shopper to help guide each guest through the store. While the main entrance leads into international fashion labels, guests can also opt for the second entrance, where they can find the Men's Store and a restaurant. If you're a real high-flyer you can also arrive by private helicopter. Walk-in traffic? There is none. A uniformed guard checks the cars off at the end of a gated driveway. But non-cardholders and the curious can take heart. In the past year, within sight of the flagship location across the Rio Pinheiros, Daslu has opened a smaller version of itself in a new luxury mall. There are no female-only floors, and a much smaller men's section, but it's still a sumptuous store.

With its coffee bars, champagne bars, two restaurants and major luxury brands, Daslu feels more like an air-kiss-filled private club. Parts of the store are also strictly gender segregated. Large ceramic Great Danes sit frowningly at Women's Fashion entrances, with NO MEN ALLOWED signs hanging from their necks. Fall in love with a blouse in the women-only parts of the store? You can try it on there at the rack—go right ahead.

The shopper can also shop by assembling her own dressing room. Point to a pair of Manolos and a Chanel suit, and they've instantly found their way to your dressing room in the right size—after all, the store personnel *know* you. The women's dressing area comes equipped with jewelry displays of all the major brands represented in the store, so accessorizing is natural. Want more-more-more? Included in Daslu's suite of services are a plastic surgeon, a salon, an upmarket drugstore, a vacation planner and a real estate department selling homes across the world.

For the guys, apparel and male toys mix and match. Model cars and trains, radio-controlled helicopters and Ferrari-branded laptops. But that's just the small stuff. Enter men's sports apparel and the toys are supersized, from Volvo SUVs to full-sized helicopters. Hey, while we're on the subject, do you happen to like boats? Buy, charter or rent one in any vacation market in the world.

As magnificent as Daslu is, it also serves as a perfect metaphor for the dichotomies of Brazil, where a wealthy population roughly the size of Belgium's is surrounded by poverty on the scale of India's.

In the past ten years, retail innovation is far more likely to have taken place outside of North America than here at home. From Migros in Switzerland to the new Mega Mall built by Ikea outside Moscow, international merchants are applying the lessons learned in North America and outdoing them in the process.

From the perspective of retail design, two critical differences separate American and non-U.S. retailers.

One is how the merchant fits into the culture. Depending on where you live in the world, the merchant's role holds differing degrees of status. In the U.S., retail is mostly a lower-middle-class profession, the price of admission being a little money to get started and a lifetime of hard work. Mr. Bloomingdale was a former schmatte salesman who succeeded beyond his wildest dreams, not a member of the WASP establishment. Sam Walton was a local Arkansas guy. Calvin Klein and Ralph Lauren? Bronx boys, born and bred. Even today, a merchant may operate a successful store, but that doesn't turn him or her into a pillar of the local country club. Not a whole lot of MBAs leave business school, or an Ivy League college, with full-steam-ahead dreams of launching a career in retail. Our business history is largely the story of immigrants who gravitated to retail as one of the few career choices open to them, which, looking back, was key to making American retail as brash and innovative and vibrant as it once was. As the immigrants moved on, however, retail drifted close to its current mostly stale state.

Across the Atlantic and Pacific, it's a different story. The retail merchant enjoys some social respectability. The British and the Dutch, for instance, have long traditions of merchant banking, or of being the middlemen in the buying and selling exchange—thus tying retail into a comfy wealthy establishment. In France you have a merchant class that for five hundred years has been selling to the aristocracy, and that rich history shows up in many different ways. LVMH, the luxury goods company that owns Louis Vuitton, Sephora and some fifty other brands and stores, operates a business school in luxury goods management and hands out the most prestigious MBA in retailing in the world. In Paris, Galleries Lafayette's marketing efforts are light years ahead of any other store in the world. The store starts marketing to you the second you board the plane heading to France. Touch down in Paris and the marketing immediately picks up steam. Arrive at your hotel and you'll be handed a map with Galleries Lafayette prominently placed among the City of Light's innumerable attractions, as well as a reminder that it's a great place for tax-free shopping. Three hours later, you walk through the doors. Do you speak German, Japanese, Dutch? Galleries Lafayette will hook you up with a personal shopper who speaks your language. They'll even change currency for you on the premises, if need be. In short, the store has anticipated every single one of your retail needs, and it does one helluva job of compelling you to shop there.

The other key difference between U.S. retailers and those abroad is topographical: Where does the store sit? Historic and densely populated urban centers create their own retail art forms, from the small to the oversized. The models of operating expenses, margins, staffing and even fixturing costs are well-concealed behind a shroud of history and fierce independence. Italy, for example, has more points of sale per unit of population than any other country in the world. There are a few streets in Milan where one goes specifically and single-mindedly to window-shop. Whenever I do just that, I'm always reminded of the French expression for going window-shopping that translates roughly to "I have to go lick the casements." The closest comparable experience may be the red-light district in Amsterdam. I'm never altogether sure what I've learned from the experience, but I sure feel privileged to have looked. Goods are sold at full price and the service can be professional and intimidating or warm and familiar—it all depends on the store. But overall, the union of window and store is unique, in part because the women on display in the windows are interacting (or at least attempting to) with the people in the street. They're active mannequins—beaming, pouting, gesturing, waving. And because the alleyways are so narrow and pedestrians are so physically close to the windows, window-shopping becomes an intimate, almost voyeuristic experience.

North America has no population concentrations where the social classes historically mix and merge. New York, Boston, Toronto, Philadelphia and Washington, DC, are as close as we get, and even those five cities have historically been in transition, with changing land and population and real estate values. But urban retailing is hot and is only going to get hotter as the American urban core gentrifies. Our American merchant class is also transforming around us. If we've given Europe giants such as McDonald's and Starbucks, well, they've got something to show us, too.

• • •

All across the world, developers are taking a long hard look at what
makes a great shopping environment work. Along with entertainment,
the shopping mall is one of our most successful U.S.-born-and-bred ex-
ports. You can now find malls all over the world, from Kuala Lumpur to
Dubai, from Tokyo to Lisbon. On the surface, some of them may look
the same as ours, but don't be fooled for a second. Every country faces
and has to cope with its own local manners, cultural codes and personal
boundaries. In South Africa, Brazil and Mexico, malls face security issues that we don't have here in the U.S., so in these countries, a mall isn't
just a place to shop and ogle other people, but, as in the high-end case
of Daslu, it also serves as a protected fiefdom, a super-insulated private
club.

Iguatemi in São Paulo is a great example of a hybrid mall—one that
links the malls we're all familiar with in the U.S. with local roots and
solutions. São Paulo is a dangerous place, so it's no surprise that one of
the first things you notice when you step through the doors of Iguatemi
are the security guards. These aren't first-timers or retired, sore-legged
guys on mall-rat patrol. These hard-eyed hawks have a martial edge
about them, and they mean business. The second thing you notice is
how inexplicably joyful you feel simply observing the human circus on
parade. It's a social setting that no American or European mall could
ever replicate. I'm glad I've come here at my age, because if I'd been a
regular visitor to Iguatemi when I was in my twenties, I know I would
have fallen crazy in love every ten minutes. It's not the stores at Iguatemi that are so interesting or special, it's the physical environment.
Within the context of Brazilian culture, most adult children live at home
until they get married. If you want to go out on the town, your choices
are limited—a restaurant, nightclub or, yes, a shopping mall. Thus, a trip
to Iguatemi offers Brazilian twentysomethings a setting in which they
can see, meet and otherwise hang out with contemporaries of a similar
social class, and in a safe place that's open day and night. U.S. malls may
provide social opportunities for the under-eighteen crowd, but it's the
rare twenty-five-year-old guy who hangs out in front of J.C. Penney or

Hollister hoping to chat up women. But in Brazil, if you're twenty-five, and you can't entertain at home (Mom and Dad are lurking nearby, ears cocked), the mall is a logical place to go.

Iguatemi is loud—gloriously loud. In part this is because the corridors and concourses are narrow, and also because in a hot climate, stone and tile flooring help keep the temperature in check. But the racket itself comes from the echo, clatter, click and clack of female high heels. I could watch Brazilians walk from here to Alaska without getting bored. They seem to have their own internal jukebox, and it's always playing some swaying, samba-heavy playlist.

Amid the high-heeled sandals, spike heels, mules, miniskirts and short shorts, Iguatemi works at being a solution to all your utilitarian needs—something an American landlord might want to bear in mind. Watch strap broken? Need a duplicate house key? Want to book a flight to the States or pick up your dry cleaning? You're in the right place.

Blockbuster Mexico, the video store, offers the same degree of security mixed in with social spectacle, family style. When you drive in, you confront a threefold line of defense: the parking lot, the door and the register. Blockbuster, like a shopping mall, is only viable here because it protects against the insecurity on the street. Latin families tend to be a close-knit bunch—they like to spend time with one another—so Blockbuster Mexico tends to be packed with extended families. In fact, the stores are jammed from early on a Friday afternoon right through into Friday evening. One time, we saw a representative from Philips showing off the company's new home theater inside a Mexican Blockbuster, simply because that's where the people are. Smart idea. Anybody in the U.S. ever considered it?

When Blockbuster Mexico asked me to come down and do some consulting work, I said sure, absolutely, but I had one request—that the executive board visit the stores with me over the course of a weekend. But, but, Paco, they replied, we've never been in a store on a weekend! We're out at our country houses!

Again, this is an issue I run into over and over—top-level execs busy crunching numbers but never even once bothering to visit the actual floor. I remember once leading the top brass of a U.S. carmaker into the ladies' room of a European dealership, where, naturally, they'd never set foot. The room was gloomy and unkempt and in overall shabby shape. "Would you *really* want your wife peeing in a room like this?" I asked. They shook their heads—no, of course not. The point here is they had no idea. Even at Dublin's Brown Thomas, led by its dynamic, straight-out-of-central-casting CEO Paul Kelly, I stumbled onto a disconnect between top brass and the actual store experience. A dazzling store, Brown Thomas, as I said, and one that, like most good retailers, made a concerted effort to focus on the unique qualities of Brown Thomas people—the staff, which makes any department store special.

Once I'd gotten the party line, Paul Kelly gave me the keys to the store and told me to go poke around and see what he could be doing better. A day later, I escorted him into the store's female employee locker room. It looked like a barracks for female Navy SEALS. Slim green lockers, stark lighting, uncomfortable benches and three narrow mirrors. Just God-awful.

Twenty minutes before the store opens, that grim locker room has literally hundreds of women in it. That's where Brown Thomas people—and Brown Thomas customer service—start. Paul even murmured that the locker room he used thirty years earlier at Trinity College down the street had more amenities. Knowing him, I have no doubt he fixed the problem.

One of the easiest ways to gauge a store's morale is to take a look at the amenities and spaces it provides its employees. This doesn't mean you have to have a paid babysitter or masseuse on staff, but it does require a little care and attention backstage.

At the start of our relationship with our Mexican office, I came face-to-face with one of the most intriguing business models I've ever seen, a consumer electronics chain known as Elektra. Today they operate about nine hundred stores, do roughly a billion dollars a year in sales and have expanded their presence into Guatemala, Peru and Honduras. In the commonly used economic rating system, with Neiman Marcus being an A and Wal-Mart hovering around the C, D and E regions, Elektra serves the C and D markets (these letters refer to the income level of the shoppers). It targets—and helps give a much-needed boost to—the hardworking poor and emerging middle class.

Bet you've never heard of it. Most people north of the border haven't, and that's no doubt because its consumer base doesn't straddle the top of the economic ladder. But Elektra has come up with an innovative lending-and-buying system I still shake my head over. Why? It's that good. And it dovetails with Mexico's growing prosperity.

In the Latin market, if someone walks in and can prove they have a home, a job and a mailing address, Elektra will lend that person the money to outfit their lives. In return, the customer agrees to make a small weekly cash payment. That said, the entire family takes responsibility for the loan. In essence, it's a bank wrapped up in a consumer appliance and department store.

The storefront is open like a garage, with merchandise spilling out every which way onto the sidewalk. The way into Elektra and the way out are pathways lined floor-to-ceiling with your next purchases, though the payment bunker, which is located far to the rear of the store, is utterly no-nonsense, with insulated walls and bulletproof windows. It's an intuitive system, and as a vehicle for social progress, it's off-the-charts innovative.

The first thing a customer might buy? A refrigerator. The second? A stove. Third comes the TV set, fourth the washing machine. Throw in a boom box, a good mattress and box spring plus a set of nice-looking furniture, and Elektra has outfitted your whole house—and given your whole family a leg up on the social and economic ladder. They've also set you up with a checking and savings account and let you choose among a full line of insurance products. Have a family member who is working in the U.S.? That person can make an online contribution to your Elektra account. Which means you can just maybe pay off your Elektra loan sooner and move up to your next purchase, whether it's that boom box or that bedside table. As you ascend the ladder, Elektra is by your side every minute, holding your hand, pointing the way.

Does the company charge high interest rates? Absolutely. But Elektra is also enabling social mobility. They're lending money not to a single person but to an entire household, including extended family.

The company's bad debt ratio? Remarkably tiny. A lot less than for your typical bank. So it's a win-win for Elektra, for Latin families, and for the entire Latin American standard of living.

Genius.

This isn't to say that all the fun is taking place abroad or that retail innovation is solely an international phenomenon.

A few promising U.S. concerns have picked up the slack. A dying mall outside of Fort Worth, Texas, has now been transformed into La Gran Plaza, a Latino mall with its own mariachi band and a former Dillard's anchor that today houses a vast and ever-changing *mercado*. It has a movie complex playing Spanish movies, a school that teaches people how to apply for mortgages and a new industry that marries a dental clinic to a jewelry store so that dental jewelry (known as a "grille" in hip-hop parlance) can be customized. It knows its market, doesn't try to be all things to all people and is an overall knockout.

Fairway on 12th Avenue in Harlem is located in an old warehouse which is shopped by a broad cross-section of New Yorkers—everyone from firemen to housewives stocking up on cheese to local Harlem mothers to businessmen bringing dinner home en route to the Westchester suburbs. Platinum Amex cards appear one moment, followed by food stamps the next. Fairway is a great show, an exhilarating adventure. Visit the coffee section and the roaster yells down to you which blend he just finished freshly grinding. Want a steak or a roast chicken for dinner? Wrap yourself in a quilted silver jacket to shop the refrigerated goods section, where instead of steaming cold cases, an entire room is one big chill.

Which leads me to a point that is always good to remember: Successful retail experiences are run by placemakers, not landlords. Whether it's peacocks, a strolling Dixieland jazz band or mermaids, they have to find a way to make their locations *exciting*. It's no coincidence that most owners and progressive developers across North America have begun knocking on the doors of marketing consulting firms. With the frequency of visits and average time spent in malls declining, they're starting to recognize that the answers aren't going to be found by crunching census data or looking at sales per square foot. Public spaces, seating, bathrooms and parking lots outside your doors are just as critical to sales as pricing and visual merchandising.

One place doesn't have to serve all people, and I'm not talking about ethnicity, either. You can have a mall that's focused on young families, a mall for teenagers and even a mall that takes especially tender loving care of its elderly. I can almost guarantee that every single member of these constituencies would thank you from the bottoms of their young, stroller-pushing or older, white-sneakered hearts.

Since this book came out in its original edition, I have had more opportunities than ever to travel. Today, I'm on the road approximately 150 days a year. One bonus of Envirosell's international licensing agreements is that I get to spend a certain amount of time with each of Envirosell's overseas licensees. Nothing could give me greater pleasure.

Today, I have more than four million frequent flyer miles, give or take a few thousand. Give me a little time off and I'll opt to stay at home. But a few days later, I just can't help it—I start to get itchy. In the world of road warriors there are people who travel more nights than I do, but I know of very few who carry off the roller-coaster time changes. The bags under my eyes are well earned, and that aisle seat over there? You can't have it, it's mine.

TWENTY

Final Thoughts

When you think about it, people have been selling, buying and trading goods since we left the caves, quarries and campsites of East Africa and set off on our various migrations across the world. A few years ago, I had a humbling experience as I listened to a Turkish vegetable cart operator tell me how he organized and laid out his daily wares. He talked about sun angles, about the order in which consumers readied their vegetables for cooking and about what was going on in their minds when they decided whether to buy eggplants or tomatoes first. He had opinions about where he should stand in relation to his vegetable cart and the best ways to interact with a wide variety of prospective customers. I could have listened to him forever. As he spoke, I could hear echoes of his ancestors, and his ancestors' ancestors. It was an enlightening monologue—all the more so since not one out of every fifty store managers I've ever encountered could have duplicated it.

It reminded me again that the science of shopping is hardly new. Along with fight-or-flight and how our brains regulate the air we breathe, shopping is practically in our species' DNA. Fact is, it may have been the first way a human could get ahead in the social hierarchy beyond competing based on size, strength or speed.

For a moment, let's consider Istanbul, a city that sits at one of most ancient cultural crossroads in history. Turks as a people come in all colors, shapes and sizes, and as you make your way through the crowded covered streets, you see evidence of a kaleidoscopic genetic mix in people's faces and inhale a variety of crisscrossing smells—body odor, hair tonic, pungent spices and aromas from countless foods, all dusted across an oriental carpet of noise—tinny music, shrill chirping children, the cloying ministrations of the young men at the shop front imploring you to come in. The Grand Bazaar is more than five hundred years old, and it's a challenge staying put in the present. Most of the store windows have elaborate displays of gold jewelry, barrels of spices, boxes of colored henna and signs. Lots and lots of signs, too—from state-of-the-art LED, to aging neon, to fly-specked lifestyle graphics that look like they've been around since the turn of the twentieth century. But one common sight you see almost everywhere is an Internet address. Yeah, the Grand Bazaar itself has its own website, which allows you to pre-shop and to contact merchants directly. The merger of bricks and clicks is right in front of you in a city that has hosted traders and shoppers for more than three thousand years.

Looking for far-flung visitors? They're not hard to spot. This city has played host to strangers since time immemorial. Turkey brushes up against many of the former Soviet republics and attracts visitors from what used to be the corners of the Ottoman Empire. Turkey is an inexpensive, go-to vacation spot for middle-class Germans (the two countries date their relationship back to the 1920s).

The Grand Bazaar merchants have also anticipated the needs and concerns of the tourist trade. The food stores advertise Iranian caviar ready to travel home with you in your checked luggage—sealed in dry-ice packages to ensure complete confidence in your purchase. The local saffron vendor even offers shoppers a course in quality, which he conducts several times an hour. He mixes different grades of saffron in bowls of water, then stands back as you coo over the various hues and richnesses of color. He moves product as well or better than any other salesman I've ever seen.

Whether it's the Grand Bazaar in Istanbul or the Gold Souk in Dubai, the rules and tools of trading are as old as the hills. I once went with a friend to fix a computer at an electronics repair shop in Ankara, the Turkish capital. We walked in, had tea with the proprietor, asked after family, talked about the weather and the local soccer matches. The price for the repair went from the equivalent of fifty dollars as we entered to seven dollars as we left.

Much of what this book is about is the eternals of shopping—and also common sense. Still, if twenty years ago you told me that someday I'd be a generally acknowledged expert on how women shop for cosmetics—and by dint of having spent countless hours observing them while they do just that—I'd have called your shrink. Ditto if you had predicted that I'd become a scholar of the dynamics that govern the fast-food drive-thru line. In fact, I'm still a little discomfited when, in a corporate conference room, I hear myself being deferred to as the senior researcher. Most people who spend their lives in retailing do so thanks to some merchant gene. Still, I'm grateful to have found a path to it. My colleagues and I have been bitten by a strange bug—none of us are businesspeople, and yet we spend an awful lot of our waking hours untangling the problems and issues that beset the world of people, spaces, products and service. We can't walk down a shopping street, read a restaurant menu or walk through an airport without deconstructing the experience and trying to figure out how it could be improved. The merchants in my neighborhood are tired of all the free advice I proffer. When Dreamboat and I go on vacations, she has to remind me to turn off the automatic analyzer device in my brain. Even then I'll end up leading us into a mall, just to poke around a bit. Unlike Margaret Mead, I don't have to go far to perform a little fieldwork.

The science of shopping is a hybrid discipline—part physical science, part social science, and only part science at all, for it is also partly an art. But it is a practical field, concerned with providing information that can improve a merchant's or marketer's edge and cut the odds of making a wrong decision. Our value lies in our ability to go beyond merely collecting data to make good educated guesses about what it means and how to respond. While I can say that most of the time we have been proven right in our interpretations, we have been wrong sometimes, too. And so we keep searching. Even our most senior management people spend ninety nights a year on the road, devoting their weekends to stores, banks, restaurants and malls all over the world. It's been hell on our personal lives, I assure you.

And even with all that, the truth in the science of shopping is transitory. The basic facts of human anatomy remain, more or less, but the store itself and the tastes and behaviors of the shopper continue to evolve. Just as the farmer of 1900 had more in common with his agrarian ancestors of a millennium before than with his agritechnician grandson of 1950, the merchant of 1900 would have a lot of catching up to do today. If we look back just to the '70s, we see that many of the leading retailers of the period are gone now or greatly diminished. Korvettes, Woolworth's, Montgomery Ward—all are now consigned to the history books, and many others will follow shortly. Might Wal-Mart stumble, will Starbucks fade, will Topshop ever go global? It's a changing world. In the olden days, the adage held that with the right product at the right price, success was assured. Today you need those elements nailed down just to hope for mere survival. Today everybody is competing with everybody else, and so the threat can come from any direction. It is dangerously narrow-minded for a store owner to believe that the only competition is from others in his or her category. In truth, retailers compete with every other demand on consumer time and money. Recently we've been hired to study patrons in movie theaters, which just reminds us that two hours and $20 spent in a cinema are forever lost to the rest of retailing. Likewise, if the experience of spending twenty minutes of unused lunch hour browsing in a computer store is more enjoyable than visiting a bookstore, then it becomes likely that some software will be sold—and impossible that a book will be. The era of the visionary retailer or the manufacturing king is over. In the twenty-first century the consumer is king. Just as fashion comes from the street up, the world of retail is about following shoppers where they are going.

First and foremost, shopping follows social change, and woe to the businessperson who fails to comprehend this. Without a doubt, the major social change playing itself out during our time has to do with the lives of women. In his lectures, esteemed social critic, researcher and futurist Watts Wacker makes the point that, based on the current evidence, men are on their way to becoming exotic household pets. Retail must pay attention to how women wish to live, what they want and need, or it will be left behind. Even the enormous changes in the lives of men and children are merely in response to the lead taken by women. It pays to listen and be humble. Shoppers are fickle today, and their loyalty to brand name—whether of a product or a store—lasts only as long as the afterglow of the most recent shopping experience.

If bad results in one fiscal quarter send shock waves through a national retail chain, two or three sour quarters is lifeboat time. The best defense against complacency is to eliminate the distance between the floor of the store and the men and women who make the decisions about what happens there. The most intelligent management decree today is to push more responsibility and authority down to the store manager level. Senior brass must develop the tools for teaching managers how to make sure the store is serving the shoppers. In 1998, I told a largely male executive group at Wal-Mart that I could tell the gender of the manager in any of their stores based solely on how recently the women's dressing room had been painted. I don't know if I am responsible, but a few months later, I noticed that lots of Wal-Mart dressing rooms had gotten spiffy new paint jobs. Male managers hate the soft goods sections, because like cosmetics, they eat up labor costs and are more likely to have theft problems, whereas hard goods such as TVs and minifridges are easier to get onto the shelf and are much easier to keep track of. Women by nature have a better understanding of how soft goods work and what they can do for the business. Ten years after I made my dressing room comment, Wal-Mart still has an underdeveloped clothing business. One simple way of improving it would be to increase the number of female store managers.

Even with all there is to be learned from the science of shopping, we recognize that there is room for a creative merchant to throw the textbook to the wind and break all the rules. You'd think a basic tenet of retail is that shoppers should be able to say the name of your store. But I have a friend who owns a highly successful web business, run out of his tiny store. It's called Mxyplyzyk, an intentionally unpronounceable appellation taken from a rather obscure character in Superman comics. It's a crowded place filled with an eclectic mix of products, from bathroom fixtures to books, and the price points roam all over the map. The checkout process is primitive and the receipts are handwritten. But I can't teach Kevin, the owner, a single thing about retail—he's invented a selling machine in his own image, and it looks like he's having a great time with it. For all the science we preach, we realize that if you've got the moxie, you might have the moves.

As professional observers, we play a strange role in the world of commerce. I joke that I'm the only person in the retailing industry who's delighted to witness shoplifting. It shows that we're able to confound the Heisenberg principle and observe people in stores without altering their behavior. After all, if someone shoplifts in front of a team of trackers, it means that person hasn't noticed we're there (on the rare occasions we get busted, usually it's by some sharp-eyed kid). Some of my most vivid memories, in fact, involve thievery. I remember studying the video of a well-dressed matron at the fragrance counter of Filene's Basement on Washington Street in Boston. She repeatedly dispatched the respectful clerk on missions to distant parts of the section while she loaded up her tote bag with bottles of perfume from the counter. Actually, we commonly see well-dressed shoplifters buy one product, then steal another. At a drugstore in Spartanburg, South Carolina, our trackers kept finding individual disposable diapers (clean ones) tucked into odd corners of the store. The mystery was cleared up when they saw a shopper filling a half-empty diaper package with large jars of a pricey headache remedy. Our most pathetic shoplift sighting involved a father who tucked a screwdriver set into his sleeping infant's diaper.

But our job is like that of the crew on *Star Trek*—we're there to observe and report but not interfere.

We preserve the privacy of those we videotape, as a way of keeping faith with our ultimate patron, the shopping public. Given that my roots as a researcher are based in public advocacy, I am very sensitive to questions of invasion of privacy in our work. I was appalled when one of the first major magazine stories on Envirosell called us "supermarket spies." A few years back, BBC radio invited me to appear on an hour-long call-in talk show. Glad to participate, I said. But when I called in, I was surprised to find they'd set up a small ambush of sorts. The other guest? An expert in consumer advocacy. The topic? Privacy.

Now, whatever you do, don't slap the George Orwell *1984* thing on me. If you believe Envirosell's store cameras are intruding on people's privacy, then let's first take a stroll through the streets of London, and we'll find our faces showing up on just a few of the city's roughly five hundred thousand closed-circuit cameras, many of which are hooked up to facial recognition software—just a small portion of the seven million cameras softly clicking away all across the U.K.

If London is outside your reach, we can log on to the web instead. In ten minutes, I can find out how much money you make, your political party affiliation, what books you've taken out of the public library, what your arrest record is, if any, and the names and phone numbers of your neighbors. Heck, I can Google-map your house from a satellite and see if there's smoke coming out of your chimney.

Our cameras are hooked up to a supermarket, department store or bank. I'm not interested in who you are, what your name is, what your phone number is, where you live or whether you own a golden retriever or a guppy or a hive of bees. All I'm interested in is shopping patterns. To me, you're Shopper #X3. You're wearing worn jeans, a Rock and Roll Hall of Fame T-shirt and a well-broken-in pair of boat shoes.

And that's it.

Some colleagues have suggested that by writing this book I run the risk of giving up all our secrets—that a company could read these lessons and skip hiring us. But this book is only a start in a certain direction. A business that pays attention to its customers probably already practices many of the things I discuss in this book. It's always more satisfying for us to work with companies that are headed in the right direction. Our clients invariably have two observations about the findings we present. The first is that our research seems to confirm what common sense already tells us about how people shop, that once we deliver our report the lightbulb snaps on and you realize that gosh, *of course* you knew (somewhere, in the back of your mind) that a shopper holding a coat and a handbag is not going to be able to select as much merchandise as one whose hands are free. It even strikes us as incredibly simple—once we've spent a few days actually observing shoppers and counting how many things they buy and then comparing that by hands-free and hands-full. In other words, once we've proven it scientifically, it suddenly seems as though you knew it all along, which is a good sign, I think. Science is supposed to make sense. Until then, however, all the common sense in the world didn't induce many retailers to improve the way they provided shoppers with baskets. This issue is still stupendously mishandled by most stores, even those owned by highly sophisticated retail behemoths.

The other common observation is that many of the recommendations we make are more like fine-tuning than dramatic renovation—but when you implement a dozen little changes throughout a store, you sometimes find you've improved an awful lot. As I like to say, in a world where marketing focuses on strategy, tactics are being ignored.

For example, I mentioned in Chapter 1 that older women were being ill-served by drugstore cosmetics sections, where less-than-glamorous products such as concealer cream were stocked down near the floor, literally forcing shoppers to their knees. In fact, we had collected some video showing older shoppers crawling in order to browse the category—images that were truly poignant, I think, and ultimately effective. While some cosmetics planograms have been changed to accommodate the mature shopper, I have footage shot in 2005 that is virtually identical to clips from twelve years earlier—the older woman struggling to get down on her knees to find her product. Yes, moving the products two feet higher has made a big difference in consumer comfort and sales. Yet even now we see the same mistakes happening over and over.

A decade or so ago, we were hired to study how people shop for flowers at a supermarket in Australia. Sales in the department were much lower than anticipated until we saw why: The method of display—large plastic vats holding many flowers—was mystifying to shoppers. No one could figure out how much the flowers cost or whether they were sold by the bunch or the blossom. And masses of blossoms in large vats gave shoppers no sense of what the flowers would look like once they got them home. In other words, the simplest matters had not been sufficiently thought out. The display was especially forbidding to the occasional flower buyer, which is most of us. A few small changes were made—individual bunches were displayed in front of the large vats, prices were more clearly marked—and suddenly flowers were flying out of the store.

The fact that a minor alteration can bring a large improvement should come as no surprise. After all, science is by and large the study of very small differences. Sometimes critical truths are discovered in this way. Charles Darwin went about measuring the length of birds' bills, which is pretty small work even by our standards. But from his studies came a fundamental shift in our theories about living things and why they thrive or fail. Darwin's main finding sounds like common sense, too—the idea that successful organisms are the ones that best adapt to their environment. In stores something similar happens, except that it's the environment that must adapt to the organism.

All this is a little high-minded for a world as workaday as retailing. But stores and shopping have never been one-dimensional. Going back even to the dawn of shopping, to the days of rudimentary barter or the open-air marketplace, there has been, for example, a social aspect to shopping that has nothing to do with buying and selling. Shopping is an activity that brings people together. When women were slaves to household work, it got them out of the house. In more primitive times shopping was an occasion for people to gather and do the things they do in groups, like talk and exchange news and gossip and opinions. Shopping still serves that purpose. Today, when people work at jobs that require

them to be out of the home and in the company of other people, perhaps there is less of a social kick in shopping. But as we wander through
the store or the mall, examining goods, we are permitted to more or less
openly examine each other, people-watching being a supremely satisfying pastime, whether in the Middle Ages or today.

Shopping is a form of entertainment, just like the movies or the
zoo. The trend today only emphasizes that function. Williams-Sonoma,
Whole Foods, or Selfridges in London—these retail sites raise the bar
every day. Once upon a time, only Woolworth's and the local drugstore
brought shopping and eating together under the same roof. Now, within
minutes of my office, I can go from a bookstore with a coffee bar to a
home furnishings store to a clothing store with a lunch counter to a
bank where there is an urn of hot coffee (gratis) for customers. When
you visit the Hard Rock Café, the Harley-Davidson Café, or a Cracker
Barrel off the interstate, it's difficult to decide whether you're in a restaurant with a gift shop or a store with food. The distinction no longer
even matters—selling (and therefore shopping) is taking place.

Great public repositories of culture and learning, museums and
opera houses and zoos, were established by the fortunes of virtuous,
civic-minded tycoons of an earlier age. As the tycoons died off, these
institutions kept afloat on contributions from virtuous, civic-minded
corporations. Today, most museums have discovered that there is a
dependable stream of independent income to be had by going retail—
that is, by creating opportunities for serious shopping, stores that offer
everything from pencils for a quarter to jewelry, art and artifacts selling for thousands of dollars. Now the shoppers get to feel virtuous
and civic-minded, knowing that their spending supports such worthy
endeavors. Still, this is simply more retailing going on, and of an innovative nature. (Cannily, museums usually locate their shops by the
front door, so that one may go in and buy without having to pay an
entrance fee or actually confront an exhibit.) Museum shopping has
become so popular among well-educated, cultured customers that we
now see businesses like the Museum Store—in essence, museum stores
without the museum.

At some level we treat stores as though they *are* museums—places to learn about what interests us, whether it's the latest manifestation of high fashion, or innovations in computer software, or the state of the art in automobile carburetors, or what's new in crime novels. To many, the arrival of the spring couture collections at Saks is akin to the opening of a new blockbuster exhibit at the Museum of Modern Art. Ten years ago, when the first edition of this book came out, I met with the CFO of Lincoln Center (our old client from Time, Inc.), who had uncovered from some dusty file the report I generated more than twenty-five years ago, the one referenced earlier in this book, about managing traffic flow and retail at his cultural complex. His point was, "We're ready now." Consider the store design trend that has forsaken distant merchandise behind glass in favor of "open" displays—tables and racks of goods that customers can browse and examine up close—and ask yourself: Is this so different from a museum? Packaging trends, too, acknowledge their thirst for learning. Never before has there been so much information printed on the boxes, bottles and jars we buy.

It is not too far-fetched to say even that stores have become places of worship—sites for the exaltation of man-made things, temples where we can express and reaffirm and share our belief in self-improvement, beauty, knowledge or fun. It's no coincidence that of the two main holidays on the Christian calendar, Christmas and Easter, it is the former—the one with the greatest shopping potential—that every year becomes less exclusively religious and more secular, not to mention commercial. For most retailers, Christmas is make-or-break—the annual arrival of a savior, if you will.

Shopping is a universal experience. But our job is still the same: to suss out the parts that are universal from Paris to Toyko, and what parts are eternal, biologically-based elements like sight, right-handedness and gender. To figure out what's changing, and why that is. The merchant community of today no longer leads but has to follow. As I mentioned earlier in this chapter, shopping is a good dipstick of social change, and even, dare I say it, social revolution. So what does it mean when H&M and Steve and Barry's both invent cheap disposable clothing that everyone wears? Why are farmers' markets booming? Women now own homes—how does that alter the landscape? What are the implications for bricks-and-mortar store design as a result of the convergence of the online world and the mobile phone?

I hope this volume has polished your glasses and that it sends you back into your own world to look at things a little differently. Thanks for reading.

ACKNOWLEDGMENTS

As I graduated from college in the spring of 1975, one whole wall of my dorm room was plastered with rejection letters from literary magazines. What would have happened if just one thing had been accepted? I wanted to be a writer.

Instead, I went to New York City and, as this book chronicles, did other things, though I still scribbled things on the side. In 1979, *Unmuzzled OX* published one of my short stories in an anthology called *The Poet's Encyclopedia*. Living in the midst of the downtown arts scene in New York, I was thrilled to have something to my name. Over the years I published articles in trade journals and wrote a chapter or two for books that have long since disappeared. My biggest literary payday was two hundred dollars. Which wasn't to say I didn't write, but it was research reports and lots and lots of proposals.

Ironically, the origins of this book are rooted in the magazine world. Two eminent journalists have been instrumental in transforming my career. Erik Larsen, author of many nonfiction bestsellers, wrote the first profile of Envirosell and yours truly for a 1993 issue of *Smithsonian* magazine. After the piece appeared, Envirosell was no longer function-ing under the radar. Then, in the summer of 1996, shortly after we moved to our new offices at the corner of Twentieth and Broadway, a slight, curly-headed man turned up at our door saying that he was a science journalist now working for *The New Yorker.* I almost called the magazine to ask if they had someone named Malcolm Gladwell on staff. As I mention in these pages, Gladwell's piece, entitled "The Science of Shopping," came out in the fall of 1996 and changed Envirosell's for-tunes for the better.

No longer would I not know how to prioritize phone messages from strangers. Hundreds of people sent in résumés asking if they could work with us. As a shy, bald, bearded stutterer (whom Malcolm describes in his *New Yorker* piece as "almost goofy-looking"), I was invited to confer-ences and seminars, and countless newspapers and magazines suddenly wanted to talk to me. And talk is what I've done. I spend eight hours a week with the press. I listen, answer questions, give facts if I know them and opinions if I don't.

In the wake of the *New Yorker* piece, the idea of a book took on a different meaning. My old friend Alexandra Anderson Spivey introduced me to Glen Hartley and his partner and wife, Lynn Chu, at Writer's Representatives and they became my agents. Their attention has been invaluable. Amid their client list, I feel like a fat copper penny in a lineup of gold doubloons. At one point they had five books on the *New York Times* nonfiction bestseller list.

Alice Mayhew has been my editor at Simon & Schuster for over a decade. I've watched her recast American history from books on the presidents to popular opuses on World War II. I've often wondered why she chooses to work with me, but never to her face. I am just glad for her wit, strong eye and steely intellect.

Bill Tonelli, a veteran magazine editor, helped make this book hap-pen. He's a stylin' guy and a kind and gentle soul. Peter Smith, the son of my favorite high school English teacher and a contributing editor at *O, the Oprah Magazine,* has shepherded this rewrite. My assistant Angela Mauro has been a patient reader and tireless contributor.

Bits and pieces of this revised manuscript have appeared in columns

I have written for *DDI* magazine and *The Conference Board Review,* under the respective editorial guidance of RoxAnna Sway and Vadim Liberman.

No one gets very far in the business world without friends and mentors. Richard Kurtz was my first market research teacher. Mitch Wolf provided early and valuable guidance. Both remain fixtures in my life. Today I have clients with whom I've worked for more than fifteen years. I appreciate the courage it took to buy our services the first time around, when we were a very exotic and risky purchase. Jim Lucas, now at Draft; Mike Ernest at Hanesbrands; Kevin Kitatkoski, now at Johnson & Johnson; Robin Pearl at Estée Lauder; Steven Smith at Hewlett-Packard; Linda Thompson at Microsoft; Tom Cook at King-Casey; Joe Gallo at Verizon Wireless; Ernesto Diaz at Sam's Club; and Kris Loukusa, now at T-Mobile, are just a few. Others, like Wilton Connor and Bob Cecil, have retired, or are just missing from this list.

The store design community and the Retail Design Institute have been seminal in Envirosell's success. Namely, Ken Nisch at JGA in Detroit, Kevin Kelley at Shook Kelley in Los Angeles, Andrew McQuilkin at RRCH in Cincinnati, Joe Nevin at Bergmeyer Associates in Boston, Denny Gerdeman and his wife Elle Chute at Chute Gerdeman in Columbus, Russell Sway from Sway Associates in Atlanta and last but not least, Monk Askew in Baltimore.

The corresponding community is made up of the designers and visual merchandisers at the stores themselves. Judy Bell at Target, Christine Belich at Sony Style, Michael Cape at Old Navy, James Damian at Best Buy, Janis Healy at West Marine, Glen Russell at Sears Holdings, Charles Zimmerman at Wal-Mart and Carmen Spofford at Federated are just a few who have tendered their support over the years.

We have a treasure chest of believers from Philips, Microsoft, Pepsi-Co, adidas and Unilever who have fallen over our transom and become part of our fiber over the past eight years. Most showed up thanks to this book, ready to hit the ground running.

As is the case with all consultants, I have colleagues with whom I exchange information, war stories and leads. Wendy Liebmann at WSL Strategic Retail is a goddess, Watts Wacker is a court jester, Marc Gobe is the eminent designer, Faith Popcorn is the trend spotter, Marshal Cohen is the retail sound-bite master, Kate Newlin is the reinventor and George Whalin is the wise coach. All are friends with whom I share e-mails, phone calls and good vibes.

I describe myself as a refugee from the academic world. That said, I have a few good friends still scattered across the teaching universe: Marianne Wolf at Cal Poly in San Luis Obispo, Doc Ogden at Kutztown University, Ray Burke at Indiana University and my buddy Joe Weishar at FIT here in New York.

In the early days of Envirosell, I quipped that the major criterion for working with me was that you had to be an interesting person, so that if we got stranded at O'Hare we'd have stuff to talk about. Three people from that first generation of Envirosellers remain: Tom Moseman, Craig Childress and Anne-Marie Luthro. I am grateful for their years of service. All three have some connection to the University of Iowa—go figure.

The international chapters in this edition profile most of our foreign partners. I have no shortage of colleagues who live outside the USA. Abdullah Sharif from Dubai, Kenji Onodera from Tokyo, Alan O'Neill from Dublin, Jean-Pierre Baade from Paris and Mark Gillian in the Philippines are, again, just a few. United Artists, our gurus' club, is made up of José Luis Nueno from Spain, David Bosshart from Switzerland, Martin Lindstrom from Denmark and Kjell Nordstrom from Sweden. We meet twice a year to eat, drink and talk. Those sessions are always the highlights of my year.

I also have the family that God assigned to me and the families I've chosen: my sister, Lisa, her husband Michael and their kids, Gabriel and Miranda; my mother, Savie; Paul and Kate Raymer and their kids; and others linked by blood and marriage. The three families who adopted and cared for me for more than thirty years are the Haymans, the Hewitts and the Lehners.

Every boy has his buds, and mine come in both genders. Joseph Guglietti, Rob Kaufelt, John Barkley, Patrick Rodmell, Hazam Gamal, Peter Kay, Stan Beck, Terry Shook, John Ryan, Rob LoCascio and Rick Moffitt are the guys, and Erika Szychowski, Haesook Kim, Sara Bowen, Dacota Julson, Medora Barkley, Susan Towers and Liz Gamal are the ladies.

My lovely significant only, Sheryl Henze, is an accomplished flautist who works nights and weekends. This book was constructed within those time periods in order to stay out of trouble.

INDEX

Ace Hardware, 113
activated fixtures, 222
add-on sales, 57, 191–92, 214–16
adjacencies, 93, 129, 154, 162, 214–19
advertising, 25, 64, 74, 220, 222; online, 235, 242; store itself as most important medium for, 25–26, 63
Aeropostale, 86
air conditioners, 179–80
airline tickets, 236
airports, 74, 127, 146
Amazon, 231–33, 237, 238, 243–44
American Girl Place, 58, 106
Anheuser-Busch, 59
Anthropologie, 86
Apple, 189, 215; iTunes and, 231, 249–51, 252
appliances, 113, 179–80, 245
arena concept, 33
art galleries, 30–31
artworks, sold online, 239
Asian shoppers, 35, 177
aspirin, 21–22, 139
AT&T phone stores, 159–60, 192
athleticwear, 148
ATMs, 145, 199
Auchan, 200
Audi, 48

baby-changing stations, 117, 135
baby products, 103, 118
baby strollers, aisle width and, 152–53
back wall, getting shoppers to, 85–87

Balkan Beat Box, 249–50
Banco Itaú, 257–58
banks, 78; ATMs and, 145, 199; in Brazil, 257–58; child-friendly, 161; mobile technology and, 246; signage in, 70–71, 72, 141; teenagers and, 163–64; waiting time in, 34, 204–5, 206
Barberena, Manolo, 266
Barnes & Noble, 157
BART stations, 55–56
barware, 110–11
bedding, 149, 172, 180, 191–92
beer, 110–12, 173, 177
bending, resistance to, 57, 126, 143, 144, 170
Bergdorf Goodman, 119–20
Best Buy, 133–34, 175, 192, 204
best-of lists, online, 231–32, 235
big-box stores, 247
billboards, 69, 76
biological constants, 39–41
Blockbuster, 161
Blockbuster Mexico, 275–76
Bloomingdale's, 59–60, 118, 241, 270, 272
Bluefly, 238
body bubble, 11–12; mobile technology and, 242–43
BookPeople, 214–15
books and bookstores, 178, 231; bargain tables in, 22–23; children and, 149, 157–58, 219; merchandising and displays in, 87, 192–93, 213–15; online sales and, 236, 237, 238; shopping baskets in, 56–57

boomerang rate, 84–85

Brahma, 112, 258

brand names, 25, 64, 152, 163, 177, 220; getting customers to pay more for, 174, 216–17; on packaging, 196

Brazil, 264; Envirosell office in, 257–60, 266; malls in, 270–71, 274–75

Brookstone, 185

Brown Thomas, 269–70, 276

Burger King, 45, 159

Burma-Shave, 69

business schools, 31, 84

butt-brush effect, 11–12, 21–22, 126–28, 196

cafeteria lines, 217

capture rate, 83

cars and car dealerships, 66, 75, 107, 108, 109, 134–35, 162, 182, 220–21, 236, 275–76

cash register tapes. See sales data

cash/wraps, 178–79, 197, 208–12; displays near, 19, 154, 205, 209; efficiency of, 17–18, 210–11; hand-allotment issues and, 51–54; men paying in, 105–6; movement patterns and, 79–80; organization of lines in, 203–4; piggybacking at, 211; placement of, 79–80, 204, 209–10; self-serve options and, 145–46, 198–99, 208–9, 211; signage near, 65, 66, 69, 205; waiting time at, 34, 169, 201–6, 210

casinos, 92

category management work, 260

CBS Records, 18–20

cereal aisles, in supermarkets, 85, 105

cereal boxes, information on, 68, 140

chevroning, 82

childproofing stores, 153, 159–60

children, 101, 108, 109, 129, 151–64; books for, 149, 157–58, 219; clothing for, 118, 149, 175; family shopping outings and, 151–52; fathers shopping with, 105, 106, 117, 154; grandparents' purchases for, 149, 158; hands-on shopping style of, 154, 158–60, 178; mobile phones and, 246; online communities for,

239; providing diversions for, 85, 160–62; restaurants and, 155–56, 159, 160; shopping carts and, 55, 154; store design and fixturing and, 152–53; supermarkets and, 12, 85, 105, 154–55; toy stores and, 158–59. See also teenagers

Christmas shopping, 237–38, 290

cigarettes, 173

Citibank, 70, 161

Clarion, 164

Clinique, 119–20

clothing and clothing stores, 33–34, 110, 172, 180–83, 236; add-ons and, 215–16; gay and lesbian shoppers and, 115–17; hand-allotment issue and, 60; jeans, 13–14, 148, 163, 257; for kids, 118, 149, 175; menswear, 103–4, 113–14, 115–16, 117; merchandising and, 215–16, 220; older shoppers and, 143–44, 146, 147, 148; overstocking and, 198; sewing machines and, 122; teenagers and, 163; touching and trying on, 104, 114, 181–83, 190, 195, 271; unisex clothing stores and, 115, 132; women's, men shopping for, 114

CNN, 74

coat check/package-call system, 59–60

coffee, in supermarkets, 60, 174

color vision, aging and, 141–42

computers and computer stores, 106–7, 109–10, 133, 134, 177, 216, 218–19. See also Internet and e-commerce

confusion index, 33, 34

convenience stores, 85, 124, 163, 177

convergence, 245–49

conversion rates, 21–22, 28–32, 181

cosmetics. See health and beauty products

counting systems, 31

coupons, 46, 122

Crédit Agricole, 164

crowding, 126–27, 169

DailyCandy, 235

dairy cases, 85

Daslu, 270–71, 274

data-collection technologies, 26–27, 56
decompression zone, 43–48, 54; greeting
    people in, 43–44, 45–46; misuses
    of, 45–46; possibilities for, 46–48;
    shopping baskets or carts in, 44, 46,
    54, 56–57
density checks, 22–23, 77, 210
department stores, experience of, 237
design of stores, 195, 197, 210
dinnerware, 58, 110–11, 118
directories, placement of, 44, 46
discounted merchandise, 47, 86, 169;
    sales and, 12, 126, 169
discovery process, 168
Disneyland, 59
displays, 26, 219–24; activated fixtures,
    222; in bookstores, 87, 192–93,
    213–15; designed without considering
    actual use, 221–24; endcaps, 81–82,
    222; labor considerations and,
    159–60, 194–95, 197; locked cabinets
    and, 189–90, 206; near doorways,
    43; power, 47; spice fixtures, 223–24;
    talking, 49, 141; in windows, 42–43,
    81, 87–88; within striking distance of
    children, 159–60
DoCoMo, 144, 246
dog food and treats, 12, 153
doll stores, 106
Domingues, José Augusto, 259
doors and doorways: automatic,
    44–45; electronic counters on, 31;
    information written on, 44, 67, 68;
    inside-outside transition and, 43–48;
    revolving, 45; walking through
    parking lot toward, 42–43. *See also*
    decompression zone
dressing rooms, 181–83, 271, 284; men
    vs. women in, 104, 114; seating near,
    93, 125
drive-in movies, 47, 48
drive-thru shopping, 202; fast food and,
    53–54, 95–96, 128
drugstores, 35, 49, 195–96, 199–200, 207,
    217, 246; hand-allotment issues in, 54;
    men's health and grooming products
    in, 119, 120; movement through,

85–86; multiple constituencies in, 21–
    22; pharmacy counters in, 85–86, 162;
    signage in, 71, 72, 75, 222–23; type size
    on packaging in, 139–40, 199; women's
    reading of packaging in, 127–28. *See
    also* health and beauty products
Dubai, 268–69
Dublin, 269–70, 276

Ear Inn, 16, 155–56
Eastern Newsstand, 51–53
e-commerce. *See* Internet and
    e-commerce
electronics and electronics stores,
    32, 87, 133–34, 175, 206, 211, 236;
    children and, 159–60; in Mexico,
    276–78; movement patterns in, 79–80;
    older users and, 146, 150; package
    design and, 83–84, 188–89. *See also*
    computers and computer stores;
    phones
Elektra, 276–78
elevators, signage in, 76
emerging countries: cutting edge of
    retail in, 268–71; mobile technology
    in, 248–49
employees, 169, 176, 181; amenities and
    spaces for, 276; bad service from, 170;
    in decompression zone, 43–44, 45–46;
    displays' impact on, 159–60, 194–95,
    197; interception rate and, 33–34; men
    reluctant to speak to, 103, 107; saving
    money on, 198–99, 206; shoppers
    searching for, 64, 205, 206; shoppers
    waiting on line and, 202–3, 204
endcaps, 81–82, 222
Envirosell, 26–27; international
    expansion of, 254–67, 279; origin and
    early years of, 16–20
escalators, signage on, 65
Estée Lauder, 46, 119
Excel, 9–10
eyesight, aging and, 138–42, 145

Facebook, 240–42, 243
Fairway, 278
farmers' markets, 55–56

fast-food restaurants: children and, 155, 159, 160; drive-thrus of, 53–54, 95–96, 128; eating in parking lots of, 95–96, 128; gender differences and, 128; older consumers and, 142, 149; signage in, 66–69, 75–76
Filene's Basement, 47
flowers, selling, 288
football, 47
footwear, 148, 183, 236
France, 137, 160, 200, 272
Frito-Lay, 49
front of store, 43–49, 87. *See also* decompression zone
Fruin, Jack, 18
furniture, 111, 218

Galleries Lafayette, 272–73
Gap, 47, 86, 115, 132, 195, 214
Gap Body, 90
gas stations, 135–36, 145–46
gay and lesbian shoppers, 115–17
gender differences, 101, 102–36, 157; changes in social roles and, 104, 107, 112–13, 117, 122–23, 124, 131–32, 284; moving through store and, 102–4; paying and, 105–6; price tag reading and, 104, 125; supermarkets and, 105–6, 123, 125; technology and, 133, 134; time spent in store and, 103–4, 108–9, 124–25; typical division of labor and, 103, 107–8, 123–24, 151. *See also* men; women
gender-segregated areas, 271
General Mills, 155, 173–74
generics or store brands, 14–15
Germany, 137, 236
gift-wrapping, 211
Gillette, 120, 186
Gladwell, Malcolm, 260
Goffman, Erving, 18
Golden Books, 219
Grand Central Station, 51–53, 55
Gran Plaza, La, 278
green concerns, Internet and, 246
greeting cards, 128–29
greeting customers, 46, 207

hair color, 49
Hallmark stores, 88, 129, 153, 192, 211
hand-allotment issues, 50–60; coat check/package-call system and, 59–60; at drive-thrus, 53–54; at newsstands, 51–53; shopping baskets or carts and, 54–58
H&M, 47
hardware stores, 113, 121–22, 130–32
Harley-Davidson, 22, 104, 119, 289
health and beauty products, 35, 49, 164, 172, 185–87, 214; female shopping behaviors and, 127–28, 129–30; generics or store brands and, 14–15; greeting people shopping for, 46; makeup demonstrations and, 127, 187; for men, 118–20; merchandising for variety of settings and, 195–96; older consumers and, 12–13, 148–49, 287–88; placement of, 12–13, 49, 217, 287–88; trying merchandise and, 94–95, 185–86, 187; type size on packaging of, 139–40; women's spatial requirements and, 127, 129–30
HEB, 145
Home Depot, 131–32
hotels, 44, 60, 76, 230; check-in and checkout counters in, 212; older people and, 141–42, 149
housewares, 107–8, 110–11, 112–13, 239–40
housing, 108, 143

IBM, 46
Iguatemi, 274–75
Ikea, 160–61
impulse buying. *See* unplanned purchases
India, 248; Envirosell office in, 264–65
infrastructure, 247–48
ink-jet printer cartridges, 190
inside-outside transition. *See* decompression zone
insight groups, 30
instruction manuals, online, 246
interactive fixtures, 160, 198
interception rate, 33–34
international perspective, 254–79;

Envirosell expansion and, 254–67, 279; retail innovation and, 268–71, 274–78; status of merchants and, 272–73

Internet and e-commerce, 150, 227–53, 281, 286; artworks and, 239; best-of lists and, 231–32; children and, 239; convergence and, 245–49; cyberterrorism and, 249; economic underpinnings of, 235, 242; as green tool, 246; local vs. global processes and, 234–35; massive amounts of unfiltered information on, 228–33; matchmaking sites and, 243; mobile technology and, 242–43, 245–49; music and, 231, 249–53; predictive processes and, 243–44; pre-shop and, 236–37; routine purchases and, 245, 247; social networking and, 240–42, 243; used products and, 238; women's shopping and, 236–38

Istanbul, 281–82

Italy, 137, 273; Envirosell office in, 255–57

iTunes, 231, 249–51, 252

Japan, 94–95, 162, 236, 253; cell phones in, 242–43, 246; Envirosell office in, 261–63; movement patterns in, 78–79; older shoppers in, 137, 144; population density in, 242, 263–64

J.Crew, 115, 132

jeans, 13–14, 148, 163, 257

jewelry and jewelry stores, 31, 114, 184, 189–90, 271

Kelly, Paul, 276

kitchenware, 112–13

KMart, 46

L'eggs, 219

lesbian shoppers, 115, 116–17

lighting, 42–43, 45, 142, 182, 197

Lincoln Center, 16–18, 290

Lindstrom, Martin, 174

lines: organization of, 203–4. See also cash/wraps

lingerie, 114, 172; male underwear vs., 89–91; seating and, 91–93

liquor stores, 75, 142

LivePerson.com, 233

living standards, 264

L. L. Bean, 104

loans, from retailers, 277–78

locked display cabinets, 189–90, 206

London Underground, 65

L'Oreal, 119

Lowe's, 131, 132

LVMH, 272

magazines, 120; type size in, 139–40

malls, 87, 93–94, 143, 278–79; overseas, 268–69, 274–75

marketing, 219–20

Mastopietro, Maria Cristina, 259

Match.com, 243, 244

McDonald's, 67, 117, 155

men, 102–20; computer stores and, 106–7, 109–10; engaging interest of, 109–13; merchandising geared to, 113–16, 117–20; shopping with children, 105, 106, 117, 154; traits of, as shoppers, 102–7. See also gender differences

Men's Health, 120

menswear, 103–4, 113–14, 115–16, 117

menu boards, 67–68, 69–70, 76, 142

merchandising, 64, 194–200, 213–24; adjacencies and, 93, 129, 154, 162, 214–19; PoP materials and, 219–24. See also displays; packaging

Mexico, 274, 275–78; Envirosell office in, 265–66

Microsoft, 9–10, 232

miniaturization, 146, 150

mirrors, 78, 168, 169, 182–83, 187, 192

mobile technology, 245–49; cash transactions and, 246–47; in emerging countries, 248–49; text messaging and, 242–43, 247

movement through store, 13, 14, 77–88, 210; bargain tables near door and, 22–23; boomerang rate and, 84–85; facing and walking forward and, 80–82; of men vs. women, 102–4; package design and, 83–84; sight lines and, 82–83; toward right, 78–79

movie rentals and sales, 95, 197, 236, 237; children and, 160, 161
museums, 153–54, 178, 289
music, 18–20, 81–82, 188, 231; falling CD sales and, 251; online resources and, 231, 249–53
Mxyplyzyk, 285

napkins, printing information on, 68, 69
Netflix, 235, 237
new products, accessibility of, 169–70
Newspaper Association of America, 51
newspapers, type size in, 138–39
newsstands, 35, 51–53, 177
Nissan, 162
Nova Scotia Liquor Commission, 175

office supply stores, 33, 183–84, 190
older shoppers, 12–13, 101, 137–50, 152; aging eyes of, 138–42, 145; boomer mentality and, 137–38; buying for grandchildren, 149, 158; health and beauty aids and, 12–13, 49, 148–49, 287–88; physical limitations of, 142–44, 145, 147–48; spatial uncertainty and, 144–45; teenagers' presence and, 21–22
Old Mutual, 269
Old Navy, 57–58
online shopping. *See* Internet and e-commerce
open sell, 176, 185, 241
outdoor signs, 81
overstocking, 198
over-the-counter remedies, 139, 222–23, 246

packaging, 196, 219, 246, 290; children and, 158; display function of, 83–84; experiencing product and, 94, 180, 186, 187–89; type size on, 139–40, 196; women's reading of, 127–28
paint, 132
parking lots: fast food eaten in, 95–96, 128; movement through, 42–43; selling merchandise in, 47–48
Pasquini, Alberto, 255–56

Pearson, 266
peripheral vision, 40, 43, 81
personal shoppers, 114
Pfaltzgraff, 58, 110–11
pharmacy counters, 85–86, 162
Philippines, 246
phones, 87, 146, 159–60, 185, 192; mobile technology and, 242–43, 245–49
point-of-purchase (PoP) business, 219–24
popcorn, microwave, 155, 173–74
population density, 242, 263–64
possession notion, 178–79
Post Office, U.S., 214; self-serve options and, 145, 198–99; signage and, 69–70, 71
power displays, 47
pre-shop, 236–37
price tags, read by men vs. women, 104
privacy, 34, 49, 128, 130, 242, 257–58, 286
Project for Public Spaces, 92
prom gowns, 106
Pryanishnikov, Alexey, 265

RadioShack, 87, 133, 143, 185, 211
recognition, desire for, 169
REI, 104
repairs, 66, 211
restaurants, 193, 208; family, 34–35, 68, 88. *See also* fast-food restaurants
Restoration Hardware, 218
restrooms, 88, 276; baby-changing stations in, 117, 135; at gas stations, 135–36; signage and, 65, 67
returns, 207, 211
Revlon, 195–96
right, movement toward, 78–79
right-handedness, 52, 80, 218
road signs, 72–73
Rockefeller Plaza, 73–74
Rodin Museum, 153–54
routine purchases, 245, 247
Russia, Envirosell office in, 265

sales. *See* discounted merchandise
sales data, 20–23, 29, 30
salespeople. *See* employees
sales per square foot, 263–64

same-store sales, 25, 30

samples, 94–95, 186; of foodstuffs, 173–74, 179, 193, 205; of songs, 250

sample sizes, selling of, 94–95, 217

Samsung, 235

Scandroglio, Giusi, 256, 258, 259

scanners, portable, 208–9

Sears, 176

seating, 91–94, 125, 145, 157

security issues, 189–90, 264, 274

self-serve options, 145–46, 198–99, 208–9, 211

selling up, 190–91

sensory aspects of shopping, 171–93; locked display cabinets and, 189–90; packaging and, 94, 180, 186, 187–89; smell and, 174–75, 179, 185–86; sound and, 179–80, 185, 188; in supermarkets, 173–74, 175–76; taste and, 173–74, 179, 193. *See also* touch; trying merchandise

Sephora, 185, 241, 272

sewing machines, 122

shoplifting, 20, 46, 100, 206–7, 209, 285

shopping bags: designs on, 58; totes for use in store, 57–58

shopping baskets, 44, 46, 54–58

shopping carts, 54–55, 58, 60, 154

shrinkage, 206–7. *See also* shoplifting

shrink-wrap, 187

sight lines, 82–83; children's areas and, 157, 161–62

signage, 26, 61–76, 127, 168, 219, 220, 221; in banks, 70–71, 72, 141; design of, 72–74; digital, 65, 76; driving and, 72–73; in drugstores, 71, 72, 75, 222–23; evaluating effectiveness of, 62–63; in fast-food restaurants, 66–69, 75–76; logical sequencing of, 68, 73; men's reading of, 107, 111; movement from back to front of store and, 86; older shoppers and, 141–42; outdoor, 81; with overly complicated messages, 75–76; placement of, 13–14, 19, 43, 64–72, 83, 86, 205; in post offices, 69–70, 71; shipped but never making it onto floor, 75; sight lines and, 82, 83;

surveys about, 24; in waiting areas, 66, 145. *See also* information fixtures

single-parent households, 108, 152

smell, 174–75, 179, 185–86

social change, 284, 290–91

social functions of shopping, 124–25, 288–90

social networking, 240–42, 243

soft drinks, 177, 222, 224

Sony BMG, 251, 252–53

sound, 179–80, 185, 188

South Africa, 269, 274

South Korea, 236, 242–43

Spain, 2004 election in, 247

Spar, 55, 56

spatial uncertainty, 144–45

spices, fixtures for, 223–24

Sprint, 185

Staples, 33

stationery stores, 88, 128–29

status of retailers, 272–73

storage areas, 176

store managers, empowering, 284

Subway, 68

supermarkets, 30, 100, 205, 219, 224, 288; adjacencies in, 216–18; beer sections in, 111–12; capture rate in, 83; children in, 12, 85, 105, 154–55; coffee bars in, 60; convenience stores vs., 85, 124, 177; coupons and, 122; dog food and treats in, 12, 153; men's health and grooming products in, 119; men vs. women in, 105–6, 123, 125; merchandise in parking lots of, 47–48; movement through, 82, 85; older shoppers and, 144, 145; routine purchases and, 245; samples and sensory stimulation in, 173–74, 175–76, 179, 205; self-scan checkout systems in, 208–9; spice fixtures in, 223–24; talking displays in, 49; time spent per visit to, 32

surveys, 23–24

table tents, 68

Takashimaya, 46

talking, atmosphere conducive to, 168

talking displays, 49, 141

Target, 114
taste, 173–74, 179, 193
technology: data-collection, 26–27, 56; gender differences and, 133, 134; mobile, 242–43, 245–49; older consumers and, 150; signage and, 76. *See also* Internet and e-commerce
teenagers, 21–22, 148, 163–64, 189
terrorism, 249
text messaging, 242–43, 247
Thomasville, 111
Three-Minute Happiness, 94–95
time, 201–7; perception of, 201–2; waiting, 34, 169, 201–6, 210, 257
time spent in store, 26, 32–33, 124; gender and, 103–4, 108–9, 124–25
Toro, 66
touch, 168, 172, 176–77, 178, 179, 180–81, 184, 185, 190, 195; artful displays and, 192–93; children's proclivity for, 154, 158–60, 178. *See also* trying merchandise
Toyota, Kaz, 261
Toyota, Momo, 261–62
toys, 32, 149, 158–59, 189, 214; diverting children with, 160–61, 162
trackers, 5–8, 285
track sheets, 5, 6, 8–9
trade shows, 48
train stations, food offerings at, 55–56
Trout, Tony, 267
True Value, 113
trying merchandise, 179–84; samples and, 94–95; security considerations and, 189–90; selling up and, 190–91; tasting and, 173–74, 179; trying on clothes and, 104, 114, 181–83. *See also* touch
Turkey, 281–82
type size, 138–41, 196, 199

underwear, 113–14, 115–16, 172; male vs. female, 89–92
United Kingdom, 78, 175, 236, 272, 286
unplanned purchases, 25, 57, 64, 87, 105, 168, 205, 209, 219; add-ons and, 57, 191–92, 214–16
used products, sold online, 238

value equations, 14–15
Victoria's Secret, 90, 109, 110, 214
videotapes: as diversion during waits, 204–5; promotional in-store, 66; in science of shopping, 5, 10, 286. *See also* movie rentals and sales
Vinçon, 58
vitamins and supplements, 196, 217

Wacker, Watts, 284
waiting areas, 66, 145, 162
waiting time, 34, 169, 201–6, 210, 257
walking. *See* movement through store
Wal-Mart, 47, 199–200, 207, 284
Walton, Sam, 46, 272
Wanamaker, John, 222
weather, 264
Wells Fargo, 161
wheelchairs, 143, 147–48
Whole Foods, 204, 289
Whyte, William H., 15–16, 26
will-call desks, 59–60
Williams-Sonoma, 112, 289
windows: displays in, 42–43, 81, 87–88; signage in, 69, 75
window-shopping, 78, 273; online equivalent of, 237, 238
wine labels, 142
women, 110, 121–36; cars and, 108, 134–35, 236; consumer electronics and, 133–34; cosmetics and, 12–13, 127, 129–30, 196, 287–88; hardware stores and, 113, 121–22, 130–32; metaphysics of shopping and, 125–26; online shopping of, 236–38; shopping as social activity for, 124–25, 288; spatial requirements of, 126–30. *See also* gender differences

younger shoppers, 13, 49, 139–40, 146, 274–75. *See also* children; teenagers

About the Author

Paco Underhill is the founder and CEO of Envirosell, Inc. His clients include Starbucks, McDonald's, adidas and Nokia. He is a regular contributor to NPR, *The Wall Street Journal* and *The New York Times.*